The *Sailing* *Mystique*

847 226 9834

BILL ROBINSON

The *Sailing* *Mystique*

The Challenges and Rewards of a Life under Sail

S
SHERIDAN
HOUSE

First published 1994
by Sheridan House Inc.
145 Palisade Street
Dobbs Ferry, NY 10522

Library of Congress Cataloging-in-Publication Data

Robinson, Bill, 1918–
    The sailing mystique : the challenges and rewards of a life under sail / Bill Robinson.
        p.   cm.
    ISBN 0-924486-63-5 : $14.95
    1. Sailing.   2. Boats and boating.   I. Title.
GV811.R5819   1994   94-8702
797.1'24—dc20   CIP

Designed by Richard Stalzer

Printed in the United States of America

ISBN 0-924486-63-5

Mystique. 1. A framework of doctrines, ideas, beliefs or the like, constructed around a person or object, endowing him or it with enhanced value or profound meaning. 2. An aura of mystery or mystical power surrounding a particular occupation or pursuit. *Random House Dictionary of the English Language.*

To all the family, through the generations, and friends, who have added so much to the enjoyment of these experiences.

CONTENTS

PREFACE

"Did you have a nice vacation?"

So often, this question was put to me by friends when I returned from a cruise in the Caribbean, South Pacific or Europe, and my answer would be a rather smug, "No. It wasn't a vacation. I was working."

I was able to combine a lifelong dedication to sailing with my profession—boating editor and writer—and while the various trips had all the pleasures of a wonderful vacation, they were actually assignments, which in my role of editor, I fortunately could give to myself as a writer. One is indeed lucky to be able to combine vocation and avocation; as a result, it was possible for me to enjoy a great many sailing experiences that I never could have had in a normal job and as a pater familias.

These experiences resulted in many magazine articles and books over a period of more than 50 years going back to my earliest adventures.

In the following pages, I have culled from all those books and magazines the pieces that best express to me the fun and rewards of a lifetime of sailing. They bring back wonderful memories, and I hope they will be meaningful to you as we share them.

Bill Robinson
Rumson, New Jersey
July 1993

I

The Rewards and Challenges

Anyone who loves sailing will no doubt appreciate, and perhaps agree with, most of the sentiments expressed here. Do you?

FOR CENTURIES, from the time man first tired of paddling his own log canoe and elevated an animal skin on a stick into the wind, sailing was the world's most important and widespread means of "assisted" transportation until in the nineteenth century, it lost out to steamships, railroads, and eventually automobiles and airplanes. It was a serious commercial business that no one ever thought of doing for fun.

Yet today, in the space age of supersonic speeds, with sail completely outmoded for commercial use, more people are taking to the water under sail than ever before in history. Why this paradox? Why did the sailboat fail to follow the stagecoach and the trolley car into oblivion when it was no longer a viable means of transportation?

There are many nuances to the answers to this question—nuances that will be explored, explained, and expanded upon as the subject matter of this book—but basically the answer is that sailing, an outgrowth of a dead method of transportation, is as a form of recreation a satisfying, many-faceted way of life, deeply challenging, deeply involving, and deeply rewarding.

Despite the serious nature of seafaring as a profession and the rugged realities of life at sea, there was a glamour and romance to sail that refused to die as its commercial importance waned. An attempt to capture these qualities, to keep them alive, brought about an upswing in recreational sailing in a rise that was a direct counterbalance to the commercial decline. And strangely, the switch to recreational sailing brought about the changes in techniques and equipment that were a radical departure from eons of status quo. Professional seamen had been content to follow in the traditions and methods of generations of predecessors, and an ancient Phoenician would not have been baffled if some time machine had transported him to one of the caravels of Columbus, or even to Nelson's ships at Trafalgar. He would have recognized most of the gear and would have known what it was for and how to handle it.

Imagine the problem, though, if the time machine had slipped him but a few decades later into the engine room of an ocean liner. Even more strangely, and sticking to sail, he would be really at a loss today on the deck of an America's Cup 12-Meter, or even on a conventional ocean-going auxiliary or a racing one-design. And so, for that matter, would Columbus and Lord Nelson.

Sailing has become a sport of multiple facets, of vast variety and scope in gear and equipment, and its appeals are multiple, too. Ranging from the relaxed delight of an escapist drifting in a quiet bywater, feet on gunwale and beer in hand, to the competitive zeal of the muscular, hard-nosed crew of an America's Cup yacht, sailing offers an amazing range of challenges and rewards of contrasting philosophies and depth of involvement. No other sport called by one generic term has more subcategories and variations, and that is its true fascination. There is something for everyone—everyone who wants to can become a sailor of some sort. There are no limitations of age, sex, size, or physical prowess, except for the very young and very old who are unable to care for themselves in routine living.

What would you like to do? Would you like to be an Olympic champion, or at least one of the better sailors in your local club? Would you like to circumnavigate the globe single-handed? Would you like to win the Bermuda Race? Or would you like to get away from the pressures of modern civilization and be at one with nature and the many moods it transmits to the world of water? How about a Bahamas cruise, a trip down the Intracoastal Waterway, or a tradewind passage from the Canaries to Grenada? Or maybe just a quietly pleasant sail of an afternoon on the waters of home, a change of pace, a chance to see the sun glint off dancing whitecaps and to find an isolated cove and anchor for an interlude of peace?

All these and more are possible to recreational sailors. All are a part of the world they enter by becoming sailing enthusiasts, and if they are dedicated enough, they just might do every one of the above, or at least to be close to a part of each sphere of action. No one facet of sailing is self-contained, exclusive, and limiting. A sailor can be one thing one day and another the next, in a complete change of philosophy and approach.

As an example, I can't personally claim achievement in every one of the above categories, but I have experienced most of them at one time or another, and the rewards, different as they may be, can be great. I have not won an Olympic title, or come close, but I have sailed in national championships against those who have, and I have won regattas; I have not circumnavigated the globe single-handed, but I have sailed alone through far-off waters and known the peculiar challenges of a single-handed passage; I have been on prize-winning ocean racers; I have cruised in most of the prime cruising areas from Fiji to the Fyn Archipelago, from the Greek Islands to Grenada, from the Bahamas to Baja California, from Penobscot Bay to Puget Sound, and from the Virgins to the Vineyard; and yet perhaps the happiest hours of all have been the quiet afternoons or moonlit evenings of poking around the unremarkable two-by-three miles of channels and tidal flats that are the waters of home. In the very familiarity there is a special sense of the rightness of belonging.

At times I like competition, and sailing has given me as much of it as I've wanted: the tense muscles, the dry mouth, the split-second decisions, the intense concentration, the thrill of winning, and the dejection of defeat. At other times, I have only wanted peace and solitude and complete release from the tensions of modern living, and these too have been easy to find in a sailboat. I have come to know my family better through sailing than in any other single way, I have made some of the best and most easily resumed friendships through sailing, and I have seen many of the world's most beautiful and fascinating places from the deck of a sailboat.

I have also spent a lot of money on sailboats; have been cold, wet, lonely, and bored on sailboats; have been seasick on sailboats; and have been scared on sailboats; but none of these prevented me from coming back at the next opportunity, and in their own way, they have been challenges that have brought some of the greatest rewards. In dealing with nature, as one always is while sailing, the variations and vagaries must be met, lived with, and mastered, and this is one of the true secrets of the hold sailing has on those who are truly devoted to it. It is a constant involvement with nature, with its contrary beauty, dangerous power, and perpetual challenge. No one who has experienced this ever forgets the satisfaction and the great sense of accomplishment, renewed through each and every day of sailing.

From *America's Sailing Book* (1976)

II

Landmarks

In every sailor's life there are certain special moments that stand in memory as a time of awakening, understanding, achievement or rare emotion. These are some of mine.

Awakening

That sudden, electric awareness that something specially yours has come into your life. This was when I was 12 at Camp Viking on Cape Cod

THE MOST exciting thing about Camp Viking for me was that magic moment when I first realized that I really knew how to sail. Later, I won the camp racing championship, greatly satisfying and rewarding, but that wasn't as important as that first critical turning point. It came in a "distance race" down

Pleasant Bay in the camp sharpies, flat-bottomed skiffs with leg-o-mutton sails, on our way to a camp picnic on a typical Cape Cod summer day of a fresh, puffy southwester. I must have been doing well enough in the sailing lessons to be named skipper of one of the boats.

As we headed down the open bay, I suddenly realized that I had the "feel" of the boat. I was reacting to lifts and headers, holding her flat in puffs, tacking on favorable shifts, and playing the waves right, as everything hit a rhythm I could sense, almost like catching on to a dance step for the first time. A wonderful glow of confidence developed as the pattern fell together, and it was a real thrill to work out ahead of the other boats, gaining each time we tacked.

When we reached the island with a lead of over a quarter of a mile on the next boat, there were cheers and yells from the whole camp, and The Skipper made the day complete by patting me on the head and saying, "Boy, Bill, you really had that boat flying. That was a great race!"

And that was it. From that sail onward, I knew that I had something that was special for me—sailing, and I was a sailor.

From *A Sailor's Tales* (1978)

Landfall

The moment of achievement of a dream; and also a clue to the practical genesis of getting there

Mar Claro closed with the islands, lying in a low black line to windward across the path of a moon newly-risen from silver-rimmed clouds. Close-hauled on the starboard tack, she heeled to a freshening breeze, which suddenly brought us a smell of sand and shallows, bared by the tide, and a faintly tropical scent of flowers, palm tree trunks, and wood smoke to replace the fresh salt air of the Gulf Stream. Key Largo, Florida, lay 15 hours and 60 miles astern, and Bimini in the Bahamas was off the port bow, deep in the quiet of a moonlit three A.M.

The little sloop surged forward to the wonderful rhythm of bow wave breaking away from the hull. She was alive and driving toward her landfall with a pleasant pressure on the tiller and a rush of water aft along the lee rail. Moment by moment, the lights of Bimini changed from a pale loom over the horizon to individual dots that popped into view, and the line of the land began to take shape under the moon. Houses and trees separated into outline from the blur, and abruptly we swept from the deep, dark water of the Stream to a luminous world of white over Bimini's bar.

Mar Claro seemed to be flying through air, so clear was the water and so sharply vivid beneath her keel were the occasional clumps of grass, starfish, and pieces of rock, set against the sand like dark jewels on a woman's skin. We felt a new sense of speed and motion as we held our course for a single tall casuarina on South Bimini.

When we were close enough to see the uneven line of foam, where the white water meets the white beach, and to hear the whisper of waves rustling over sand and sliding back again, we started sheets and made the 90-degree turn to port for the harbor entrance, which opened before us to the north. The bright lights on the piers glared at us. When we finally slid inside South Bimini's point and past the fishing boats moored at the piers, the hum of their generators added a note of latent, poised power, of activity suspended for the quiet hours, while their tuna towers and outriggers cast eccentric shadows against the tracery of palms in the background.

To port, we saw an empty berth at a pier and eased into it. The whisper of water along *Mar Claro*'s sides abated, and the soft thunder of her luffing sails stilled by degrees as we lowered and furled them. While we followed the familiar routine of securing her, the air moved over us, warmly gentle and pungent from the mangrove cays, coral outcroppings, and bonefish flats, which stretched far to the eastward until they blended with the Great Bahama Bank. Behind us on the beach we heard that rhythmic rustle that can only come from a sea breeze stirring through palm fronds. Somewhere in a cluster of native huts, a cock crowed. *Mar Claro* had made her first foreign landfall.

We had bought *Mar Claro* for many reasons, but the thrill of sailing her through Gulf Stream moonlight to the Bahamas had been only the wildest kind of a dream. We had done it in a 24-foot sloop, which we had intended to use primarily for day sailing on a shallow bay in New Jersey. Thus our arrival in Bimini was like an approving punctuation mark, an exclamation point of delighted surprise, after all the months of planning, and my crucial pitch to Jane.

Armed with folders and pictures, I made the best and driest martini in the world, settled Jane in her favorite spot on the sofa, in front of a blazing driftwood fire, and prepared for a long heart-to-heart talk.

It was one of the shortest pitches on record. Over the rim of her glass, Jane's eyes rested on the folders beside me, and before I could say a thing, she did.

"I know. You're getting a new boat. That's fine, but I want a clothes dryer."

P.S. She got the dryer.

———

From *New Boat* (1961)

On the Great Bahama Bank

A once in a lifetime sensing of a strange rarity—total silence, in a passage in a friend's motorsailer

On *Rolling Stone*, we crossed in a calm so complete that the surface was devoid even of the gentlest heave or aftermath of previous swells. Not a ripple marred the glass-smooth sheen while we watched our shadow slide over the bottom off the port bow. The sky was as clean as the water, with not a wisp of cloud, as the sun gradually sank off the starboard quarter. About halfway to Sylvia, we were startled to feel the ominous bounce of keel on sand. We were right on course, a course that was supposed to be clear for six feet of draft at any tide, but we have since learned that this was not an unusual situation in periods of especially low tide. The tide and its currents are capricious on the Bank and are not charted or predicted. Wind plays an important part in the flow of water, and the strong west winds of the previous few days had evidently pushed water off to the eastward. Boats have made the Bank passage with as much as eight feet of draft, but they must have had high tide under them in several spots. We only bounced and didn't run hard on.

From Sylvia the course is due east for forty-six miles to Northwest Channel Light. About ten miles beyond Sylvia Buoy (since replaced by a platform light), the red sun set over the blank horizon astern, and the skipper decided to anchor for the night. Night crossings on the Bank are tricky, as native workboats can be operating there without lights, and unpredictable cross currents can make navigation difficult. Without the visual piloting that helps in the daytime, it is possible to wander off into areas of coral heads and shifting sand bores. Unless it is really rough, anchoring in the uniformly shallow water is no problem. In fading twilight, we dropped our anchor in twelve feet, and its bubbly descent was clearly visible. Even in the moonless hours of the night, it was possible to follow the chain down through the eerie glow of the water and spot the dark blob of the anchor in the sand.

I have never experienced a stranger sensation afloat than that night at anchor on the vast silent platter of the Great Bahama Bank. Below decks, the boat was completely quiet and steady, more so than in most marinas. On deck there was absolute stillness and a tremendous sense of space. After the others had turned in, I climbed to the flying bridge and sat there for a long time in awe of the rare scene. How often in a lifetime does anyone experience total silence? Thinking back, I could not remember the complete absence of some sort of sound, but here, on a motionless vessel on a still sea, thirty miles from any land, there were long periods without a detectable sound. It was so quiet that I could hear the blood moving through my ears. Overhead, the stars filled the faultless sky in greater numbers than I had ever seen.

Now and then a fish would break the surface, and the gentle flip-flop of its splash sounded like an explosion. In the calm the boat was hardly heaving or settling, and every few minutes the faintest gurgle or slap of water told of the hull moving imperceptibly. I almost jumped overboard when the generator whirred to life on one of its automatic starts.

When it subsided again, the stillness returned. There was a complete suspension of sound and time and the loneliest awareness of the vast spaces in nature that I have ever felt. I might have stayed there all night gazing through the luminous Bank waters to the bottom throwing back the ghostly white of the Milky Way and at the star-speckled sheen of the surface stretching off to a barely defined meeting with the sky, if a whisper of breeze that drifted in for a moment hadn't broken the spell long enough to send me below to my bunk.

From Where the Trade Winds Blow (1963)

Night Passage

Out of the memories of many great sails, one still stands out: St. Barts to Antigua

There are two possible routes from the "in-between islands" to Antigua, where we were headed to make plane connections for Martha and John and to pick up our next two crew changes. We could make a direct run for it from St. Bart's, seventy-five miles on a course of 140 degrees, or we could hop down the chain of St. Kitts, Nevis, and Montserrat—a great circle course with the longest leg about fifty miles. It all depended on the wind direction. With the wind anywhere south of east, it was a rugged slug to make the direct run—one reason Antiguan charter skippers seldom wanted to head into this area. Even the island-hopping route could mean plenty of hard thrashing to windward.

When it came time for our departure, we were in St. Bart's, and the wind was well north of east, just right for a straight reach. It was an opportunity not to be missed. The plan was an evening departure for a dawn landfall on Antigua, so we left the harbor of Gustavia at 1800 to clear its spider web of anchored boats before dark and then jogged around the outer roadstead under power while we had dinner in calm water. By 1915, it was completely dark, the dishes were done, and the trade was gusting off the hills in uneven puffs. We made sail, mainsail and jib, and headed out between the rounded rock called Pain de Sucre (Sugarloaf) and the main island on course for Antigua.

As soon as we cleared the lee of the island, there was real, steady heft to the wind, and I felt that a reefed main and both headsails would be the best combination. Reefing the main would do little to cut our speed in a breeze over sixteen, it reduced a touch of weather helm, and there was easy flexibility in the two headsails. It was a dark, clear night, with that full, horizon-to-horizon display of stars that is always so startling to someone who has spent most of his life around cities. As ever, our friend Orion, the easiest constellation to identify in all the vast panoply, was up there as a focal point, and at this time of year there was that wonderful juxtaposition in late evening of the Southern Cross on one horizon and Polaris and the Big Dipper above the other one.

There were periods of darkness when a batch of clouds would scud swiftly in from the northeast and blot out the stars. We would charge on through a blackness broken only by the phosphorescent rush of whitecaps on the port quarter, shining briefly as they hissed under us, the unearthly glow of the starboard running light flashing against the rhythm of the bow wave, and the little circle of white from our stern light spreading over the nearest foam in our wake. The lights of St. Bart's dimmed rapidly astern, and, well off to starboard, faint pinpricks in the gloom showed where St. Kitts was.

To me, emotions and perceptions are always heightened in night sailing, perhaps because of that primeval fear of the dark that crawls through our sensibilities no matter how matter-of-fact the surface approach might be. Whitecaps, ignored in the noonday sun, have an ominous authority as they suddenly burst out of the void with a swooshing crash, waves look blacker and bigger, and sound is magnified. The rush of water alongside, the hiss of waves and wake and their slap against the hulls, and the orchestration of wind in the rigging are heightened; the sense of speed is intensified; and euphoria is tinged with an anxiety, a presentiment fostered by darkness that something unknown is lurking just beyond the borders of consciousness.

Since our memorable thrash to the Caicos, our night passages had all been under power; this sailing was a wonderful contrast and one of the most exhilarating sails I have ever had, with the pleasures sharpened by that anticipation of the mysteries that might be hidden in the black of night.

There was also a warm spot of encouragement glowing behind the sense of blank blackness, in the knowledge that the late moon would be up before the night was over. Somehow, this prospect makes night watches in darkness better than the ones that follow the setting of a waxing moon half way through the night. On those, dawn seems so far away, but dawn loses its importance when the late moon lights the long hours after midnight.

By the change of watch, the breeze had come up, perhaps to eighteen or a bit more, and I felt that she would do better minus the staysail and still not lose speed significantly, so we doused that and swept on under reefed main and jib at about the same clip. Jane and I were off for the midwatch, and, while it was bouncy and noisy below, there was a marked contrast to the sense of strain and urgency there had been on the passage to Caicos. Just the few degrees change in wind direction, from a close reach to a beam reach, made all the difference.

The moon was up when we came back on at 0400. We were still tearing along at close to hull speed, but the sense of rushing blindly through blankness, alone with the little circle of our own running lights and the nearest breaking waves, had been washed away in the silver flood of light that glittered and danced across the wavetops out to the horizon. The lights of St. Kitts and Nevis, faint at best, had faded in the moonlight, and it was an empty ocean under the moon for a short spell until the first lights of Antigua came up on the bow at 0430.

As we approached them, a new set of lights came into view on the starboard quarter; we realized that they were not from an island, since they were closing with us rapidly and looming brighter as they did. Soon the red and green of running lights could be seen too. With the earliest glimmer of dawn across the water, the big white hull of a cruise ship took shape around the lights, and we could see the distinctive athwartships twin stacks of the *Doric*, a ship we had taken from New York to Bermuda several times. She passed about half a mile off on her way into St. John's, the deepwater port of Antigua, looming over the waves like a great, mobile apartment house. She was a majestic sight in the growing light when she swept on by, and before long her lights had blended with those on Antigua as she closed with the shore.

Rather than envying her passengers their luxury, I pitied them for being asleep at such a beautiful moment. Sunrise at sea, with its message of reassurance and renewal, is a lovely time of day—the freshness of new light on damp decks making you forget the dry, chalky taste in your mouth and the grainy feel in your eyes—and this was one of the most beautiful dawns I have ever seen. Antigua had a crown of clouds on its southern end, and Montserrat, off to leeward and more mountainous, had collected a great tower of cumulus. Smaller puffs of trade-wind scud were marching in from the east, and the sun, still below the horizon from our height of eye, was already sending shafts of color against the masses of clouds over the islands. Its slanting angle on Antigua picked glints of gold and paler yellow out of tumbled black and white, while Montserrat's cover, more down-sun, was bathed in glowing salmon. The colors shifted, grew brighter, faded, and glowed again, while the sun fought its way through small clouds on the eastern rim of the sea, and Antigua went through mutations of misty mauve and darker grays under the cloud shadows, gradually turning to tropical green as the sun rose and the day broadened.

We had Sandy Island off St. John's abeam at 0700, seventy-five miles in just over eleven and a half hours, and the pace of the passage slowed noticeably in the full light of day as we moved out of the trade-wind seas into the protection of the island and the lighter wind of its leeward side.

I had just relaxed in preparation for going off watch, and Jane was taking the last of her wheel trick, when I felt a strange lethargy overtake *Brunelle*, as though she were caught in molasses. I looked over the stern, and, sure enough, there was a Clorox bottle float bobbing around abaft the rudder. Shades of the Gulf of Mexico! We had caught another pot. Under sail, this is nothing like the problem of getting one on the prop under power. We killed the jib and let the main luff, and John and I took turns at cutting away. He made the crucial deep dive to get the last two turns from around the prop, and we were free again. A shallow shelf extends well to leeward of Antigua, and it is liberally speckled with pots. From then on, we kept a good lookout for them as we sailed around the southwestern tip of the island and beat our way eastward along the south shore inside Cade Reef.

Through previous cruises here and two sessions in Antigua Race Week, I was familiar with the waters. Such familiarity is always a reassurance, especially since Cade Reef, which extends for several miles and is less than a mile offshore, is a wicked collection of coral that has trapped many a vessel on the approach to English Harbour.

The entrance to it is marked by a strange natural sculpture on the high cliffs outside. A set of columns that look manmade, called the Pillars of Hercules, are set deeply into the cliff face, and if it were not for their distinctive profile, it would be easy to sail right by the narrow dogleg that leads into English Harbour. In the days of colonial warfare, when Lord Nelson based the British fleet here, this hidden entrance, and the ease of fortifying the heights around it, made it one of the best naval bases in the West Indies. Now, under the pressure of the yachting boom, boats spill over from the inner harbor and fill up Freeman Bay, the outer end of the dogleg, and the approach is not so secret any more.

One of the big, scruffy, rust-pocked schooners that run "dude cruises" through the islands was anchored on the outer edge of Freeman Bay, giving an instant identification. The rest of the bay was chock-a-block with boats at anchor when we nosed in and picked an empty spot off the beach in the officially designated quarantine anchorage. Still glowing in the pleasures of one of the more memorable sails of a lifetime, we put up our Q flag and settled down to wait for the port officials to come give us clearance.

From South to the Caribbean (1982)

The Extra Dimension

The continuing joys and special rewards of waterfront living

Last night I stood by the window as usual and gazed at the water. Except where faint reflections from houses on the other shore quivered across ripples, there was unbroken blackness until a sudden, thin shaft of white signalled that the flashing buoy at the turn of the channel was still in place. I counted out its rhythmic pattern several times before turning to bed. In a few days it would be taken away for the winter.

The buoy, with its friendly wink, is one of many water-front elements that weaves a special pattern in the fabric of our suburban existence. Inlanders envy us our summer delights and pity us our northeasters and floods, but these are the obvious things. After years of daily routine beside a salt, tidal river through all the seasons, we know and live with an extra dimension that can only be measured in the flash of a buoy, sunlight glinting on water, tide swirl, and the hum of a sea breeze through our windows.

In a house whose back door faces a suburban street and whose front gives on tide wrack, sedge bank, whitecap and fog, we are able to get back-to-nature amid the familiar pattern of commuters bound for the city, children on their way to school, and housewives driving off to the supermarket. It is a happy compromise of two conflicting worlds.

We did not have to take to the woods or cut ourselves off from the conventional life of our times, and yet, at our very doorstep, we have all those intangibles whose lure clogs highways each weekend and colors the dreams of civilization's prisoners.

And this is so, even though the river that flows by can lay small claim to the exotic and would attract little notice on a wilder stretch of coast. Here, however, in a booming New Jersey county crossed by the steel and concrete threads of a commuters' world, its microcosm of wider horizons is thankfully cherished.

The Shrewsbury River is tame as bodies of water go, small and often marred by man-made flotsam. Though called a river, it is actually a tidal flat, since its source is the sea and not the brackish creeks six miles inland, where the thrust of its tides is spent and ebbs away. Along our street it is just beginning to fan out of the narrow entrance channel from Sandy Hook Bay to a wider span of three-by-three miles. Here its shallow fingers weave southward through sandy islands, sedge banks, and salt meadows. Separated from the Atlantic by the sandspit where the houses of Sea Bright huddle together, the Shrewsbury mirrors the moods of the open sea in softer, subtler tones.

Though tame, the river dominates still. In the morning there is always a moment's pause on arising to gauge the day's promise from the color of the water, the drift of wind ruffles across its surface, the pattern of cloud reflections, and the clarity of the emptiness that means the ocean is out there beyond the houses silhouetted on the Sea Bright strip. It is with us from that first dawn glimpse till the last flicker of lights across the midnight water. It is with us through all the seasons, from the blue, white, and gold of summer to gray and dun under winter clouds, but strangely, amid nature's constant presence, a man-made sign gives us the most obvious omen of a new river year.

Spring arrives later near the water. Daffodils and forsythia bloom inland but a few hundred yards, but the ocean, slow to lose warmth in the fall, lags also in absorbing the early season rays of the sun. Blossoms and buds hesitate before the sea breezes and fog that often curtain us from a warm inland day. Not until a Coast Guard buoy tender chugs up the river in April to sow her bright, new crop and take away the ice-scarred veterans of winter, do we have tangible evidence that a new season is at hand. On the first night after the inanimate can buoy at the turn in the channel has been replaced by our familiar flasher, we stand an extra time at the window and watch the rhythm of its pinprick of light.

Nature has its own seasonal signs on the river besides the burgeoning of plants. Great rafts of broadbill that wintered between ice floes in the side channel have swept into the sky for the last time in an awesome rush of air and wing flickering, leaving only strays and native mallards behind. Flounders and eels nose their way along bottom mud on the flood tide of warm days, shore birds pause on their great migrations, and a gaggle of stately geese settles in a shallow behind an island. Osprey nests, deserted for the winter, are re-occupied in the third week in March as the birds sweep back and forth, trailing twigs and grass for repairs, and snowy egrets come to take their poised, lonely stance along the sedge banks.

Man reacts first to the fish, with heavily-bundled floun-der fishermen as the earliest arrivals. The striped bass season is open, but the initiated know that the greenheads are fur-ther south. One day, though, the casting genius who runs the tackle shop will sense the moment, after following re-ports of the northward surge of the fish, and the word goes out. Then, like a rumor come to life, the hum of outboard motors fills the newly warm air, and orange, blue, and green rowboats from the rental docks swarm to the narrow band of river that swirls under the Sea Bright drawbridge. Here, at the magic moment when the tide's seemingly unstoppable surge slows and then ceases, and the water balances in pond-like stillness for the time it takes to row a boat across it, fishermen troll and turn. They know that it is in this pause, when worms and bits of clam stop tumbling with the tide and swirl upward in the suddenly stilled waters, that the bass lunge for their food. In brief frenzy, rods curve and tremble, reels sing, and glittering green and gold fish flash their last struggle into the sunlight. Then the flow of water gathers speed in the other direction and boats head back to the dock to await another slack tide.

Ashore, there is an aroma of new rope, varnish and cop-per paint, as winter covers are peeled from boats and own-ers work in their front yards on fitting-out tasks. One by one, skiffs, bass boats, small cruisers, and sailboats slide from their cradles and bob on the surface, ready for the new sea-son.

Spring has other moments of magic by the water, as on an evening of high, still moonlight when the river runs by like liquid glass, its gurgle and murmur hushed with the night under the faintest drift of air from the sea. In the suspension of sound, even the roar of ocean surf has ceased, and then, high and clear, a faint tolling brings an awareness of a bell buoy, three miles at sea. As it heaves slowly on the gentlest of swells, its endless clangor penetrates the world inshore. Barely above an imagination of sound in the inner ear, its slow vibration seems to chime with the glance of moonbeams where a channel marker parts the tide. No steeple can be sending this hint of music into the night sky, and yet it is not a supernatural echo of quivering moonlight.

More often, the sea has a brusquer way of bringing its sound and smell to the land. When clouds scud over the sun with falling barometer and wind from an easterly quarter, the surf's tumble doubles the roar of the gale, and rain lashes the houses in bursts. Backed into the river by the weight of water thrust up on the coast, the tide rushes in with wide-shouldered power, burying buoys under its headlong rush and lapping above its usual limits of barnacled slime on bulkheads and pilings to seek strange paths across lawns and flower beds. Tide and wind funnel against each other in the narrow channel, building an awesome overfall of whitecaps.

In contrast are the blue and white days of full summer, with the faces of new cottagers a part of the scene. Our semi-suburbia has become a full resort, and we share the river with those who only know its summer aspect.

These are days of sun and breeze, of sailboats crowding down on the turning buoy in a race, of powerboats in constant passage on the river, wakes curling, flags flying, crews waving, and red and green lights flashing by after dark. Hot humming mornings give way at noon to the trade wind, cool sea air starting as a sudden ruffle across the water, until it builds to an afternoon breeze that whistles through window screens and flecks the river with whitecaps. At sunset it fades with the light, as gulls fly in high procession upriver to their night nest in the islands.

Now our life is on the river much of the time. We race the family catboat, picnic in island coves we like to think of as our own discovery, crab, clam, and fish. We sail in brisk southerlies, puffy northwesters, hot westerlies and clammy easterlies and, perhaps the best time of all, at twilight, sliding home from supper cooked on an island fire of driftwood.

While colors blaze and pale overhead and reflect in the water till it fades to a luminous, night-absorbing gray, we listen to the sounds that carry through the twilight. Our bow wave makes the softest of gurgles, and, high in the sky, sunset's last ray glints briefly on the wing of an airplane from Kennedy that climbs into the west, its drone throbbing down distantly. As it fades away, there is a void until the bark of a dog sounds from Rumson, and a lone gull cries on its flight to the islands. Two miles astern, off Little Silver Point, an outboard whines on a speed run.

Once again all sounds fade, then a whirring of wings and a soft, swift quacking sweeps by overhead. Streaking across the band of light in the west, mallards from a mainland pond head toward the Gallilee marshes for the night. As one, they veer momentarily away from the loom of our sail before steadying again on a gradual descent to the marsh. Suddenly, right alongside, a fish tail slaps the water. As we close with the shore, the high insect murmur of a summer night, the beep of car horns, and the sing of tires on a hot street close around us.

Summer moves along, and there are a few dragging days when the sea breeze deserts us and land-born heat smothers the atmosphere, but most of it passes to the breezy tune of the south wind. There are vacation hours when time is ignored as we prowl tide-bared sandbars, dragging a seine net through their intricate shallows and pouncing on the killies, shiners, baby snappers, garfish, crabs, jellyfish, shrimp, and "solly growlers" that jump and quiver in a shimmering blob when the net is lifted onto the sand. We scrabble after the disappearing necks of steamer clams in muddy sand, net crabs, and troll for the ravenous snapper blues. Soon the snappers are bigger, the south wind is stronger, and Labor Day is upon us.

Then we stand and watch the cottagers stuff suitcases, scuffed beach toys, and cardboard boxes full of seashells into their cars for the trip back to the city. They take with them the spirit of the resort, and we turn soberly to school and more rigid commuting. We are suburbia again, but the river still flows by, ours once more as boat traffic thins out, sailing races end, and each day sees fewer cars parked at the rowboat rental dock.

Autumn's lingering warmth makes up for the harshness of our spring. A deeper blue in the sky and the water brings a new sense of space. Now the sun wheels lower in the southern sky. By early afternoon its light slants across the marsh grass plumes as on a rippling cloth of gold, and its path on the water almost fills the river with a flood of brilliance. Early in October, color magic seeps into shore foliage, but in subtler shades than the reds and the yellows of the uplands. Bluish haze that legend calls smoke from Lenni Lenape campfires softens the purple and rust shoreline, and it seems to recede into distance until the river is wider and more open than ever before. These are the best days of all in a river year. They dwindle in frequency and in their own hours of sun, and the intervening ones of wind from the sea, carrying the moan of foghorns and the rumble of surf, come more often. The shoreline blends to a uniform brown, and gray is the dominant color of sky and water. Instead of autumn leaves swirling by, we have seagulls scudding in broken flight, their cries more piercing and mournful, and high swift vees of southbound ducks against the clouds.

When there are days of sun, their breeze fades at dark and a motionless night of dampness and low-hanging stars thunders with the crash of waves from some distant storm shattering themselves on the ocean beach. The lighted buoys are taken away, and we bow to the season by bringing the boat ashore to her winter cradle, fleeing northeasters and ice that will hurry by with the tide in heaped, broken floes.

Mornings come alive with the roar of shotguns, as ducks zigzag in panic over suddenly lethal marshes. When the guns are finally stilled, a dead period sets in, unless rare conditions produce iceboating and skating. Now, except for an isolated warm day when we rig the dinghy for a short sail or tramp island beaches gathering driftwood for the fireplace, the river recedes from active partnership in our lives, though we watch it still and know its moods.

We see it angry under storm-lash, smiling and gold-plated in the clearing northwester, forbidding on a day of rain and swiftly moving ice, and changed most of all when snow clouds sweep down and lose themselves in its blank grayness. The extra dimension is always there, and on those misleading mid-January days when a stray breeze from the south jumps the season by three months, we stand on the bulkhead and breathe in the soft, salt promise of the new year. Downriver we can almost hear the chug of the buoy tender.

From The Sailing Life (1974)

III

Early Days

There had to be beginnings and lessons learned

Learning to Cruise

Eager neophytes are quickly given a lesson

TWO AUGUSTS of Baby Rainbowing at Nantucket completed my preppie days, and the next three summers saw me working at summer jobs to help finance college. Uncle Billy was my tuition angel, but I had to work to earn spending money and I spent two fascinating summers as an office boy at the McGraw-Hill publishing company on West Forty-second Street in New York. I learned a lot of things that have nothing to do with this book, but I had no chance to do any sailing.

At the end of junior year, I had made enough money from student employment jobs to convince me that I didn't have to spend what loomed as the last free summer of my life working in New York. I figured I would never have the whole summer off again, and this was my last chance to do some real sailing for quite a while. Dad thought I was crazy, but Mother, romantic enough to go along with the idea, overrode him, and I went ahead with plans.

I signed up two classmates, Gordy and Frank, to split the month of August in ten-day and twenty-one-day stints, and then went looking for a boat. Through a broker in Mamaroneck, New York, at the western end of Long Island Sound, I found *Bona*, a sturdy twenty-six-foot gaff-rigged sloop of indeterminate age for the sum of $105 for the month (including broker's commission). She had been bought on the strength of a bonus the owner had received, and his son, who was taking Latin at the time, had insisted on feminizing the word for a boat name.

I was checked out by the owner and family on a Sunday afternoon, and the poor man looked as though a potential rapist was taking off with his daughter, but he still was pleasant and helpful. Gordy arrived the next morning, and, eager to be off, we threw luggage, groceries, and odds and ends of gear down the hatch helter-skelter and chugged out of the harbor into a placid Sound. As we cleared the entrance buoy, a whisper of a southwester ruffled the oily surface, so we made sail and settled back with all the confidence of Ferdinand Magellan, even though I had never handled a boat this big and Gordy had hardly sailed at all.

Throughout the warm, hazy day, the southwester built beautifully, and we swooped eastward, enjoying ourselves to the hilt on a glorious sail. I had no plan on a destination. The sailing was too great to worry about that, and we would just keep surging down the Sound, munching peanut-butter sandwiches and drinking beers. What a life!

What a life until the sun began to lower into the coppery smog on the western horizon, and I came to the realization that, as captain and navigator, I should have a port picked out for our first night's stop. By now we were passing New Haven, and I became aware, as I scanned the chart, that we had just about run out of good harbors. We had to get into some harbor before dark or sail all night, and I didn't think we were quite ready for that.

Finally I found Branford on the Connecticut shore, and that seemed to be it, though the channel was tricky-looking, winding through rocks and reefs, and it was dead downwind. That would mean several jibes, so I decided that we had better get sail off and power in. Gordy was very firm about the fact that he had no idea what "all those strings" were, so I gave him the tiller, told him to head straight into the wind, and went forward to work the halyards.

At full throttle we rounded into the seas that had been curling nicely under our transom all afternoon, and suddenly they were monstrous, steep cliffs, crashing down on us in close order in the shallower water near shore. We rose high over the first one, crashed down on the second, and went right through the third, almost washing me overboard. I shouted to Gordy to throttle her back, and started fighting the sails down as spray followed by green water continued to sweep across me. With two jibs and a gaff-rigged main, there were all sorts of strings to handle, and, between holding on as we charged over and into the seas and fighting the flailing sails, I managed to let about half of their ends go to tangle around the lazy jacks.

Somehow I managed a semblance of a furl, and we turned back toward the harbor entrance, almost rolling our bottom out as the seas came abeam, then yawed our way in past Cow and Calf and made the turn hard to starboard by Blyn Rock. The seas built higher against an ebb tide, threatening to poop us, but finally we made the entrance to Branford River and breathed a great sigh of relief in calm water, the turmoil behind us on the other side of Indian Neck.

We were inside, but there was still a tricky fore-and-aft moor to make between stakes along the edge of the channel, and it was pitch-dark by the time we had backed and filled enough to get our lines out and secure everything. It didn't help to have people on other boats watching us in tolerant amusement.

Ravenously hungry, we finally fell below to find disaster personified. The ports had never been shut, and we had not stowed our clothes or provisions. The lights didn't work, but one glimpse in the beam of a flashlight was enough. Clothes, bread, eggs, binoculars, charts, shaving cream—the works— made the most ungodly jumble imaginable. I snapped off the flashlight and we collapsed onto the sodden bunks.

As I fell asleep, I had to admit to myself that there was more to this cruising than I had realized.

From *A Sailor's Tales* (1978)

The Cruise Ends

Despite all the snafus, a great time was had—and a lifestyle confirmed

As the end of August neared, it was time to get *Bona* back to Mamaroneck, but we were having such a good time in Nantucket that we waited until the last minute to leave. We only had three days to make it, but we planned on pushing through hard.

The first day went well, with a fresh, clear northeaster giving us a fast reach to Edgartown. We weren't the fastest boat out there, though. The big seventy-two-foot yawl, *Baruna*, glossily black and the center of all admiring eyes after winning the Bermuda Race that year, had been at anchor in Nantucket when we left. We took the Tuckernuck Shoals route, and halfway across we saw her tall sails appear on the horizon behind us and rapidly sweep by to the eastward on the deep-water course via Cross Rip Lightship. When we surged into Edgartown, going about as fast as *Bona* could, *Baruna* was already snugged down at anchor looking as though she'd been there all summer.

When we left Edgartown, the motor refused to start. My father's opinion of my mechanical abilities was all too valid when it came to fixing engines, and Frank, although he had passed an ROTC course in engine repairs, had no better luck. There was a good breeze and we had no money left, so we figured we would just have to sail through, standing watches at night. I'd never done any night navigation, but I was feeling pretty salty after a month as skipper and didn't expect any trouble.

A southeaster took us around the Vineyard, and late in the afternoon we passed Vineyard Lightship and began the twenty-five-mile openwater passage to Point Judith. I decided to hit the sack for awhile before starting night watches, and I went below without telling Frank the course change to make at the Lightship.

We should have come right about 25 degrees but never did, and the resultant confusion when I came back on deck soon after dark was classic. It was a very clear night, and we were headed right for a long string of lights that stretched well to seaward of our course. I thought that it was Point Judith and that we were heading well inside it. This prompted those classic words, "This compass must be off," and we corrected our course to port to head outside the last of the lights. From then on, I couldn't make anything work right. No light or buoy agreed with any identifications I wanted to make, and I was too inexperienced to backtrack to a known spot and figure out what might have gone wrong.

Also, I never gave Block Island a thought. On our way

up, smoky sou'wester weather had kept Block Island hidden as we passed between it and Point Judith, and I mentally placed it far out to sea like Nantucket.

It was a long night's sail as the breeze lightened and we headed a bit south of magnetic west into "mystery land." As far as I knew, we were anywhere between Providence and New Haven and I was completely lost, but we just made sure there was nothing ahead of us that we could bump into. Visibility turned bad in the small hours as a damp haze settled over the ocean, and it was something of a shock when the sun came up and burned the stuff away to find ourselves outside Montauk Point on the open Atlantic. It was Block Island whose lights had confused me, and we had gone to seaward of it.

With the dawn, the breeze stopped, and it took us a full twenty-four hours to drift around Montauk and across Gardiner's bay to Plum Gut and into the Sound. We were just off Horton's Point at the next dawn, barely stemming the tide. Since we had planned to stop at night originally, we hadn't stocked up on food and had intended to buy just what we needed for the last days, so sustenance was now a real problem. In fact, all we had aboard was strawberry jam and Rice Krispies, and we had three meals of a mixed glom of them, made all the more unappetizing by the sight of an Eastern Steamship Lines ship on her way in from Nova Scotia steaming serenely by while visions of the meals being served in her dining saloon tantalized our minds.

It was a long, slow, muggy day of drifting westward u..til a southerly came in late in the afternoon and we began to make some knots. Through the evening, it headed us gradually and became stronger, until we were skinning along the Norwalk Islands hard on the wind and pounding. The inshore waters were full of oyster stakes, and, though we kept the best lookout we could, most of them only appeared when they were abeam and could be seen against the shore lights. Fortunately, we avoided being impaled.

Midnight brought a series of thunder squalls, with lightning bouncing around us and thunder filling the air. They lashed us briefly with torrents of rain and enough wind to have to shorten down to a reefed main for a while. Midnight had also brought the legal end of the charter and the end of the insurance coverage on it, and it was an anxious time of slugging into a nasty chop and keeping track of where we were. Sleep was forgotten and even the Rice Krispies were gone, so it was a bleary, weary crew that finally brought *Bona* into Mamaroneck on the failing breeze of a humid dawn.

Sounds terrible, doesn't it, but would you believe we'd had the time of our lives?

From *A Sailor's Tales* (1978)

Sailing Sitters

The practical aspects—and fun—of getting our young family into sailing way back when (1949)

One summer afternoon as the Robinson family was returning from a sail on the Shrewsbury River, the neighbors were taking the sun on their bulkhead with visitors from some inland New Jersey town. Sweeping in before the onshore breeze, we first impinged on their drowsy awareness with the unavoidable flying moor amid suddenly dropping sails, frantic grabs at pilings and a chorus of shrill squeals and barks. Then we brought them up standing with the disembarking routine that ensued.

In the approximate order, the following were transferred to the bulkhead from the cabin and cockpit of the 18-foot *Maiwara III:* one male Robinson, age 5, one female Robinson, age 3, one female friend, age 4, one lunch basket, six sweaters, two fishing poles, three toy boats, three pairs of sneakers, one pair of rubber boots, one hamburger grill, one knitting bag, one dachshund, one camera, four pieces of driftwood, eight clam shells, one broken piece of tiling, two dolls, one woolen koala bear, two thermos bottles, three empty coke bottles, three kapok cushions, one jib, one mainsail, one skipper, and one wicker basket containing three wet and two dry diapers, four rattles, a plastic duck, and an empty baby's bottle. Finally the skipper's wife stepped out carrying one female Robinson, age six months.

As each item appeared, a little gasp escaped from a gray-haired lady who was one of the visitors. When at last mother and baby climbed on the bulkhead, it was too much for the good lady.

"Oh my goodness," she cried. "You had a *baby* in there, too!"

Had she been a regular denizen of our waterfront, she would have known that there was nothing unusual about the procedure she had just seen. Every one of the many sails between May and November entails a similar operation, give or take a diaper or two. It has become second nature to us to go through a routine that would horrify many a salty character for the simple reason that we could not go sailing otherwise. The family budget barely squeezed in *Maiwara III* herself, leaving no allowance for hiring a sitter for the brood every time we wanted to take a sail. Finances aside, we happen to enjoy the family voyages, and the kids do too. There are few other pursuits in which we could all be together so pleasantly.

Friends often envy us our windjammer excursions and shake their heads when we tell them they should follow suit.

"I don't know how you do it," is the answer. "We couldn't possibly manage it with the children."

Perhaps some people would find it not worth the trouble to combine boating with raising children in the age group under 8 or 9. We do find it worthwhile, and we are far from alone, to judge from the juvenile population we see afloat while we are out in our boat. In the process, though, we have learned a few lessons on the art of keeping the family yacht a reasonably pleasant place to be, instead of an armed camp. Major sins to be avoided are staying out too long, taking risks with the weather, making too many restrictions on board, and combining a family outing with entertaining childless or otherwise nonunderstanding adults.

All our experience has been under sail, but this is no place for a sail-vs-power argument. In general, though, there are fewer physical problems in managing children aboard a powerboat, but less variety and excitement to keep them permanently interested. The whole subject of boating with children has as many variables as there are babies, but an analysis of *Maiwara III* and her usual routine might illuminate some factors that can be generally adapted and applied.

She is a round-bottom, lapstrake, 18′ x 7′ x 1′8″ keel sloop with inboard ballast, cuddy cabin, four horsepower aircooled engine, and slightly under-rigged at 140 square feet of sail. That draft figure is not a misprint. Her long, shallow keel draws a maximum of 20 inches but is efficient enough for windward work. She will never win any races, and it takes considerable coaxing to bring her about, but this is a minor disadvantage compared to the joy of handling her draft in the shallow Shrewsbury River. One of our great delights is to beat past the clam diggers standing in water not much over their knees on the flats. Many a plug of tobacco has been swallowed at the sight of our cargo of towheads breezing gaily by on the wind, and the bug-eyed look becomes complete when a small voice pipes, "Gettin' many today?"

Aside from providing opportunities for conversation with clammers at work, *Maiwara*'s underbody is ideal for beaching. She can be run right into shore on an even keel for picnics and exploration trips. Centerboarders have the same ability, but we are free from the cluttering nuisance of the trunk, with its propensity for pinching small fingers and its lure as a dropping hole for items like spoons and bottle openers. When we run aground, which often happens on the flats, the routine is for the entire family to climb onto the forward deck while the skipper goes overboard to push. He never gets his shorts wet in summer, and in colder weather hip boots are high enough to keep him dry.

The good beam and lack of centerboard make for a roomy cockpit despite the cuddy, and that small space itself is a godsend. In addition to its remarkable capacity for absorbing most of the paraphernalia listed above, as well as a portable icebox which remains there most of the time, it assumes numerous other functions. The baby naps there in peace, the older kids play house in it, and it keeps everything and everybody except the skipper dry and warm when the weather happens to take a turn for the damper or chillier. We have yet to use it for overnight sleeping, but the eldest has been promised a cruise for this summer.

The inboard rig, free of running backstays and other complications, is easy to handle, an important consideration when the skipper must always have one eye for the ship and one for his crew. An auxiliary engine of some sort is a must. An engine does away with the uncertainty of the time element, an important consideration when sailing with children, as a long, becalmed, be-gnatted wait in the evening twilight with a bunch of tired kids who should be home in bed is something to be avoided. It was also a comfort to have an auxiliary when the three-year-old stepped on a rusty nail on an island during a picnic. Civilization was dead to windward, but under power we had her at the doctor's getting a tetanus booster within 20 minutes of her first yelp of pain.

There is no room for a marine head in the cuddy, of course, and a galvanized bucket has to serve. Actually, it is much simpler to move the mountain to Mahomet than vice versa in this problem, but so far no solution has been found for preventing crises in this department from arising at the most inopportune times, such as when making a mooring, tacking in a narrow channel, or starting the engine.

So much for the boat. She is far from the only kind of boat that can be used for family outings, but her special characteristics should point up solutions to the situation. Now for handling the younger generation on board.

The number one rule, and one that is never broken is: always wear life jackets. We are horrified at the number of times we see children without them on passing boats. They are a must. Our older two can both swim enough to keep themselves afloat for a few minutes, but not long enough for us to come about and get back to them should they fall over. They accept jackets without protest as a natural part of going in the boat. We made a special effort to have them swim early so that they would respect the water without fearing it, and they can also swim around with jackets on. Until they are older and are proven distance swimmers, though, we will insist on jackets. With them on, the kids can move about the boat freely without disturbing parental peace of mind. The added freedom, both of motion and from the nagging plaints of "be careful" makes for a lot more fun for all hands. A favorite post is the forward deck, where they lie with their heads over the bow watching the stem cut through the water, and they work off surplus energy by making a circuit of deck, cockpit, cabin, forward hatch, and foredeck playing pirates or just plain chasing each other. With jackets on, this can go on with a minimum of adult twinging, but in heavy weather, of course, everyone stays in cockpit or cabin.

We keep a couple of extra jackets for young friends who come along. Bringing their friends makes a special treat out of the sail for our kids and for the visitors, and in most cases they serve to entertain each other, taking the burden off the grownups. Surprisingly, we have found that most children will mind better on a boat than they will on dry land after being forewarned of the sacred status of the captain and the heinous horrors of mutiny. This is provided, of course, that you have seen enough of the friend to know that his parents are not believers in unlimited "self-expression" for their little darlings.

Naturally we play it conservatively on wind and weather. Some of our outings on blustery autumn days are one-tenth sailing and nine-tenths picnic in the lee of a clump of bayberry bushes on an island. We also have to forego venturesome voyages to distant parts in favor of protected waters close to home. In our case, we have yet to make the passage through the river and Sandy Hook Bay to the ocean because of our juvenile cargo. Wider horizons will have to wait, and we are lucky to have a protected river, filled with uninhabited islands, at our doorstep. The islands make wonderful spots for picnics and exploration, and they are also important because they provide an objective of some sort for the trip. Breaking it up with a landing party is a good idea.

Sometimes we anchor and fish, but the patience needed for real angling comes a little later in life than the age we have been dealing with so far. A diversion that usually causes excitement is to heave-to near a turning buoy when the Lightnings and Comets are out racing to watch the rounding maneuvers. Another favored pursuit, especially when there are friends to swell the volume of sound, is to line the cabin top to cheer and wave wildly at all passing craft, climaxing the greeting with synchronized whoops as each wave of the other boat's wake hits us. Towing toy boats astern sometimes helps to keep them entertained.

There are times when all these fail, life gets a little dull, and the group gets whiney and restless. This is the moment for the icebox to be opened, as a strategically offered bottle of soda and a couple of cookies tide over many a minor crisis. In more serious straits, the skipper sometimes has to tell sea stories, and sometimes, to the consternation of all clam diggers to leeward, we end up singing.

The baby presented special problems that were solved progressively in her first summer. Before she could sit up, she was no problem at all, reposing peacefully in a basket in the cuddy. Before the season ended she had advanced to a car chair that was suspended from the cockpit coaming as it would be from the back of an auto seat. She seemed to enjoy herself as much as anyone else. She was too small for a life jacket, and her mother was specifically responsible for her in the "abandon ship" bill. Another summer will find her in the life jacket set, too.

We make very little effort at formal nautical instruction. The terminology comes through repeated hearing of it. (Certain other terminology that occasionally comes to the surface when the engine won't start is something else again). As the whim hits them, they sometimes ask to steer or hold a sheet, and they are allowed to do it for as long as they want to, if conditions permit. They are told when they are doing a good job; errors are corrected by telling them the right way, without censure. We want the process to be painless over several seasons, with a sort of osmosis doing most of the work. The son and heir, to get into the act, has asked for such jobs as handling the anchor (a $4^1/_2$ pound Danforth) and the jib halyard, and rowing the dink to and from the mooring. He was given them as his province once he was doing them right. In time, Pop expects to give just one order: "Let's go sailing today."

So far it has been fun. We feel sorry for those who tell us their children keep them off the water, and we think they are missing something. Each year has brought so many changes, though, that one can never be sure of a permanent solution. Now that we have the cowboy craze to consider, and now that the baby has changed from a stay-put basket case to a scrambling, ambulatory, unreasonable whirlwind of 18 months, the sequel to this article just might turn out to be "How to Make a Flower Box Out of an Old 18-Foot Sloop."

From *The Sailing Life* (1974)

The Next Generation

And so it continued; Sam, herein, is the son of the 3-year old in the previous piece

One of the best times I have ever had with a member of the younger generation was in taking grandson Sam, just before his eighth birthday, on a "cruise" in our 18-foot catboat, which is our home waters daysailer. It was just an overnight affair, with a day of sailing out in Sandy Hook Bay to start. This means a trip down river from our home pier, negotiating two drawbridges, one of which has to be blown for, always a thrill for a kid. Once out in the bay we had a fine sail, with the skyscrapers of New York on view to the north, big tankers going by in the Sandy Hook Channel, freighters in sight in Ambrose Channel farther out from us, and Navy ships at the long ammunition pier for Earle N.A.D. There was all sorts of traffic, mostly in sportsfishing boats in and out of the river, other sailboats, and a few commercial fishermen. Sam took the tiller for longer than he ever had before, really excited by the feel of control. I think it was the first time he had ever had the real feel of steering a boat under sail, always a thrilling moment.

Late in the afternoon, we powered back up the river past our house and had a late sail on the way to an anchorage in one of the creeks at the very head of the Shrewsbury.

Sam also handled the outboard, which was another new experience for him, and I think he enjoyed steering under power almost as much as the sailing. We anchored in a quiet dead end of the creek, with sedge grass on the banks surrounding us and the sun lowering over marshes and trees inland. No other boats were near us, but some resident boats rode quietly to moorings further out the creek. After cocktails, a Seven Up for Sam and a martini for me, I cooked hamburgers and canned peas on a portable Sterno stove, and we settled in for the night with Sam playing with the shortwave bands on the portable radio, excited at claiming to have Japan tuned in. After breakfast in the morning, we headed home after one of the best times, a proof of how that age reacts.

———

From *Cruising the Easy Way* (1990)

Cruising with Teen-agers

Adjusting to making cruising en famille work during these often difficult years

Doesn't anyone ever cruise with teen-agers?

Over the years I have noted the existence of a vast literature on how to handle children under ten in a boat, but there has been silence about the next decade in a family's growth. We are heir to reams of advice on how to rig a kiddie coop in the cabin and the best way to clear zwieback from the bilge pump, but what of the terrible teens?

How to cruise successfully with, in our case at the moment, a boy 17 and girls 15 and 12, or any combination thereof? They like to cruise, we like them with us. No longer, though, does a walk from the harbor to the drugstore for an ice cream cone rate as the big treat of an evening in port, and we can't get away any more with having them chase mallards round the anchorage in the dinghy as a cocktail hour dodge.

Do the mothers who write articles in starry-eyed confidence about life afloat with toddlers get fed up with togetherness and subside, punch-drunk, into silence when the dreaded teen years approach? When we entered that era, we found we were on our own. With the Dr. Spock years astern, no ready reference was available, yet I know parents do take teen-agers along. We have even seen Dr. Spock cruising with his. To fill the gap, then, and to warn parents who think they have it made when there are no longer diapers drying in the rigging and plastic toys underfoot, here is a father's report on the strangely neglected subject.

As I see it, a cruise with teen-agers is possible, and can be successful, if it is planned to go from movie to movie via restaurants, with rock-and-roll music (I guess that's what it is) available on the radio at all times. Each passage should start in mid-morning (or later), end in early afternoon, and include a stop for swimming and snorkeling. At least every third day should be spent in port.

To show how their minds run, here is a typical afternoon conversation between one of the girls and me as we are lazing comfortably along in, say, Nantucket Sound. She has been reading—a novel or underwater adventure book, perhaps; a comic book more likely. The other one is doing her hair curled up on the forward bunk and strange wails and slurping sounds issue from the radio, which she has cradled next to her tummy. Mother is reading drowsily.

"Where are we going in tonight, Dad?" Alice asks.

"Vineyard Haven, maybe." (I would have preferred Hadley's Harbor and its quiet, uncivilized isolation, but I know better.)

"What's it like?"

"Well, it's a little old town at the head of a big harbor with lots of boats. It's where the ferry from Woods Hole comes in."

"Have you ever been there?"

"Yes."

"When?"

"Oh, a long time ago."

"How big is it?"

"Maybe a couple of thousand."

"Has it got stores and things?"

"I think so."

"What kind of stores?"

"Drugstore, grocery, gift shop, you know."

And this game can go on for hours, but at this point I usually break down and end it by saying, " . . . and I don't know whether it has a movie."

"Do you think it might?"

"Yes, it might."

Meanwhile, Martha has stopped doing her hair for a moment and has turned down the volume on the radio. She takes my wallet down from the bunk shelf, pulls out the Diner's Club booklet and starts to leaf through it.

"Massachusetts, Massachusetts—we're not back to Rhode Island, are we?" she asks. "What place did you say?"

"Vineyard Haven."

"I don't see it anywhere."

"Guess we eat aboard then," I say.

"Oh, gee," the girls sigh.

The conventional cruising guides do not have all the vital information for this kind of operation. They do not give radio schedules (I mean disc jockeys, not navigation beacons), or the location of movie theaters, bowling alleys, and amusement parks. Never mind about the type of holding ground or the availability of ice and fuel. How near the waterfront is the cinema palace?

Your idea of a perfect cruising harbor may be a snug cove with not another boat in sight and a shoreline unmarred by signs of human habitation, but don't go there on this kind of voyage. You'll want to see signs, preferably neon, as you move into the harbor entrance, and one of them had better read "Pizza," come to think of it. Also, as the cruise progresses and the wallet grows thinner, that chaste little Diner's Club sign on the door of a restaurant becomes an increasingly important one. Eventually, it always ends up as the only way we can eat ashore.

Scenery is "nice" to teen-agers, but they can take it in very quickly, and then they want to get ashore and do some exploring. The psychology is akin to liberty in the navy. Each new port is a challenge. Even after a passage of a few miles there is a great itch to get ashore there. If it only offers sand dunes and empty beaches, it passes as a lunch stop, but once the sun goes down and the lights come on, there had better be some sort of lights on shore.

A cruising boat must be big, and have excellent reading lights for each individual, to keep teen-agers happy aboard in the evening. We have cruised on everything from 24 to 80 feet with ours, and even after a couple of nights in an 80-footer in the Exumas, they were ready to get back to some sort of activity ashore. Hours of skin diving and snorkeling made them sleepy enough to cut down the restlessness for a few evenings, but then that "liberty port" psychology began to set in.

While under way, teen-agers take care of entertaining

themselves pretty well. The stratagems for keeping tiny tots happy need not be employed. Gone are the coloring books, the stuffed animals, and the plastic toys. They enjoy most ship's business, including wheel tricks, and can be fed a modicum of practical navigation. If properly instructed, they can be as good as most adults and better than some in line handling, anchoring, sail handling, and other such maneuvers. When things are quiet, they can be kept happy with a supply of soft drinks, books, and cards. Our girls can play one or two games of cards, chess or checkers before the hair-pulling starts, and our son is one of the more accomplished sack artists in America. And then there is the radio.

Don't think you can avoid rock-and-roll music just because you're getting away from that station that drives you nuts at home. When we trailed to Miami to cruise in the Keys a couple of years ago I smiled smugly when the New York stations faded from the dial. At last I would be rid of "that" station and its pack of idiot announcers. Miami, however, had not one but several that sounded just like it, only worse. The kids have shown a remarkable knack for locating such outlets in places like Providence, R.I., Cleveland, Ohio, and Kingston, Ont. Even in the far reaches of the Exumas they exhibited a second sense that could tell when ZedNS in Nassau was going to play American music that sounded as though we'd never left home. And Miami came through at night, of course.

Housekeeping afloat with teen-agers is difficult, especially in something as small as our 24-footer. The jumble that can develop in a few minutes in the cabin of a small boat has to be seen to be believed, and it is enough to keep a mother in a constant state of helpless defeat. The kids seem content to live like trader rats for the whole time they are aboard, burrowing into their own little pile of supplies for whatever is needed at the moment, but adults have to keep this sort of thing under control if they want to hold on to their sanity.

We provide one bunk-net for each person. They are always organized with the greatest of care when the cruise starts. But as each day goes by and more objects have been stuffed into them hastily when Mother says "all right, let's pick it up," they become great bristling, bulging lumps. The clothes are balled up into odd shapes, with books, magazines, towels, hair curlers, foul weather gear, souvenir postcards, sea shells, fishing lines, make-up kits, diaries, stationery boxes, and many more mysterious objects jammed together. Each search for an object produces a more complicated jumble, and a deepening of the crisis. By the last couple of days it is impossible to lie on the bunk when the net is rigged, and the nets are therefore placed on the floorboards next to the bunks, making the cabin sole at bedtime resemble the back room of a Salvation Army depot. Sometimes it gets so bad the nets have to be completely reorganized.

Starting out in the morning, when the cabin is a solid mass of bulging bunk nets, can present its problems. I have been known to slip up on deck at daybreak, make sail by myself, and have several hours of quiet sailing before the others wake up. If I get up with the others and wait to get under way until they have everything organized, it can mean that we never do get going. Of course, the weather has to be good for this solo stuff, but I enjoy it, everyone else appreciates the sleep, and I don't have to help pick up the cabin. Sometimes we even anchor for a late breakfast after several hours of sailing.

Cruising with female hairdos is one of the biggest problems a skipper has to contend with, and when the females are in their teens the situation is at its most serious. Fresh water is a must at frequent intervals, curlers and bobby pins turn up in every corner of the boat, and almost every maneuver calling for help from the crew is ill-timed because someone is putting her hair up or down. For this reason, one of our most successful cruises was on Lake Ontario, where the girls spent a good part of the trip in the lake washing their hair. We didn't get much sailing in, but we sure used a lot of soap.

As can be seen, most of the teen-age problems we have had have been feminine ones. When everyone was younger, we all cruised together, but a 17-year-old boy has plans of his own, as well as summer employment. When he did cruise with us, he objected mildly to being a "sailing babysitter" and having to go to the movies with his sisters. He was much happier on nights when he could go exploring on his own. Now he uses the boat by himself with schoolmates for crew, and I sometimes join them for a stag operation. They make a raffishly effective racing crew, and there is no problem about entertaining them afloat or ashore. They have their own world, and all they need an adult for is a bit of cash now and then.

When we were all on board together, we not only had the problem of hitting a port where there was something to do on shore. Sometimes we also had a hard time getting away from one. After two days at Ocean Reef Club on Key Largo, for instance, the children had made so many friends ashore there that it was difficult to tear them away. The young man had found himself a lady love and was seldom to be seen, and the girls entered into the group of youngsters there as though they were staying for life. For a couple of days, in order to use the boat at all, we had to just go day sailing out to the reefs, inviting new-found friends along and come back in at night. The girls were just as loath to leave Nantucket after a few days there on another cruise, but we finally were able to tear them away when the Dreamland Movie Theater had to shut down because the films failed to arrive on the steamer.

Each family has its own systems and operational methods, and teen-agers can vary as much as adults. There may be some who love to go off for two weeks of isolated cruising with nothing but seashell collecting on empty beaches to keep them happy, but I have yet to meet them. It might seem, from some of the problems outlined here, that it is hardly worth it at all to cruise with kids during the difficult years. Strangely enough, we have enjoyed each expedition and keep planning on more.

As I plan, though, I am engaging in a secret search. I am looking for a cruising area out of range of disc jockeys.

From *The Sailing Life* (1974)

IV

Our Boats

Background on the boats that kept the Robinsons afloat and happy over the years

Choosing a Boat

Some lessons we have learned about what to look for in choosing our boats

Putting it all together for a "perfect cruising day" doesn't just happen. The days when everything goes right can only be the product of thought and preparation, of the working out of many details and compromises.

It is an absolutely valid cliché about cruising boats that every boat is a compromise, or we would have one stock design instead of the multiple choices available in sail and power. My experience as owner of four cruising auxiliaries between 24 and 42 feet, and frequent cruiser under the OPBYC (Other People's Boats Yacht Club) burgee, almost all under sail, has been that every time I board a boat to cruise,

I am instantly aware of the truth of the cliché. Every inch of every boat, from bow to stern, is made up of compromises of some sort, and they must be balanced in evaluating and choosing a boat.

The first consideration is the type of cruising to be done, ranging from marina-hugging in apartmentlike power-boats to world-girdling passagemaking of the hairiest chested variety. The boat must be suited to the purpose in the best way possible. For most of us, the bulk of cruising is done, of course, in local waters for weekends and vacations, and the dream of far horizons can be answered, in a way, by chartering in more exotic areas. More and more people, however, are taking off for extended cruising over long periods of time. They may be retirees released at last from the daily grind and taking advantage of newfound free time, but many cruising sailors are doing this at an early age, not waiting for the "golden years" before they bust loose.

And so these are the starting considerations in choosing a boat:

Cost, both of purchase and operating
Suitability to area
Suitability to those who will be using her
Comfort in relation to performance
Looks vs. function
Rig
Draft (governed by hull form)

And so the compromises that affect an individual situation must be considered and met as well as possible. The first one, naturally, is a personal matter. It is folly to fall in love with a boat that will be a financial burden, crimping plans right from the start. Cost is not just the price tag on the boat itself. Unless the vessel is fully found, the cost of outfitting her must be considered, and then the running cost of operating expenses, maintenance, and insurance. For those who cut all ties from house and home, these can be considered cost-of-living expenses, not just the price of recreational pleasure.

Many long-distance voyagers and live-aboards still in their vigorous years supplement their income by interrupting continuous cruising and taking temporary jobs in different areas. Perhaps the top skill in making this sort of arrangement possible is to be a good mechanic. They are in demand everywhere, and an enterprising sailor can do quite well as a free-lance mechanic. I am the opposite, always in need of help for anything more complicated than changing a light bulb, and I have been delighted to hire such free-lancers in out-of-the-way harbors when trouble developed. The fully retired of a more elderly stripe might find it harder to get temporary work, and the whole project should thus be suited to the retirement budget. Nonetheless, it is always helpful to be a do-it-yourselfer.

There are basic compromises to balance: comfort and ease of handling vs. performance; looks vs. function; rig; draft; construction method; use of space for specific purposes; total number of berths possible for the actual living space. These are major, but each boat has many more minor ones throughout the layout. Bill Lapworth, one of the 20th century's most successful yacht designers, has had a basic rule in designing boats of any size: Boats are for people. Whether it was a Cal-20 or a 60-footer, he has kept this in mind as a rule of thumb, and his boats as a result are always comfortable to be aboard, above and below decks, for the right number of people. Some designers have ignored this, scaling the proportions of a good-looking 40-footer down to a 24-footer that might be lovely to look at but would be about as comfortable as a dog kennel.

It is surprising how often a love affair with a boat's looks ends up in ownership of an unsuitable choice. People who sail on shallow bays or inland waters end up owning husky cruisers such as a replica of Joshua Slocum's *Spray* or a Tahiti ketch for sentimental reasons, and severely limit their use. Other sailors have taken off on world voyages in cockleshells that should be confined to inland waters. Sometimes they make it, sometimes they don't. My own boats have been chosen for function and have not always been the most beautiful boats around, but "handsome is as handsome does," and function comes first for me. The reverse of this is the practice of completely ignoring looks in an attempt to get full headroom in a 20-footer, for example, with a monstrosity as a result. And, as an aside, hotshot ocean racing boats built to beat the International Offshore Rule measurement can sometimes come out looking like a nightmare distortion of a decent sailboat.

Powerboats are even more likely to suffer distortion in the interests of space and accommodations, often seeming to be higher than they are long, or giving the impression that someone forgot to append the after half.

Accommodations and layout should make sense in relation to how the boat is to be used. A family with young children, doing mostly weekending, can benefit from the practice some builders have of cramming as many bunks as possible in a minimum space. Everyone knows everyone and the situation can be kept well in hand. If several adult couples try to fit into the same layout, chaos can result, with someone suddenly realizing that he is brushing somebody else's teeth instead of his own. If the plan is to have guests aboard frequently this should be considered, with privacy a governing factor. If a live-aboard couple wants as much room as possible for themselves and guests be damned, a completely different type of layout should be chosen. I have seen a 50-footer that was laid out expressly for one couple, with a great big stateroom and a roomy lounge, and only one head, where the only sleeping space for guests brash enough to remain overnight was a convertible settee in the main lounge.

Offshore passagemaking calls for very different bunks from the kind of coastal cruising in which stops are made every night. In fact, offshore passages call for special considerations in every department, and an entirely different breed of boat.

In the "good old days," a cruising boat and an ocean racer were one and the same. In fact, the basic philosophy of the early ocean races such as the Bermuda Race, the Transpac, the Mackinac, and the occasional transatlantic race, was to prove that cruising sailboats could safely venture offshore. Today, the breeds are mutually incompatible, and the cruising boat owner who wants to race has a difficult time of it. The IOR made it impossible for a well-found, comfortable cruising boat to do well in offshore racing, which led to the development of the IMS (International Measurement System) in an attempt to rate all types of boats for distance racing. It has allowed some older cruising boats to be competitive, but as soon as designers start turning out boats for the IMS, the well-rounded boat will again be in trouble.

At a level below the grand prix ocean racing events, it is possible to combine cruising and racing when a rating formula like PHRF (Performance Handicap Rating Formula), which rates boats on the basis of past performance of the type, is used. Many clubs use this for local racing, and the term cruiser/racer is no longer an anomaly. This is a solution that many owners are comfortable with. Another solution is to own a boat that has one-design racing as a class, a growing trend in many areas, as more and more sailors become fed up with the complexities of rating systems and the rapid obsolescence they foster. Because so many IOR boats have to be quickly discarded like so many squeezed–out toothpaste tubes, the trend has been to PHRF and one-design.

It is still a fact that the amenities that make a boat right for cruising, such as bow-chocked anchors, big refrigerators, extra heads and well-built, solid lockers, bulkheads and other below-decks fittings, are all wrong for getting the ultimate speed potential out of a boat. However, the extra fractions of knots that eliminating these features accomplishes are really not that important, so performance ratings and one-design racing can be thoroughly rewarding. For ultimate speed, choose a high-tech catamaran like the San Diego Yacht Club's America's Cup defender in 1988, but expect no other useful purpose to be served. A cruising boat owner needs a well-rounded boat.

And speaking of catamarans, there are multihulls that are used for cruising, and they have some fanatical devotees. Circumnavigations have been made in catamarans and trimarans, and they can obviously be made to go faster than monohulls if that is the intent. In general, they are cheaper to build than monohulls of similar overall length, and they can be fitted out with cruising amenities quite easily.

That's the good news. The bad news is that they have one serious, basic safety flaw: they can capsize. Once capsized, they cannot be righted. Other drawbacks are the need for strong construction of the connections between the hulls, as failures are common here, and the amount of space they take up in mooring areas and marinas. If all yachts were multihulls, marinas would require much more space than they do now for the same number of boats. Also, multihulls are extremely sensitive to excess weight, which means that every ounce of cruising amenities counts.

Rig is of course one of the major considerations in choosing a cruising boat. By far the greatest number of cruising boats are single stickers, which is only natural. Divided rigs have their adherents, and often with good reason, but they are in the minority.

In my opinion, a divided rig on a boat under 40 feet

overall is not necessary or advisable. There may be certain areas, circumstances, and special purposes where a ketch, yawl, or schooner this small has strong points, especially in cat-rigged boats, but not as a general rule. The extra stick gets in the way of the cockpit; extra sails, spars and rigging cost money; and sailing performance is not usually as efficient as on a single-masted boat in this size range.

The advantages of a divided rig are in the smaller size of each sail, which makes for ease of handling; the greater number of sail combinations possible, both in crowding on sail and in reducing it by stages; and the heavy weather practice of using two very small sails, such as jib and jigger (mizzen). All these advantages become much more obvious and helpful the larger the boat is, while the bigger a single-masted boat is, the harder it is to handle the main and headsails. In the 40-foot size range the choice of rig is wide open, and either single mast or divided rig can be easily handled, but if a cruising boat is bigger, the divided rig has more appeal and usually makes more sense.

Divided rig almost always means ketch nowadays in the cruising boat field. The yawl, with its minimum mizzen mast, was mainly developed as a rule beater under some ocean racing rating formulas of the past. Some sail area was "unpaid for" on yawls, which made them attractive for ocean racing, but for cruising, the larger mizzen of a ketch makes more sense. In that favorite heavy weather tactic of divided-rig sailors, jib and jigger, there is better control and power with the large mizzen. I must say that I have had some delightful heavy weather sails jogging along on a reach under that combination, with everything nicely under control, and good speed, while the wind howled. In light air, it is fun to add a mizzen staysail and feel the extra power, but all this only makes sense in larger boats.

The schooner is a rig that still delights traditionalists, and it has its points, especially in its power off the wind. It is not as easy to shorten to a two-sail combination in a schooner as in a ketch, nor is the balance as good. Schooners have never been noted for their windward ability, and this is particularly true in smaller ones. When a big schooner is barreling along on a broad reach in a good blow, however, there is a wonderful feeling of controlled power. One of the most exciting sails I have ever had was in the replica schooner *America* (108 feet LOA), hitting 14 knots on a broad reach in a 30-knot breeze in the Baltic.

A modern version of the schooner, developed in Europe but now seen in all waters, has a rig of two masts of equal height with equal marconi sails. This is a fairly efficient sailing rig, with easily handled sails, and several easy combinations for reducing sails in a blow. For this rig to be efficient, however, the boat should be in the 50-foot range or larger.

———————

From *Cruising the Easy Way* (1990)

Our Four Boats

The Robinson yachts and why we chose them—and enjoyed them

The Sanderling Catboat

The catboat concept probably offers the most cubic feet of usable space per foot of overall length of any small cruising boat, and it is a wonderful compromise until the sail area becomes too big for efficient and safe handling. I would say that 18 to 22 feet is the ideal range for catboats to be used for cruising. Over that, if you happen to be caught in a

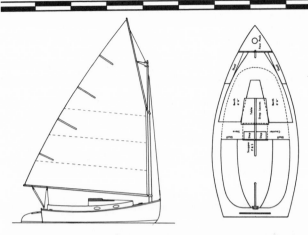

The Sanderling 18-foot catboat 18½" x 17'9" x 8'6" x 1'7"

squall or in an increasing wind on a run, handling the sail can be anything from a problem to impossible.

Our 18-foot catboat *Polly* is a Sanderling, the class name given to the specific model developed by Breck Marshall of South Dartmouth, Massachusetts, who also designed a 22-footer on the same principles. He took the classic Cape Cod cat, a design going back to the early nineteenth century, and adapted it to modern materials. The weakness of the old Cape Cod cat, which was designed for offshore fishing single-handed out of the shallow bays of the cape, was in the weight of the solid wooden mast placed right in the bow. This required a broad, flat bow to support the mast, and thus the boats were poor to windward. Also, the weight of the telephone pole mast made them root and broach on a run or broad reach, causing a heavy, sometimes impossible, weather helm. By using a hollow aluminum mast, Marshall could make the bow much finer, with hollowed sections, and the Sanderling's windward performance is very good.

Downwind control has also been improved, and the Sanderling is a lively, able sailer. She can take rough seas better than most boats her size.

As an 18-footer, she has cabin accommodations equal to many 22-footers, with sitting headroom, a head, and a shelf that can be used for a portable stove. There is stowage under the bunks, and shelves could be added above them for more stowage if desired. Water bottles and an ice chest have to be portable but can fit under the cockpit seats, and lamps and running lights are also portable and self-contained.

A six-horsepower outboard is about right for power. Bigger than that, the power is wasted, and the motor is too hard to manhandle on and off the bracket. We have used a four-horsepower motor with perfectly adequate performance, perhaps a half knot less than boats with a six, and it is a joy to handle on and off the bracket and to stow under a cockpit seat or on the cabin sole when not in use.

For camp cruising in areas like Cape Cod, Great South Bay, Barnegat, the Chesapeake, and the Florida Keys and Florida west coast, this kind of boat makes a lot of sense, and I would love to have one in the Exumas some day for the ultimate in gunkholing.

There are two sets of reef points. It is not all that easy to put in a reef while underway because of the long overhang of the boom beyond the transom, but once a reef is in she handles like a baby. I have only had a double reef once, in about a 30-knot breeze, and again she handled beautifully.

Some modernists look askance at a gaff rig, but it makes much more sense with the mast right in the bow, where no shrouds are possible. Also, there is the old-fashioned advantage of "scandalizing" the sail by dropping the peak if a sudden emergency arises, reducing the sail area by one-third.

In our home club, the Sanderling is raced as a one-design and provides extremely even competition, and there are extra dividends in comfortable day sailing, supper parties and picnics under sail, overnighting, and cruising. For family camp cruising, a cockpit tent can be rigged to make bunk space out of the cockpit seats. Our club members have ranged as far as Cape Cod and the Chesapeake in their boats.

The Amphibi-Ette

This 24-footer, smallest of the Controversy type promoted in the 1950s by Farnham Butler and Cy Hamlin of Mount Desert Island, Maine, was the first cruising boat I owned, launched in March 1958, and I literally wrote a book about her (*New Boat*, published in 1961 and long since out of print). I don't propose to do that again here, but she did have a lot of interesting, and at the time innovative, features (and incidentally, her fourth owner was going strong with her entering the 1980s).

We owned *Mar Claro* for nine years and she suited us

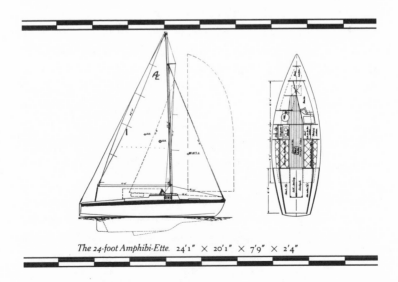

The 24-foot Amphibi-Ette. 24'1" × 20'1" × 7'9" × 2'4"

well at the time, both financially and nautically. Our children were in their teens and all five of us could manage to fit into her at the same time, with the three females tripling up in the very ample double bunk forward. She was trailable and we were at an adventurous age, taking her to the Great Lakes, Maine, southern New England, Florida, and the Bahamas, mostly on the strength of her trailability.

It was the idea of Butler, who conceived and promoted her, and Hamlin, who did the specifics of the design, to produce a light-displacement, trailable boat that would be inexpensive (since weight governs the price of a boat to a very large extent), and much roomier than conventional boats her size through the use of reverse sheer and a convertible cabin hood. (This type was called Controversy because the ideas were contrary to tradition.) Since conventionally planked wooden boats that needed caulking and dried out when out of water were not adaptable to trailing, she had to be of seamless construction (this was in prefiberglass days). Her bottom, a rounded hull flaring to a hard chine, was strip-planked, and her topsides were a specially coated plywood. In the nine years we had her she never leaked a drop, and she was no more difficult to maintain than a fiberglass boat since painting her topsides was no more of a problem than keeping a fiberglass boat waxed, and all boats need antifouling on the bottom. The biggest maintenance problem was the canvas hood, which gave her full headroom in the main cabin, and a double cockpit, with or without navy top, in good weather. This tended to deteriorate and had to be replaced twice while we owned her. The modern pop-top used in quite a few boats in this size range is an outgrowth of the Controversy hood.

As I have mentioned, I like to keep equipment as simple as possible, so she had no running water, a Sterno stove, and an icebox compartment that was built to take a portable chest. She was livable if simple, very little ever went wrong, and we spent as much as two weeks at a time in her in adequate comfort. Without the full headroom under the hood, I doubt if we would have wanted to stay aboard this long.

Her keel-centerboard underbody, with a draft of 2 feet 4 inches, allowed real gunkholing, and she was the best boat for the Exumas we've ever been in. She sailed well enough to windward with her keel, so that we only used the board when racing. She was fast enough to win her share of races and regattas, including a first in Off Soundings once; able enough to handle a 55-knot squall in the Gulf Stream with no difficulty; and stiff in a blow since she was relatively underrigged. On a broad reach in a blow, her chines picked her up on a semiplane, and she could go well over hull speed, often staying with 40-footers boat for boat.

She would look old-fashioned now, despite her reverse sheer, against modern fiberglass slickers, but she was ahead of her time when she was new, and a lot of the ideas in her that were new then have since become accepted as standard.

The OI 36

The Morgan Out Island 36 was developed from the mold of a Morgan 38 that was designed as an ocean racer under the Cruising Club of America Rule. When that was replaced by the International Offshore Rule in the late 1960s, use was made of the now-outmoded oceanracing mold by adapting an Out Island layout to the 38-foot hull. The result was a cruising boat that sailed remarkably well in comparison to most boats with the same number of accommodations. The OI 36 failed to achieve wide popularity, however, because the main cabin was not quite roomy enough to ap-

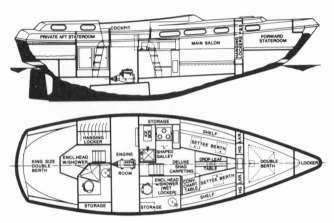

The Morgan Out Island 36. 35'10" x 28' x 11' x 3'9"

peal to motorboat owners who were switching to sail. They wanted saloon-like space and had no idea about sailing qualities, and this was the market the OI line had to appeal to. After the OI 36 went out of production, enough people had learned of its special qualities to make it a sought-after used boat.

We owned the OI 36 *Tanagra* for five years and were very pleased with her on almost all counts. We chose her for the same reasons that led us to the CSY 37—size range, two private cabins with separate heads, shallow draft, and sailing ability. We cruised in her from Cape Cod to the Exumas over several seasons and found her livable and able. We did agree that the main cabin was small, as was the forward stateroom, and the cockpit could also have been a bit roomier, but the after cabin was very roomy and comfortable. On the few occasions when we cruised with six people, conditions were quite crowded and it is always inconvenient and awkward at breakfast time to reconvert the dinette from night duty as a bunk.

In an attempt to overcome adverse reactions to the dinette version of the main cabin, Morgan came out with a layout that put the galley to port and the head to starboard immediately forward of the cockpit. The main cabin was forward of this and had good room at a drop-leaf table for meals and entertaining, but the settees were too narrow to be real bunks, and the "forward cabin" was just an undersize double bunk in the peak, with crawl-in access. This layout was fine for in-port entertaining, but no good for sleeping anyone but kids or midgets, except in the after cabin, which was unchanged from the original layout.

Despite its shortcomings, the original OI 36 layout provided a great deal of accommodation space in 36 feet, and the boat had good performance qualities under sail and power. She made about 7.2 knots using just under one gallon of diesel fuel per hour with a Perkins 4-108 engine. With 60 gallons of fuel and 175 of water, she had a better than average cruising range of more than four hundred miles under power. The main water supply of 100 gallons of pressurized water was supplemented by a 75-gallon tank under the forward bunk that was on hand pumping only, so there was good backup should the pressure water system fail.

Entrance to the engine room was awkward, but the space itself was quite large, and once you had made it through the small door, most of the equipment was reasonably accessible.

The rig was easily handled, and the roller-furling jib was especially handy. It was set up on its own luff wire, there was a separate headstay on which other jibs could be hanked, and the roller furler could be lowered on deck if there was any problem in getting it completely furled or some other form of jam. The high boom allowed sailing with the Bimini up.

The OI 36 deserved to be more popular than it was—it was popular with me.

The CSY 37

She ended up as our choice for the latest Robinson family yacht. I point out, with the layout plan in view, how the tricabin set-up has been ingeniously worked out, with the very real help of the raised-deck feature. I have never been partial to this from an esthetic point of view, but it is a wonderful practical feature. In handling it, I would have liked the forward corners of the raised deck, at the break above the foredeck, to be contoured rather than sticking out as a sharp protrusion. They stick out farther than any other spot on the boat and have a proclivity for encountering pilings in landings that are not perfectly executed.

The CSY 37. 37'3" x 29'2" x 12' x 4'9"

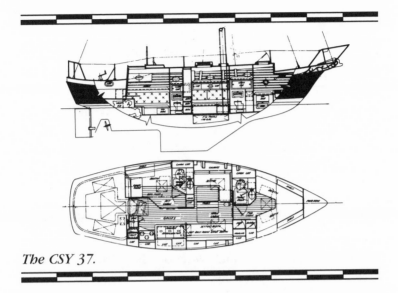

The CSY 37.

Also, the step down from the raised deck on each side of its after end tends to be a water catcher when on the windward side in rough going, since the scupper is on the outboard side. This doesn't happen very often.

Below, no one cabin is very big, so there is no great sense of space anywhere below decks (in contrast to the other version of the boat that has a big main cabin), but I still prefer this layout for our use. The great number of hatches (six) is a real plus in the tropics. We are glad we chose the shallow-draft model as we haven't noticed any problem with sailing ability, and the less draft the better when poking through areas like the Florida Keys and the Bahamas.

One addition to the sail plan that I ordered belatedly (and am glad I did) was a Flasher, the poleless cruising spinnaker developed by Charles Ulmer and since adapted in their own version by other sailmakers. This has worked very well and has added real zip to downwind performance. It will not stay full dead before the wind, but is effective from a broad-off, quartering reach to a point where the apparent wind is just forward of the beam. It is rigged like a drifter, with the tack attached at the bowplate and a collar holding the tack pennant close to the forestay. It's a relatively light sail, not intended for winds above 12-14 knots, but it is a good solution to those downwind blues many cruising boats suffer from, On *Tanagra* we had a pole for winging out the jib, and while it worked pretty well it was a nuisance to rig and had a narrow range of effectiveness.

A design feature that contributes to added living space is a V-drive for the Westerbeke 4-108 diesel through a Warner two-to-one reduction gear. I have found engine access very good through a big cockpit hatch and through the companionway stairs, which slide back from the opening. As designed, there was no insulation for sound in the engine compartment, which made for a high noise level, especially with the Bimini top rigged, but material was added, greatly reducing the problem. A removable dodger that snaps onto the front of the Bimini has been a great help in one or two rough passages, but it hampers movement forward out of the cockpit. As I said before, it's always a case of compromise, but the ones made here have worked out well for us.

From *Cruising: The Boats and the Places* (1981)

V

Some Yachting History

Some background, and personal coverage of memorable events

Origins of the Sport

There were colorful beginnings and their influence carries on

IT HAD to start with royalty. The pomp and circumstance, the aura of regal splendor that surrounded yachting in the era of the great yachts, and the later traditions they fostered, could only have been inspired by royal example. Cleopatra, of course, had her barge, Charles II is traditionally credited with owning the first real yacht, the *Mary*, in 1660, and Queen Elizabeth I had preceded him with a small sailing vessel oddly called *Rat of Wight*, but they had no ordinary yachtsmen to inspire.

Not until 1817, when the Prince Regent ordered sent to the newly formed organization known as the Yacht Club at

Cowes, England, a note saying "you are to consider this an official notice of His Royal Highness's desire" to become a member, were the prerogatives of royalty joined with the pretensions of lesser mortals in the pursuit of pleasure afloat. The club promptly raised its dues, doubled the size of the requirement for membership to a minimum of a 20-ton yacht, and changed its name to Royal Yacht Club. Later to become known as the Royal Yacht Squadron, also at the request of the Regent, the first yacht club to come down to modern times in a direct line of operation thereby acquired the trappings of royalty, and they became a traditional part of the sport.

It took some time for the yachts themselves to acquire much distinction, and two souls, who certainly can be called rugged in their individuality, had much to do with this. They were a peppery gentleman known as Thomas Assheton-Smith and Queen Victoria. The early yachts were little more than floating houseboats, rigged only for sail, and one candidate for membership in the Squadron was supposedly black-balled because his vessel had taken two months to sail from London to Cowes and also had brick bulkheads in the cabin. Mr. Assheton-Smith, who had built five sailing yachts in the early days of the Squadron, and whose cutter *Elizabeth* took part in the club's first race (and lost through a dismasting), tired of sailing vessels and, in 1829, decided to go to steam. He tried to get approval for a steam yacht, was turned down and even accused of possible commercialism in building one, and as Peter Heaton reports in his *Yachting, A History*, "withdrew his name from the club." His first steamer was *Menai*, of 400 tons, costing £20,000, and he went on to build seven more as a real pioneer of the genre.

He remained an unfashionable pioneer, however, with the antipollution forces of the day decrying the "murky vomitings of the furnaces," until Queen Victoria was won over to the convenience of a power-driven vessel. The Regent, who became George IV, had been using a ship-rigged yacht called *Royal George* for his lavish entertaining, but the plush vessel was not to Victoria's liking, especially when she often saw steamers passing the becalmed or tide-bound sailing yacht. A woman known for getting her own way, to put it mildly, she had the *Victoria and Albert*, a 200-foot steamer, commissioned in 1843 and promptly set off cruising, visiting such friends and relations as King Louis Philippe of France and King Leopold of Belgium.

It was the second *Victoria and Albert*, however, in 1855, that did much to influence yachtsmen who followed in the Queen's wake. She was 300 feet long, 2,342 tons, a handsome, able paddle-steamer with two stacks. Her interior was designed by Prince Albert personally in a motif of white with gold relief and a chintz wallpaper with moss rosebuds on a white background. In an era in which yachting flourished, along with the heyday of Empire and the freeswinging aftermath of the Industrial Revolution, she was the dominant vessel, a familiar sight at yachting and naval spectacles (and a vindication for Mr. Assheton-Smith).

Sailing yachts became mere racing machines, and the desire to emulate the royal way of life burst forth in a series of steam yachts ever more magnificent and regal. And Americans, stripped of the traditions and trappings of royalty at home, perhaps even tried to outdo the less impressionable British and Europeans in the splendor of their new yachts.

An empire builder, American style, was one of the first to start the tradition. Cornelius Vanderbilt, who delighted in the unofficial title of Commodore, built the first big American steam yacht, *North Star*, and in 1853 dramatized the tradition of the "grand tour" of European harbors with an epic voyage, epic in the scope of its undertaking in those days. Years before him, George Crowninshield of Salem, Mass., had used the fruits of a pre-Industrial Revolution fortune to take a "grand tour" of Europe in 1817 in *Cleopatra's Barge*, popularly called America's first yacht. This sailing vessel was well ahead of her time, and in spirit she was a forerunner of the steam-yacht days.

Commodore Vanderbilt was not to be left alone in his glory for long. Once the distraction of the War Between the States was left behind, the way was clear for a wide-open race for prestige and glory as millionaires vied with each other to produce the most luxurious and fastest yachts. Speed was as important as luxury, especially for New Yorkers when they headed down Long Island Sound for Newport, R.I. Many a yacht went up for sale quickly when she suffered the indignity of having a faster vessel come up astern and pass her on the way to the fashionable watering spot. Mortification was rampant on the fantail of a yacht when an owner had to face his guests as a rival vessel surged on by, leaving a gritty trail of smoke for those on the slower boat to inhale.

At first, the steam yachts of the second half of the nineteenth century were merely sailing yachts with steam added. They had the low, rakish hulls of the schooners popular at the time, clipper bows and several masts that were rigged for sailing, though seldom used. An English adventurer, Sir Thomas Brassey, did conduct a circumnavigation in the brigantine *Sunbeam*, making long passages under sail and using her steam engine for moving through calms and in and out of harbors and rivers.

A yachting historian of the day, Edward S. Jaffray, belittled the *Sunbeam*, however, by pointing out that her best speed under steam was only about 8 knots. She would, he said, "cut but a poor figure in a run up the Hudson or the Sound in company with our better class of yachts." He went on to say that "Every man who gives an order for a steam yacht directs the builder to make it a little faster than any previous vessel, and thus the ingenuity of the enterprising builders is taxed to the uttermost, and excellence is the natural result."

This race to magnificence was started not so much by *North Star*, since she was put into commercial service after her grand tour and was not really considered a bona fide yacht by the yachtsmen of the day, as by William H. Aspinwall, president of the Pacific Mail Steamship Co. To test whether a new invention, a single paddle wheel in the interior of a vessel, could be applied to his commercial ships, he had a 60-footer built. The wheel was a flop, but he kept the boat, put side-wheels with feathering buckets on her, named her *Fire-Fly* and began using her as a yacht for commuting from his country place on Staten Island to his Manhattan office. His son John caught the bug, and in a little over thirty years built thirteen steam yachts, working them himself as engineer, pilot and captain. A forerunner of the grander vessels to come was *Sentinel*, a 103-footer. Through these years Jacob Lorillard, who began a policy in 1868 of building a yacht a year and selling her at the end of the season, was also spreading the gospel. His largest was *Tillie*, a 105-footer.

As these gentlemen raced around New York Harbor, up the Hudson and up the Sound at speeds up to a then-astounding 17 knots, they began to attract the attention of men with bigger ideas. E. T. Gerry bought one of Aspinwall's boats, then sold her and build the much fancier 178-foot *Electra* to act as flagship of the New York Yacht Club.

Electra was quite a vessel for her day. The niceties of life were already being considered. Her double smokestack was arranged to carry off the cooking odors from the galley. She had fifty-eight Edison electric lights of 16-candlepower each and 100-candlepower masthead and running lights, a machine that could make 56 pounds of ice a day, ventilation blowers and independent fire and bilge pumps.

In 1881, George Osgood of New York astounded his friends by breakfasting in Newport at 7 A.M. and taking off for New York aboard his 185-foot yacht *Stranger.* At an average speed of 15 knots, he arrived in New York in nine hours, dining there that evening, the equivalent of lunch in London and dinner in New York in the jet age. She was the fastest yacht that year, but the old urge had started, and soon the same builders, William Cramp and Sons of Philadelphia, had turned out a larger and faster yacht that eclipsed *Stranger*, and her sistership, the first Morgan *Corsair.*

This was Jay Gould's *Atalanta*, a 248-footer capable of more than 20 knots, built in 1883. She also stepped up the luxury of her appointments, which, in her builder's words, were "magnificently fitted up with hardwood saloons and staterooms." Not only that, but she finished 11 minutes ahead of *Stranger* in a 95-mile race from Larchmont to New London when fresh from the yard, and the yachting fraternity had still another standard to meet.

William Astor at least met it in 1884 with the first vessel to use the famous name *Nourmahal* which, incidentally, means "Light of the Harem." Jaffray called this 232-foot Harlan and Hollingsworth production "a queen among steam yachts." A steel vessel, with provisions for sail as a bark, as well as steam, the custom in these early yachts, she was designed for ocean use, and her looks were especially pleasing. Rakish bow, elliptical stern and a long, lean midships section made her shapely as well as sea-kindly, and her glossy, black steel topsides were noted for the smoothness with which the plates were joined. Her female figurehead and the delicate gold tracery at her bow were also admired.

She had one large, black stack, and, as a reminder of what went on in her innards to make the gracious living topsides possible, she had eight coaling ports. Jaffray said she was "of strength sufficient to laugh at the fitful moods of the ocean."

Even these free-wheeling new millionaires had to give some thought to cost, however. Everybody knows what J.P.

Morgan, Sr. said when asked about the cost of running a yacht, but it is not so well known that he said it in answer to a question by Henry Clay Pierce, who had made his money in oil. Clinton H. Crane, one of the top naval architects of the period, and a man who designed many of the major steam yachts of the early twentieth century and got to know their owners well through his dealings with them, gives a post-script to Morgan's famous answer that "you have no right to own a yacht if you ask that question."

Pierce, even though he asked about cost, gave no evidence of worrying about it as he planned his new vessel with Crane. He wanted special food compartments in the hold, including an elaborate refrigerating plant, and he also had his quarters done by a Boston interior decorator all in silk panels with gold-plated hardware, gold fittings in the bathroom, and altogether some 150 special items. Smelling trouble, Crane had an order signed by Pierce for every item specified, which stood him in good stead when the owner finally got the bills. Forgetting Morgan's dictum, he howled in anguish and turned the whole batch of bills over to his attorney, but Crane was covered by the signed orders and the bills were paid.

Morgan, Astor, Gould, Gerry and their friends first came out with their big luxury yachts as the nineteenth century was drawing to a close. The salaries they paid their large staffs sound laughable in our inflationary times, but the total bill still came to a tidy sum by the standards of any day. Seamen and firemen received about $30 a month, which was, of course, all found with board and uniforms, and their conditions were much better, in pay and housing, than those of merchant seamen. It was a premium job to work on a yacht. Owners could pick and choose, and most of the crews were Scandinavians with a fine seafaring background. Mates and engineers could get from $45-100 per month, and captains as high as $200. Stewards rated $60-100 and waiters the same as seamen and firemen. The chef could usually command his salary on a personal basis with the owner, who would keep it a secret.

With up to fifty men in the crews of the larger yachts, the monthly payroll could run about $2,500, and it would cost $1,500 to feed them. James Gordon Bennett's *Namouna* was kept in commission year-round, Bennett entertained lavishly, and she was maintained in top condition. She probably cost him about $150,000 a year to run, which is a good solid figure even at Gay Nineties prices. Gould and Astor were said to spend only slightly less, mainly because they didn't entertain as much.

Townsend Perry, writing in the New York *World* of November 8, 1885, summed up an article on the costs of operating a big yacht by saying, "I don't know which will eat a man up the quickest, an extravagant wife or a steam yacht, but think of a rich man with both." The answer to this, however, came from a wealthy yachtsman, who gave this heartfelt endorsement. "My yacht, it is true, has cost a large sum, but it is worth every dollar of it. It has made a new man of me. Before I built it, I was constantly suffering from dyspepsia and other troubles arising from too close attention to business. Now I am a well man."

And so, as a balm to dyspeptic millionaires and an expression of their desire for regal trappings and ego-extensions, yachting had become a colorful facet of the life of the era by the time the nineteenth century gave way to the twentieth. The America's Cup competition made yacht-racing a glamorous sport, virtually the first international one, and the figures involved in it received as much attention as movie stars, TV stars, and sports champions do today, becoming almost household words. In fact Sir Thomas Lipton did a fantastically astute job of making his name and his tea one, in a public relations performance that was far ahead of his time, and still ranks as one of the most effective from both a sporting and a commercial standpoint.

The luxury yachts that trailed in the wake of the glamorous Cup yachts also became famous in themselves, a part of the American scene, and a true expression of the country's prosperity and growing economic power. The Goulds, Astors, Morgans, Vanderbilts, Gerrys, Bennetts, Lorillards and their fellow members in the club didn't just become famous because they owned big yachts, but their vessels kept them in the public eye, glamorized them and gave them a status that business figures had not known before.

With their luxurious craft, they set a style and established traditions that flourished and increased through those last "days of innocence" that preceded World War I. Luxury yachting reached a peak in these years that it was never to know again on the same scale.

The sport had grown enough for three monthly magazines devoted to yachts to set up shop: *Rudder* in 1890, *Motor Boating* in 1906 and *Yachting* in 1907. While they paid attention to the small launches and sailboats that were coming into use as pleasure craft, the luxury yachts were what filled their pages with a fascination like that of the movie magazines of the 20s and 30s. Few could climb the companionway up the glossy sides of a *Nourmahal* or *Corsair*, but they could glimpse the wonders of her interior in the pages of the magazines.

By 1914 a tradition had been established, one that was to continue to grow for another thirty years, and then change and mushroom in very different fashion.

From *Legendary Yachts* (1971)

Early Long-Distance Voyagers

The pioneers, whose traditions are still being followed

At dawn on September 17, 1925, Alain Gerbault, a romantic French tennis champion who was one of the first single-handers in small boats, was 48 days out of the Galapagos in the Pacific in his 39-foot cutter *Firecrest*, approaching Akamaru in the archipelago of Mangareva. He had been lying to all night, waiting to make his entrance by daylight, and now with the breeze fresh, he hoisted all sail and headed for the channel.

Never reticent about his emotions, this is how he described the experience in his book *In Quest of the Sun.*

. . . I stood at the tiller drenched in spray. There was no need to look at my charts. Every detail on them was engraved on my memory, for I had pored over them many a long hour, taking delight in repeating to myself the sweet-sounding names of the various islands.

I left on my port the islands of Kamaka and Makaroa, the latter looking like a ship, and threaded my way through the girdle of reefs until I was so near the cliffs of Makapa that spray was dashed on *Firecrest*. When I had doubled the point, Akamaru was abreast, quite close, and I could not help exclaiming aloud in admiration. There it was, Polynesia! All the descriptions of my favorite authors faded before the more beautiful reality!

A dazzling white coral beach was bordered by great plantations of coco-nut trees, whose branches were swaying in the wind. As a background rose the slopes of the mountain-side covered with the fine and picturesque foliage of ironwood trees . . . from the whole island emanated an atmosphere of calm and tranquility beyond description.

Phrases like these have since become the clichés of the travel folders, so often have they been restated by others, but Gerbault's wonder and rapture, comparatively fresh and uncommon in 1925, are a perfect expression of the lure and the rewards that have created a strange new breed of modern-day adventurer, the small-boat voyager. While man has progressed into the jet age and on into space, these individualists have willfully turned back the clock to another era, escaping from civilization and its pressures by facing unnecessary dangers, obstacles and discomforts. They have created these hazards for themselves, and their kind has multiplied in almost exact ratio to the lack of practicality of such ventures. The easier travel becomes and the further we move from the days when passaging under sail was a necessary means of transportation, the greater the number of romantic idealists who have set off across open seas in small sailboats, either alone or with a companion or two. The single-handers are the purists, the complete escapists and the final expression of this special form of rugged individualism, but the state of mind is the same for the married couples or the oddly assorted individuals who have linked together for such an adventure.

Captain Joshua Slocum started it. Just as small boys of the late 1920's all wanted to soar through the clouds in romantic freedom as a result of Lindbergh's flight to Paris, so did an earlier generation at the turn of the century dream of escaping by small boat to exotic lands and faraway islands after Slocum's unprecedented feat of sailing alone around the world in the 36-foot *Spray*, variously rigged as a sloop or a yawl.

Slocum was far from the first to go to sea in a small boat. Many nineteenth century stunt men tried to gain fame and fortune by making odd voyages. Some were lost and some crossed the ocean in tiny boats—two fishermen even rowed across the Atlantic—but there was a certain form and neatness to Slocum's feat, a round satisfaction in having completed a world circumnavigation. As he sailed, the press kept track of him. In each new port he entered there was more publicity on his progress, and he became a worldwide celebrity. His book, *Sailing Alone Around the World*, was a best seller and is a classic in its own right.

It has become a familiar story. Perhaps the best-known incident of all is his account of how he finally achieved a night's sleep in the hostile Straits of Magellan, where he had to be ever on guard against attacks by Indians. Wearying of constant vigil, he sprinkled carpet tacks on his deck and retired. When an Indian crept aboard during the night, stealth gave way to his startled yowls, and Slocum was bothered no more. Why he should have had carpet tacks on *Spray* is another question.

Slocum was a fine seaman and boatkeeper, and he actually rebuilt *Spray* from a derelict oyster sloop sitting in a pasture at Fairhaven, Massachusetts. She was given to him almost as a joke when he complained that he no longer had a ship after years at sea as a captain, but he took the gift seriously and rebuilt her plank by plank and frame by frame. She would never have won an ocean race, and romantic souls who have had replicas of her built have not had much by modern standards, but she was a sturdy, able boat for his purpose.

After returning a celebrity in 1898, Slocum, aged 54, then enjoyed a few years of fame, but his restless later days were not particularly happy ones. He was eventually lost at sea in 1910 after setting out in *Spray* for the Amazon. No trace of him was ever found.

He left a heritage that still lives, however. Devotees of long passages in small boats have formed a Slocum Society, and the list of those who have figuratively followed in his wake is a long, evergrowing one. Certain routes have become so popular for small-boat passages that they are even called milk runs, and an arrival of a small boat after such a passage creates about as much stir as the docking of the Staten Island Ferry. The most popular route is from Europe to the West Indies via the Canary Islands. Azores or Cape Verdes to Barbados, Antigua, or one of the other Lesser Antilles, a trip of something over 2,000 miles, mostly in the Trade Winds. A longer, less-traveled but still familiar route is the Panama-Galapagos-Tuamotus passage before the equatorial Trade Wind system in the Pacific. The Panama Canal has eliminated such difficulties as Slocum's in negotiating the Straits of Magellan, though there are still small-boat voyagers who go around Cape Horn by preference.

Just as Lindbergh opened the floodgates for a host of other fliers trying for various firsts, so did Slocum bring on immediate imitators. One of the first was Captain John Voss of Vancouver, British Columbia, like Slocum a beached professional seaman. His voyage started in a spirit of straight commercialism when a newspaperman offered him money and a share of the royalties from a resulting book if Voss would sail him around the world in a smaller boat than Slocum's. Voss's choice of vessel was an unlikely one, an Indian dugout canoe. He had limited finances, and was able to obtain this boat at a good price by getting her Indian owner drunk. At 37 feet she was longer than *Spray* by a foot but smaller in every other respect, and she made a strange sight when Voss fitted her out with a cabin and a three-masted rig.

There were very few who thought that *Tilikum* would make it, but after a continuous series of misadventures and mishaps, she did, and she is now on exhibit in a park in Victoria, British Columbia, hard by the harbor which saw her start and finish. The newspaperman didn't last long, evidently deciding there were easier ways to write a book. A constant victim of seasickness and fear, he jumped ship after a couple of Pacific stops, but Voss persisted without him and ended up writing a book himself. Called *The Venturesome Voyages of Captain Voss,* it makes entertaining reading, though perhaps not always in the way the author intended.

Voss tried to train the unhappy newspaperman in shipboard duties without much success. Things went well in practice but it was a different story when actual crises arose. The neophyte had been taught how to go forward and shorten sail so that Voss could remain at the tiller in a blow, and did it well enough in calm weather. In the first real storm at sea, however, Voss called his sleepy companion topside and sent him to lower the foresail. Just as he reached the forward deck, an immense wave loomed up astern of *Tilikum,* and instead of working the halyard as he was supposed to, the frightened man shinnied up the mast like a cat being chased by a dog. Not only did this put a dangerous burden on slender *Tilikum's* stability, but it also meant that Voss had to leave the wheel and talk the climber back down to deck.

With the departure of the scribe, Voss picked up various companions as he went. Native seamen from the islands, stranded professional sailors and eager novices all went for part of the way, and tragedy struck when one of them was swept overboard from the cockpit while Voss was below. Despite all this he carried on, gaining funds by lecturing and putting *Tilikum* on public exhibition.

As Slocum had before him, Voss received a great deal of attention in Australia, where *Tilikum* took in quite a sum in exhibition fees. At one inland park where she was on display, a stream of Aussies paid their shilling to troop aboard and have a look at her cramped quarters, and Voss was disturbed to see one stout matron settle down on the cockpit seat. She didn't budge for hours, and she was still there at closing time. When Voss finally got up his courage to ask her to leave, she crossed her arms firmly and said, "I'm not going until the boat does."

She thought she had paid for a boat ride, not just an inspection, and was determined to get her shilling's worth. Voss finally convinced her that conditions weren't exactly right for boat rides, since the nearest water was miles away.

Voss and some other commercial travelers in the field did little to make small boat voyaging more respectable, but it continued to receive publicity. Jack London brought even more with his beleaguered project to sail to the South Seas in *Snark*, a venture that cost him $30,000 at 1905 prices. Despite such troubles, the fascination of such a venture lured even more sailors. Thomas Fleming Day sailed his little yawl to the Mediterranean in 1911, but World War I brought a hiatus. After it, in a spasm of renewed escapism, small-boat voyages proliferated. The voyagers before World War I had mostly been professional seamen seeking gain, or at least a means of returning to the only life they knew. Yachtsmen in those days were mostly wealthy and mostly concerned with competition in large racing machines in coastal waters. Sailing alone around the world would have been as inconceivable to them as hiking from New York to California.

Cast loose by the war, a newer generation of yachtsmen had other ideas. The first bona fide yachtsmen to complete world circumnavigations were two taut-ship Britishers, George Mulhauser in the 62-foot *Amaryllis* going in a westerly direction in 1920-23, and Conor O'Brien in the 42-foot ketch *Saoirse* going the other way in 1923-25. Both were old-school-tie types who had constant trouble with paid and amateur crews. Conor admitted he "didn't suffer fools gladly." But they contributed much technical know-how to passaging lore, as they were both fine seamen.

One of the most publicized and persistent of global circumnavigators was Harry Pidgeon, an Iowan who had never seen the ocean until he moved to California at the age of 18.

In 1921, aged 51, he set out on Mulhauser's route in *Islander*, a 34-foot Seabird yawl of the same type Day had used for his 1911 crossing to Gibraltar. Pidgeon built *Islander* himself, starting in 1917, for a thousand dollars, and she took him two and a third times around the world—twice in the 1920's and a last time in 1947, when, aged 77 and with a new bride as crew, he got as far as the New Hebrides, where *Islander* was blown ashore and wrecked in a hurricane. The bride and groom were saved, however. Many of his predecessors had been compulsive loners, but Pidgeon was primarily an adventurer who took his time in the islands he visited and made many friends with the unassuming simplicity of his manner. He too became a public figure through publicity at home.

Gerbault was the most compulsive loner of all. He went voyaging because of his inability to settle into postwar civilization, but after every long, lonely passage he would come ashore to find increasing public adulation and overwhelming attention that only served to turn him seaward once more.

His first long passage was across the Atlantic to New York, a desperate saga of storms, calms, failing equipment, poor food and extreme personal hardship. He took 101 days to sail from Gibraltar to New York, partly because of rotting sails and partly because the old-fashioned *Firecrest*, a deep, narrow, plumb–stemmed cutter, was highly unsuited for single-handing.

Driven to sea by persistent invasions of his privacy and by all sorts of pleas from men and women who wanted to go with him, he finally ended up in the South Pacific, where he would turn up occasionally for short visits in port before disappearing again. He and his vessel were early casualties of World War II in the Pacific.

The Depression of the 30's gave a new impetus to small-boat voyaging and one book title from that era, Dwight Long's *Seven Seas on a Shoestring*, is symbolic. Long is typical of the latter-day voyagers who made heroes of Slocum, Voss, Gerbault and London and set out to follow their tracks. He had as many adventures as most of the others rolled into one, as he was young, curious, and not very experienced, but he finally got back to Seattle to complete his circuit after six years, surviving dismasting, piracy, local wars and shipwreck in Long Island Sound in the 1938 hurricane.

Two of the most literate and colorful voyagers of that era were William Albert Robinson (no relation to the author) and Richard Maury. Robinson sailed the 32-foot ketch *Svaap* around the world in three and a half years, starting in 1928. He explored many out-of-the-way islands the others had bypassed, with a Polynesian native, Etera, as his faithful crew. He started out again in *Svaap* in 1933 with his bride Florence for the Galapagos, and became the center of a highly publicized incident there when he was stricken with appendicitis, the number-one bugbear of the small-boat voyager. Luckily there was a fishing boat in the harbor which radioed for help to the Navy in Panama. Following radio instructions, he was packed in ice from the fishing boat in an attempt to keep his appendix quiescent while two Navy surgeons flew in to operate and a destroyer steamed out at flank speed to take the Robinsons aboard. *Svaap* had to be left behind and was wrecked there, but Robinson continued to follow the sea.

For a while he operated a shipyard in Massachusetts, building replicas of traditional sailing ships, but after World War II he went back to the South Pacific in *Varua*, a 70-foot brig he had built in his own yard, and he has been sailing those waters ever since.

Maury, a descendant of the great oceanographer Matthew Maury, had a truly romantic approach to seafaring and the ability to put it in words. His *The Saga of "Cimba"* is one of the best written of all passaging books in its expression of the excitement and challenge of going to sea in a small boat. His boat was a 25-foot Nova Scotia schooner, a miniature version of the famous fishing boats there, and when he bought her, the only white boat in the harbor. Despite continued misfortunes and accidents to prospective crew members, Maury set out with Dombey Dickinson as crew in November, 1933, for the South Seas via Bermuda. On the way *Cimba* went through a massive storm and survived a 360-degree capsize, but she was eventually wrecked on a wicked reef at the entrance to Suva in the Fijis. She was salvaged and repairs were started, but Maury finally lost her in a continued battle over red tape. Repaired and jauntily sitting at a mooring as the governor's yacht, she was in the harbor of Suva during World War II in strange contrast to the war convoys stopping there.

The only yachtsman who ventured to sea on a long passage during World War II was the Argentinian Vito Dumas, another of the breed who want only to get offshore and don't seem to care much for landfalls or harbor visits. In the double-ended 31-foot ketch *Legh II* he made a 20,000 mile passage mostly along the 40th South parallel, the fabled "Roaring Forties" of sailing-ship days. In his 230-day passage in 1943, he stopped only in Cape Town, South Africa; Wellington, New Zealand; and Valparaiso, Chile. As a neutral in those waters, he was not bothered by the war, but he had to carry complete supplies for the voyage from the start because of wartime restrictions in the ports he visited.

The end of the war brought on a new era of voyaging in which small boats sailed off over the horizon by the hundreds instead of only two or three in a decade. The breed became a brotherhood—and a sisterhood—and used everything from boats smaller than 20 feet to luxury yachts. As commercial sail had disappeared from the sea lanes, the tiny white dots of the small-boat voyagers were the only vestiges left of the way man had crossed the oceans for centuries. What had been remarkable became routine—about the only vessel not tried for long passages was a pair of water wings.

Irving Johnson, who had started a series of planned, businesslike 18-month global circumnavigations out of Gloucester, Massachusetts, in the pilot schooner *Yankee* in the 30's, with 18 or 20 paying guests as his working crew, began making these trips again with a 98-foot steel brigantine, also named *Yankee*. He showed how to combine adventure and romance with very efficient planning and ship operation. In contrast kayaks and rubber rafts were used for long ocean passages, and *Kon-Tiki's* well-publicized drift from South America to Polynesia also raised many a nautical eyebrow.

There was also a trend to smallness. Back in the 20's a Barnegat Bay sailor named Slade Dale had demonstrated how seaworthy a small sailboat could be by circumnavigating Cuba in the 23-foot sloop *Postscript*, but it wasn't until World War II turned loose a new generation of shoestring adventurers that small boats became more and more common on long passages.

A record was broken in 1953 when two young Englishmen, Pat Ellam and Colin Mudie brought a little 19-foot lapstrake sloop across the Atlantic to dramatize the capabilities of the miniature ocean racers known as the Junior Offshore Group in England. *Sopranino*, designed by Laurent Giles, was the smallest modern boat to have made the passage by then, and she did much to popularize what became known as the Midget Ocean Racing type in the United States. She was fine for passaging, but Ellam and Mudie found her very cramped when they were in port if they both had to go below at the same time. Mudie later emphasized his affinity for strange forms of transportation by attempting to cross the Atlantic in a free balloon.

Another version of *Sopranino*, John Guzzwell's 20-foot yawl *Trekka*, which he built himself in British Columbia, became the smallest vessel to circumnavigate the world via a long, interrupted voyage starting in the late 50's. Guzzwell, a quiet, retiring man who was an excellent workman and fine seaman, spent much time in New Zealand on his way around the world, and was in no hurry wherever he went. He even broke off his own voyaging to sign on as crew with Miles and Beryl Smeeton in their 45-foot double-ended ketch *Tzu Hang* bound eastward around the Horn from Australia to England. On her he became involved in one of the most bizarre disasters in the history of yacht passaging.

In the far reaches of the South Pacific on the edge of the Roaring Forties, *Tzu Hang*, running before a gale in immense seas, pitch-poled and capsized at the same time in a corkscrew motion. Below, Guzzwell and Smeeton were tossed around with the cabin contents like dice in a cage and Beryl, at the helm, was washed overboard. The boat was dismasted, with her deck and hatches swept clean, but all miraculously survived. Beryl was rescued despite her broken collarbone, and eventually with great ingenuity and fine carpentry by Guzzwell, a jury rig was assembled that brought the battered vessel safely into Chile.

Tzu Hang's remarkable experience is a good clue to the unexplained disappearance of small craft that have failed to complete voyages. In addition to *Cimba* and *Tzu Hang*, two other vessels are on record as having survived 360-degree capsizes at sea. Marcel Bardiaux, an ebullient Frenchman who pulled the switch of financing a global circumnavigation by writing a book beforehand telling what he was going to do, had this experience in his sloop *Les Quatre Vents* as the first single-hander to round Cape Horn east to west.

In bitter cold weather approaching the Cape in the Atlantic, he was forced to heave to under storm trysail in a strong gale that was blowing from the south directly against a five-knot southward–flowing current. The opposing forces built a steep, wicked sea, and huddled helplessly in his cabin while the little ship took care of herself, Bardiaux was horrified to feel her flip off the top of a wave and turn completely over. The trysail was now underwater, and for a while it held the boat upside down, acting like a keel, while Bardiaux bounced around on the cabin carlings amid hot coals from the stove that were scorching the wood.

Suddenly she flipped again and the sail broke free from the water. The release was so violent and the keel spun back to its normal underwater location so quickly that the boat did another complete flip and was upside-down again. The second time the sail came up and it stayed there, however, and fortunately the rig held. Bardiaux finally battled his way into the Pacific, but was hospitalized with frostbitten hands before he moved on to warmer climes. He almost lost his boat again on the vast complex of coral reefs out of sight of land off Noumea, New Caledonia, but was able to get his battered vessel off and keep going.

The other recorded 360-degree capsize dismasted the 39-foot centerboard ocean-racing yawl *Doubloon* in the Gulf Stream off Cape Hatteras on her way north from her home port in Florida to the 1964 Bermuda Race. Like *Les Quatres Vents* she was caught in opposing wind and current, with a hurricane-force northeaster blowing against the Gulf Stream. The steepness of the waves caused her to flip completely while quartering before the seas with centerboard down under bare poles. Both masts went and skipper Joe Byars, rushing topside, could not find the helmsman, Gene Hinkel. He threw a life ring with a lighted buoy in the water and called to Hinkel against the roar of the storm, but saw no trace of him. He went below in horrified dejection, thinking he had lost one of his crew.

His reaction 15 minutes later can be imagined when Hinkel's soaked form suddenly appeared in the hatch and clambered below. He had been caught in the rigging alongside and the noise of the wind and waves had prevented Byars from hearing his shouts.

Doubloon may have been tripped over by her board, which Byars had lowered to increase steering control. She did one more complete flip during the wild night, but her watertight integrity held, and she was eventually towed into port by a freighter after limping along under jury rig.

These misadventures that were survived and reported are an indication of what can happen to even the best-planned voyages, but there have been hundreds of passages carried out without mishap or even dramatic incident. Every year a boat or two is lost at sea without a trace, and an accident like one of the above or a collision with a big ship, which would never even be felt on the ship on a rough night, could account for the disappearances.

Except for an occasional loyal wife who went along submissively in some of the adventures of the 1920's and 30's, passaging was mainly a masculine world until after World War II. Mrs. Erling Tambs had accompanied her husband, a Norwegian novelist and complete novice as a sailor, in a trouble-beset voyage from Norway until they lost their boat *Teddy* in New Zealand, going through two pregnancies en route. Sometimes a European, very often a refugee from the advance of Hitlerism, showed up in the West Indies in some small craft with his wife as crew, but they were exceptions, and lady skippers were non-existent.

Ann Davidson changed this in the 23-foot sloop *Felicity Ann*, in which she was the first woman to sail alone across the Atlantic. A complete novice, she had started out on an earlier voyage with her husband, only to have him lost overboard in a shattering experience that would have sent most women far into the mountains for the rest of their lives. A female of fiber and determination, however, she took the opposite approach and decided to do alone in a smaller boat what she and her husband had started out to do together.

She made it across in 1953 after some harrowing experiences, and while she didn't exactly start a fad as the Amelia
Earhart of the sailing world, she gave many women enough
confidence to at least accompany their husbands on long
voyages. Some had already been at it. Sten and Brita Holm-
dahl, tiring of restrictions in socialized Sweden, took off
from Marstrand in the 32-foot ketch *Viking* in 1952 and
made a very seamanlike world circumnavigation in two
years. Bill and Phyllis Crowe of Honolulu were another married couple to circumnavigate the world, in the 39-foot
schooner *Lang Syne*. *Lang Syne* was home-built, and *Viking*
was converted by the Holmdahls from a fishing boat. Both
these couples were awarded the Cruising Club of America's
Blue Water Medal, which has gone to many passage-makers
for outstanding voyages.

Two other married couples have also completed world
circumnavigations and been awarded the Blue Water Medal.
Eric and Susan Hiscock in the British cutter *Wanderer III*
have been around twice, and Thomas S. Steel has also been
around twice in *Adios*, a 32-foot ketch, the first time as a
bachelor and later with his wife. Al Peterson went around
solo in the double-ender *Stornoway*, then took a wife for
continued voyaging.

Wives don't always take to the joys of long passages. Bill
Murnan, a Southern Californian, started out with his wife
soon after World War II in an aluminum Seabird twin-screw
yawl, probably the only twin-screw sailboat ever to go
around the world. After one long Pacific passage she decided
this wasn't for her and wanted off. Murnan put her ashore at
an island with air connections and bought her a ticket to
Cape Town, South Africa. "You go there and wait for me," he
said. "I'll be along in a while."

Obediently she got a "temporary" job there and settled
down to wait. True to his word, Murnan showed up—three

years later—and she rejoined him for the passage up the Atlantic to the States.

Not all the companions afloat are married. The ports of Southern Europe are not strangers to adventurous girls willing to sign on any vessel going across to the West Indies, and some of them manage to make it. Edward Allcard, a reticent Britisher who has been one of the most persistent singlehanders in the world during the post World War II era, even found a girl stowaway aboard his ancient 30-foot yawl *Temptress* a day out of the Azores on the way to the Mediterranean. A young Portuguese girl anxious to get to the mainland, she reportedly was quick to learn the duties of an able crew.

Some of the voyagers attract a great amount of publicity while others go their way anonymously, content to be alone at sea. Such a one is Jean Gau, a wiry, middle-aged Frenchman who lives only to sail. In order to finance solo world circumnavigations, he lives on his boat at Sheepshead Bay in Brooklyn and works on the night shift as a chef in a New York hotel. When he has a stake saved up, he takes off around the world. He has done this three times now, and has made some shorter transoceanic passages as well. On a circumnavigation of the globe which started in 1964, his 30-foot Tahiti-class ketch *Atom* grounded on a reef far out of sight of land in the treacherous Torres Straits between Australia and New Guinea. While exploring the reef at low tide looking for the best way to get his boat out of what seemed a hopeless situation, Gau came on a gruesome discovery. Another vessel had been wrecked there, and her rotted rigging and shattered planks were strewn over the coral. Tangled in them were several human skeletons, and the graphic reminder of what his fate could be made Gau work all the harder to get *Atom* off, which he managed to do that night. From there he sailed non-stop on the 7,000 mile passage to

Durban, South Africa, in 113 days, one of the longest such solo stints ever accomplished.

As long passages became more and more common-place, the only voyages attracting much attention were the out-of-the-ordinary ones. Another solo woman, Mrs. Sharon Sites, made it from Los Angeles to Honolulu in the summer of 1965, and a 16-year-old, Lee Graham, set out from California in 1965 to be the youngest world circumnavigator. He was also the first to make the trip in a stock fiberglass sloop, an L-24.

Robert Manry, the Cleveland, Ohio, copy-desk editor who forsook the green eyeshade for a sou-wester and took off from Falmouth, Massachusetts, for Falmouth, England, in the $13^{1}/_{2}$-foot *Tinkerbelle* in the summer of 1965, caught the public fancy. For a while he was "lost," simply because no one could spot his tiny vessel on the vast expanse of sea, and the story suddenly caught on in the mass media. When he finally unlimbered himself from his tiny prison after 78 days, he was a surprised international celebrity.

While he was at sea, an even smaller boat was breaking his record sailing in the opposite direction. John Riding, a 6-foot 4-inch Englishman, who towered over his tiny craft like a lighthouse over a buoy, sailed the 12-foot *Sjo Ag* in slow stages from England to Newport, Rhode Island, via Spain, the Azores and Bermuda. He designed her and had her built to be the smallest boat that could possibly carry a man and the supplies needed to keep him alive on long passages. Her egg-shape (*Sjo Ag* means sea egg in Norwegian) is intended to give the least resistance to rough water, and it has worked. She stayed afloat even when picked up by a wave and dumped back over her own log line. One of Riding's greatest difficulties was with amorous whales who followed him, nuzzling the hull. He finally scared them away by putting the end of a mouth-operated fog horn under water and blowing it at them.

Single-handing has developed into such a science that there have been two single-handed races across the Atlantic in recent years. With any rig or size of boat allowed, both races have been won by well-organized, hard-driven boats. Francis Chichester, a British publisher, won the first in *Gipsy Moth III* in 1960, then reduced the record he set from 40 to 33 days in a non-racing passage in 1962. In the 1964 race, he was second to a muscular, dedicated French naval officer named Eric Tabarly, who did a remarkable job of keeping the ketch *Pen Duick* going at good speed for a 27-day, one hour and 56-minute passage. Smaller boats, like a 23-foot Cap Horn, struggled into port safely but much more slowly.

The long voyagers have built up their own techniques and traditions. They are an international brotherhood that keeps in touch through chance encounters and grapevine news, running into each other every few years in Las Palmas, Antigua, Panama, Honolulu, Sydney or Cape Town. They have made twin staysails an accepted passage rig and have worked out some ingenious self steering devices. They have learned important lessons in provisioning small boats for long passages, and they have proved time and again that it is not the size of a boat that makes it seaworthy.

They have their own jokes and oft-repeated tales, like the time in Majorca a sailor named Peter Tangvald asked a Scottish friend to help him remove a balky engine from his boat. They sweated the greasy hunk of iron up on deck, where the Scotsman thought that Tangvald was going to make repairs. Instead he placed a foot against it and gently shoved it over the side, where it disappeared with a great splash.

"What did you do that for?" the Scotsman asked, his sense of thrift outraged.

"I don't want anything on my boat I don't understand." Tangvald answered. "I don't understand engines, so I won't sail with one. I don't understand heads either, as a matter of fact."

Whereupon he went below, removed the head, and also tossed that in the harbor. He has been sailing without both pieces of equipment ever since.

The long voyagers respect the loners and the moody members of their fraternity, laugh at the characters and help the unfortunate. John Riding described their psychology when he said, "It is a state of mind. It is more of a psychological excursion as opposed to a yachting venture."

It is a state of mind that has been spreading since Joshua Slocum first looked at that derelict hull in the pasture, and it will long remain one of the most fascinating facets of the yachting story.

From *The World of Yachting* (1966)

The 1962 America's Cup
The brash Aussies brought new life and color when it was needed most

Disappointment over the *Sceptre* fiasco could have brought another hiatus in *America's* Cup activity as long as that for World War II, but fortunately a new element was soon injected into the picture, and the most exciting and interesting challenge, at least since 1934, if not in the history of the series, resulted.

Australia, anxious to prove itself in world competition from its far-off location in the Antipodes, emerged as a potential challenger soon after the 1958 series ended. The Aussies had long held their own in tennis, cricket, swimming, and track and field, despite their location and small population, but they were not as well known to the "other side of the world" as international sailors. The general impression was that they enjoyed sailing over-canvassed dinghies in heavy air for cash prizes and wagering, and that they were also rugged offshore seamen, but that was about all.

At Newport in 1958, two bachelor brothers, slightly eccentric and apparently wealthy sheepherders named Frank and John Livingston, had been very much in evidence, talking to all and sundry about the problems of an *America's* Cup challenge. They owned the largest racing yacht in Australia, *Kurrewa IV*, about the size of a Twelve, and they expressed a strong interest in becoming involved in future competition. As they talked to more and more people, however, they became more and more disillusioned about the realities of staging a challenge from their isolated homeland, and they departed in October, leaving the impression that they had given up the idea and that Australia was only a talking possibility, not an actual one.

There was great surprise, therefore, in October 1959, when those interested in the Cup matches, wondering which of several British yachtsmen would be the first to renew the series, suddenly learned that *Vim*, the underdog heroine of the 1958 trials, had been chartered for four years, with an option to buy, by the Australian publisher Sir Frank Packer. Australian Olympic Finn sailor Colin Ryrie, in the United States for some Finn competition, had quietly negotiated with Capt. Matthews on Packer's behalf, and before anyone was aware of this interest, the graceful "superboat" of 1939 was on her way Down Under. All of this had nothing to do with the Livingstons.

This was followed in January by a visit to the United States by Alan Payne, Australia's most successful designer of ocean racers, and its only full-time practicing yacht designer. He visited with New York Yacht Club officials and with the towing-tank crew at Stevens Institute in Hoboken and quietly and efficiently established a working arrangement "in case" he was selected to design a challenger. It was agreed that he would be able to use the facilities at Stevens, which had played such a vital part in the two most recent defense efforts, and which had never been used by a challenger before. Payne pointed out that there were no similar facilities in Australia, and that a Twelve-Meter had never been designed or built there. *Kurrewa IV*, which Packer had once owned when she was called *Morna*, was an old Scottish-built Fife design.

Rumors began to fly concerning an "Empire challenge," with the Duke of Edinburgh as coordinator. Supposedly, he was to try to pull various Commonwealth nations together into a common effort that would produce several candidates, a sail-off, and an eventual challenge that would have a stronger competitive background than the ill-fated *Sceptre* effort.

While these rumors were flying about, New York Yacht Club officers were startled to receive, on April 20, a direct challenge from the Royal Sydney Yacht Squadron for a series in 1962. Evidently word had come through to Packer that the Duke's letter was being formulated, and the Royal Sydney Yacht Squadron challenge was quickly sent off before receipt of any royal communication. After careful consideration by New York Yacht Club officers, Commodore George Hinman announced on April 28 that the Australian challenge had been accepted. At first it was thought that the Australians might cooperate with possible British candidates, but this notion was soon brushed aside, and the yachting world looked forward eagerly to an entirely new chapter in the *America's* Cup history.

The 40-year-old Payne, quiet, earnest and self-effacing, promptly became one of the world's busiest men as he tackled the monumental task of creating a Twelve-Meter from absolute scratch in a country of ten-million population, where no one had ever before attempted the building of a sailboat anywhere close to the complexity of a Twelve. In one great leap he had to investigate the industrial potential for making such items as masts and winches as well as sails and all sorts of sophisticated fittings. And he also had to try to catch up to the acknowledged genius of Olin Stephens, who had first designed a Twelve-Meter over 20 years before, and of other designers who had the benefit of the availability for study of the U.S. Twelve-Meters that had been built.

The question of sailcloth had not come up before and was therefore never spelled out in the conditions governing the boats, but in order to make sure that the Aussie challenge was competitive, it was interpreted that sails were not an item that had to be "built in the country of origin" of the challenge. It was agreed that the Australians could use American-made sails if they felt the need, and of course the Stevens Institute tank had been made available to tank-test designs. These two concessions literally made the Australian challenge a practical possibility.

While Alan Payne bustled, and the brash, cocky Australian character bristled with pride, there was little early reaction by way of defense candidates in the U.S. In 1959 it developed that the Shields brothers, well-known senior sailors from Larchmont, N.Y., would be taking over *Columbia*, with Paul as owner and Cornelius, who had been called in to help *Columbia* in 1958, as advisor, and Corny, Jr., better known as Glit, as skipper. Doctor's orders kept Corny, Sr., out of the cockpit, but he was a strong, key figure in the effort. The boat had been given a new veed keel shape and less ballast.

The Henry Mercer syndicate decided to rejuvenate *Weatherly*, altering her according to some ideas arrived at by her builder, Bill Luders, and her original designer, Phil Rhodes. When Bus Mosbacher was announced as her skipper, she immediately became a formidable contender. She was being lightened a great deal, including having her stern bobbed, her underbody was altered to reduce wetted surface, and ballast had been added to her keel. *Easterner*, slightly modernized and modified, was to be sailing again, but was still a family affair, without the high-pressure effort expended on the other boats.

The only new contender for this campaign aroused a great deal of interest when announced. Sponsored by a syndicate headed by Boston yachtsman Ross Anderson, she was built in considerable secrecy, even unto her name, in Graves' Yard in Marblehead, Mass. The brainchild of sailmaker F. E. "Ted" Hood, she embodied a sailmaker's ideas of an efficient sail-carrying platform. He had only designed a few ocean racers, but, with his father Steadman, known as "The Professor," as astute adviser, and with his reputation for success as a sailor and as the key man in Twelve-Meter sailmaking, the laconic Ted's boat was considered a formidable front-runner for the defense berth even before she was launched in late May.

In a late evening ceremony under a full moon, to get the benefit of the highest tide, she slid down the ways and her name was finally revealed as *Nefertiti*. (The name ever remained a controversial one and the subject of continual parody.) The stage was now set for the defense campaign.

Meanwhile, cautious optimism was growing on the other side of the world as the new Aussie yacht took shape. Named for Packer's late wife, *Gretel* was beautifully built by the Lars Halvorsen Yard, run by brothers with a top reputation in ocean racing. *Gretel* hit the ways in February 1962. By early March, her gear and sails had been assembled, and she was taking short trial spins around Sydney Harbor. The tough, eager sailors who, as two rival crew units, had been working out on *Vim* for almost two years, itched for a chance to try her in action.

Their chance came unexpectedly on a cloudy Sunday in March. Packer, a large, forceful man famous for his business methods, and complete dictator of the *Gretel* campaign, had given orders up until then that she and *Vim* were under no circumstances to sail in the same water at the same time; but with a group of luncheon guests assembled on the lawn of his waterfront house, he decided on the spur of the moment to put on a show. It was only *Gretel's* fifth shakedown sail, but he ordered the two boats to stage a brush in the eastern arm of the harbor just inside its entrance at The Heads.

In an atmosphere electric with excitement and anticipation, they headed south on a close, port tack reach. *Vim* was to windward and about a half length astern, and both boats had their wind clear in a 12-knot breeze. At first they seemed tied together, but, gradually, inch by inch, *Gretel* began to move ahead. She was moving smoothly, with a noticeable absence of quarter wave, and standing up a bit stiffer than the older boat. When they reached the end of the three-mile straightaway in the vicinity of Packer's house, *Gretel* had moved out by about 100 yards. On the strength of this, no one could exactly claim that the Cup was as good as won, but there were broad smiles all around, and, as the boats moored for a lunch break, the remark "At least she's no *Sceptre!*" was heard repeatedly. From that moment on, there was a real undercurrent of optimism and excitement in the Aussie campaign.

It carried right on to Newport, where the colorful *Gretel* contingent practically took over the town. Despite the tremendous hours of hard work they put in, as much in altering *Gretel* as in sailing her in rather meaningless practice starts and buoy roundings against *Vim* under orders that Packer boomed over the voice radio, they made friends all over town. Bars became "pubs" and their infectious enthusiasm lent a gaiety and a great sense of anticipation to the summer as the four American boats went through their eliminations.

At first these promised to be wide-open battles, potentially as exciting as the *Vim-Columbia* set-to in 1958. *Nefertiti* took some early races and became the darling of New England, but gradually a pattern emerged that took most of the suspense out of the summer. *Easterner* again showed flashes of natural speed, but she never developed into a truly serious contender. *Columbia's* gang was never able to settle down, as personnel changes became more and more frequent in a belated attempt to find a winning combination, and the lack of previous Twelve-Meter experience showed up in her handling. At times she was dangerous, but too often she took herself out of contention with mistakes.

This left it to *Weatherly* and *Neffy*, and it soon became apparent that Hood's creation was great on some points but was not a well-rounded boat. Her sail-carrying power really told in a blow, especially on reaches, and sometimes no one could hold her, but she paid for her beamy power with too much wetted surface and she was ineffective in light and moderate airs to windward and on runs.

Mosbacher, with by far the most hours at a Twelve-Meter helm of anyone in the competition (he had sailed *Easterner* for one summer after all the time spent on *Vim* in 1958) and with a demonstrated genius for molding a highly efficient, loyal crew that knew collectively that each job was secure, barring a monumental lapse or loss of enthusiasm, was soon demonstrating his ability to dominate any given match race. In the selection series in August, *Easterner* and *Columbia* were soon to be eliminated, and only one heavy weather loss to *Nefertiti*, when she broke two spinnaker guys and blew out two spinnakers, kept *Weatherly* from being undefeated.

This came after four wins, and matched her 4-1 against all comers with *Neffy's* 3-2. Each added a victory that eliminated the other two, *Weatherly* soundly trouncing *Columbia* in a fresh breeze to dramatize how much better in a blow her changes had made her, and then, with the choice down to the last two boats, *Weatherly* ran off three straight wins in moderate air. Mosbacher controlled the starts when it counted, and the blue-hulled Mercer boat was even able to hold off *Nefertiti* when a windward-leeward course turned into an all-reaching one in freshening breezes. On August 25, with the score 4-1 for *Weatherly* in their own series, after a 5-minute, 39-second win, Commodore Henry Morgan and his committee came alongside *Weatherly's* berth in the fading twilight to inform Bus and his happy crew that *Weatherly* would be the defender.

All this time, Packer had been switching crews, failing to pick a helmsman (much less a "skipper" who could mold his own crew à la Mosbacher) and running odd, sketchy drills between the two Aussie boats. Never once did they stage a formally simulated full race over a Cup-type course. Payne, slaving day and night on the fantastic number of details to bring a Twelve-Meter to top racing pitch, had almost worked himself into a state of exhaustion, and the crew was beginning to tire of the meaningless sailing drills and a rugged physical-education regime that had been clamped on it. But not much of this was visible to the Newport townspeople and the yachtsmen crowding into the narrow, hilly streets of the town.

Over Labor Day weekend, the Aussies did something which startled everybody, including some of their own syndicate members who arrived in town for the first time and found *Gretel's* mastless hull lying in her slip almost completely gutted. To correct a weather helm, Payne had finally convinced Packer that the mast had to be moved forward 19 inches (the maximum the frame structure would allow), and the boat was virtually rebuilt amidships and completely rerigged in less than a week. It was a monumental effort and typical of the dedication of *Gretel's* personnel.

Finally Packer named Jock Sturrock as helmsman for the Cup series. Sturrock, a bluff, fun-loving man in his mid-40's and a proven winner, still had no power over crew selection or other policies and was therefore one of the most relaxed men in Newport as the September 15 starting date approached. "It's just another boat race," was his grinning comment when asked for his reaction. Packer's dictatorial policies reached a climax the morning of the opener, when he removed the navigator, put in his alternate helmsman, aging Archie Robertson, as a cockpit observer, and gave navigational duties to Magnus Halvorsen in the cockpit crew.

Sturrock therefore had to face the world's most experienced Twelve-Meter helmsman, in point of hours of actual racing, and a crew that had been virtually intact since the spring through two dozen tough races, with a crew that had never before sailed in the same combination, and he himself never having once sailed a Twelve-Meter race "in anger."

That *Gretel* made it close is a remarkable tribute to the effort that produced her out of nothing; to Payne's design, which made it possibly the fastest Twelve in the world at that time; and to the enthusiasm and fighting spirit of the crew. To beat this combination would take an equal amount of fighting spirit, cool control and skill, and fortunately for the defense of the Cup, *Weatherly* had all these.

The tremendous interest that the build-up had aroused was made all too evident on the bright, clear, breezy morning of September 15 when a spectator fleet that dwarfed the impressive opening-day assemblage of 1958 swarmed all over Rhode Island Sound. Unfortunately for the Coast Guard in its attempts to handle this mammoth armada, the wind was northwest, off the land, which meant that the course had to be laid out toward the direction from which the spectators were coming. If the breeze had been from the sea, the fleet would have been behind the course, but as it was, they formed a massive clutter all over it, and the start had to be delayed as Coast Guard cutters dashed hither and yon, sirens screaming and bullhorns roaring, trying to clear the area.

The sea would have been quite smooth if it hadn't been for the bobble created by the wakes of this fleet that was estimated as close to 2,500 boats, ranging from cruise liners jammed with passengers to outboards and small day-sailers.

Finally, at 1:10, over an hour late, the race got underway over a twice-around windward-leeward course of 24 miles. Under mainsails only, with jibs ready to break out, the adversaries circled like wary dogs in Mosbacher's favorite starting pattern for most of the ten-minute preliminary period. Bus came out with the advantage, at just the right moment, of what had appeared to be a standoff, forcing *Gretel* over the line just before the gun, so that Sturrock had to tack back for the line and was late. As the gun sounded, *Weatherly* was away and winging, with her wind clear, a telling demonstration of the gap in combat experience between the two skippers.

The advantage of several lengths she gained in this way was gradually increased as the wind backed to the west a bit and allowed *Weatherly* to reach the lay line after two tacks. She had a lead of 1 minute, 28 seconds at the stake boat, and this was the race to all intents and purposes. *Gretel* did close the time gap a bit as they ran back to the start in a freshening breeze, both with blue-topped spinnakers. On the next beat, with the breeze increased from the eight knots that prevailed at the start to a fresher 15-18 knots, *Gretel* suffered from sailing with a light weather main, and also from some internal troubles resulting from her makeshift crew setup. Without a full-time navigator, she overstood the mark a bit, and slow reactions by her uncoordinated cockpit crew caused a backstay fitting to fail, calling for a quick, unnecessary tack to take the strain off it while it was being replaced.

The result was a 3 minutes, 43 seconds victory for *Weatherly* as the huge gathering gave her a thunderous ovation of whistles and sirens, and it almost looked like the same old story as the boats headed for port in the slanting late-afternoon light. *Gretel* signaled for a layday, which was to be her calculated policy after every race. Payne later explained that this was decided upon to give the maximum time after each race for making adjustments according to lessons learned in combat. After all, this was her first formal competition of any kind.

A very different complexion on the series emerged with the second race, which wasn't until Tuesday, since Sunday was not a scheduled day and Monday counted as the layday. The weekday spectator fleet was perhaps 700-800 boats on a sunny, breezy day, with a 15-knot W by N breeze kicking up a lump of sea and freshening to more than 20 before the race ended.

What developed became one of the great races of Cup history, beginning with the usual merry-go-round start that put *Weatherly* into what has emerged over the years as Mosbacher's favorite spot, a safe leeward with wind clear.

Soon the close-winded American boat was feeding bad air back to *Gretel* and Sturrock had to tack. *Gretel* had a flatter Hood sail than her loose, opening-day main and was going well, but Mosbacher was still gradually eating up to windward as they stood off on a long port tack. Then came one of the most concentrated periods of action in all the years back to 1851, when Sturrock began a short-tacking duel. Within ten minutes, there were more than a dozen tacks, as the crews belted into the coffee-grinders like football linemen blocking out opposing tackles. It was a slam-bang affair, with the Aussies working themselves into a competitive frenzy as they flipped their boat about and whanged her flailing genoa home time after time. The yoked winches Payne had developed were paying off, and *Gretel* had almost halved the distance between the boats when Mosbacher decided not to play the Aussie game in quite the same way and broke off into a loose cover. It kept him ahead by a boat length at the first mark of the eight-mile-legged triangle, 12 seconds on the clock, and the margin remained exactly that as the boats roared southeastward on a reach as though yoked together.

At the turning mark, the already exciting race erupted into one of the great moments of Cup history as they jibed around the tug and squared away for a run almost directly downwind to the finish. *Weatherly* was a bit slow in breaking out her heavy weather chute, a blood red affair, and Mosbacher allowed Sturrock to shoot up on his weather quarter during the rounding into a position that cast *Gretel's* wind shadow over the leader. *Gretel's* spinnaker was the first to fill, a pure white orb that burst instantly, without a flutter, into sculptured marble. Just as it did, her long lean hull surged up onto a big Point Judith roller, and suddenly the deep-displacement hull was surfing like a planing dinghy. Sturrock felt the wheel quiver and go slack as the boat surged forward, and the whole boat began to vibrate, her bow soaring into space as she rode the crest. Standing at *Gretel's* mast, just having secured the spinnaker halyard, burly Norm Wright, whose early sailing had been in the hotly competitive 18-foot dinghies, couldn't resist an old custom of eighteen-sailors, a blood-curdling war-hoop they always let fly when they feel a boat pick up on a plane.

His exultant "Yeeee-hooooo" almost frightened Sturrock out of the cockpit, as he thought the mast must be going, and the cry also froze *Weatherly's* crew for an instant as it hurtled down the breeze to them. *Weatherly's* chute was just filling as *Gretel* surged by, but it was too late, and the Aussie boat took the lead in this one swift instant.

Just as *Gretel* swept by, *Weatherly's* spinnaker guy chose to part, and her pole whanged forward against the headstay and buckled like a broken lance, ruining any chance she had of fighting off the flying *Gretel*. They paraded to the finish, where the Aussie margin was 47 seconds, to a tumultuous ovation, and the series stood at 1-1.

It was at this moment that the critical decision was made to stick to the layday-after-every-race policy, creating one of the great "might-have-beens" of the *America's* Cup story. The next day brought a carbon copy of the fresh westerly, and *Gretel*, now a proven performer, might have once again beaten the shaken Americans, but this was not to be. Instead, after one of the most riotous celebrations in the history of yacht racing, the next day was spent puttering in port. The night before, the Aussies had taken over their favorite waterfront "pub," the Cameo, which they dubbed the Royal Cameo Yacht Squadron, and staged an all-out bash that will never be forgotten by those hundreds of celebrators who managed to wedge through the doors. "Waltzing Matilda" rang from the rafters time after time, along with many less-printable ballads; beer flowed down throats, over heads and cascaded along the bar and across the floor; and the decibel level was unbelievable.

As it turned out, this was the high point, although there was one more splash of drama before the series ended. The third race didn't provide it. The westerly had faded to a whisper and veered to N by E at about 6-7 knots of a warm, quiet day, and the only excitement was at the start. Sturrock seemed to have the ring-around-a-rosy advantage and forced *Weatherly* to tack away just before *Gretel* started on the port tack at the leeward end of the line. Mosbacher was late but had his wind free on starboard, then tacked to port, and when Sturrock tacked over to cover, he crossed *Weatherly's* bow and tacked back on top of her, losing his advantage, as Mosbacher still had his wind free. This was all he needed to work out ahead in a faltering breeze, and the long twice-around windward-leeward race degenerated into a drifting match, with the last two legs becoming reaches as the wind turned fluky. *Weatherly* ate it up, *Gretel* wallowed, and the margin was as much as 23 minutes halfway through the race. As the breeze freshened late in the day, and the boats began to move faster, *Gretel* cut down some of the distance and also the time margin so that it was 8 minutes, 40 seconds at the end, a far cry from the exhilaration of the second race. Again the layday request went up, and again the Aussies missed a fine sailing breeze by so choosing.

This put the fourth race on Saturday, a week after the start, and another big fleet came out to watch a triangular race in a moderate southerly that filled in nicely as the afternoon went on. *Weatherly* took another safe leeward start after the preliminary circling and worked steadily out to a windward advantage during the whole leg, with Mosbacher refusing to respond to Sturrock's attempts at a tacking duel, maintaining a safe, loose cover. He had a 1-minute, 31-second margin at the mark, and the rest of the race was a thrilling cliff-hanger as *Gretel*, slightly faster off the wind, tried to close the gap. On a spinnaker reach she whittled it to 55 seconds at the second mark, and then kept coming on as they jibed and squared away for the finish on the port tack. At first they both flew spinnakers, but, with *Gretel* inching up on his quarter, Mosbacher sailed higher and shifted to a genoa. *Gretel* followed suit, and many thought that she had been "psyched" into dropping an effective sail. She stopped gaining and soon shifted back to spinnaker, driving off to leeward until she was almost abeam of *Weatherly*. Before she could break through, however, *Weatherly* put her spinnaker back up and also began to drive off on a slightly lower course for the line. This gave her enough of a better sailing angle to keep her ahead by 26 seconds, which is the closest official time margin in Cup history, though some boat-for-boat finishes were closer in the days when handicaps determined the time margin. When she finally made it, tension released in *Weatherly*'s crew like a kettle blowing its top.

Unfortunately, after another two-day layday brought on by an intervening Sunday, the fifth race was a distinct anticlimax before a greatly diminished spectator fleet. This was another twice-around windward-leeward, the last one to be used in Cup competition, on a hazy day, in a moderate southerly. This time Sturrock took the safe leeward, but it availed him naught, as Mosbacher worked up from his trailing windward position until Sturrock tacked first and Mosbacher flipped to a safe leeward on port that soon had command. That was the race and the series, as he built on the lead with a loose cover, with the long, lean, light-blue hull loping easily over the ground swell. Nothing *Gretel* tried produced any significant gain, and the two-minute lead the defender had at the first mark increased slowly to a final one of 3 minutes, 40 seconds.

Although this series ended more with a whimper than a bang, it had been a lively, relatively dramatic one and it restored some semblance of competitive interest to the *America's* Cup. It also aroused dreams of possible glory in the heads of many potential challengers and no doubt assured a good future for the competition in Twelve-Meters. If the far-off Aussies could come this close from scratch, couldn't others feel that they might do even better?

From *America's Cup Races* (1970)

Niña Wins the Bermuda Race

One of the most heart-warming results in ocean racing annals

When DeCoursey Fales, 74-year-old skipper of *Niña*, moved front and center at the prize awards ceremony to receive the Bermuda Trophy for winning the Bermuda Race, the ovation that shook the rafters of the big shed along Hamilton Harbor where the ceremony was held was the loudest, longest and most heartfelt ever heard in the history of the race.

The crowd had been a gay, noisy one, and most of the speakers awarding lesser prizes were afforded scant attention. When Sir Julian Gascoigne, Governor of Bermuda, handed over the big silver replica of St. David's Light to Fales, however, every man and woman turned to with a full-throated roar. This storybook ending to what had otherwise been an undramatic race for most of the participants, touched a chord of response in all of them.

The statement most frequently heard all over the island as the crews joined in the usual round of festivities was, "If I couldn't have done it, I'm glad it was the Commodore." Over the years, the anachronism of a schooner built in 1928 and sailed by a white-haired gentleman who might reasonably have retired from racing before most of today's ocean racing sailors were out of junior classes, has captured the imagination and gained the respect of all competitors. Here was the perfect answer to all the talk, the charges of rule-beating, the feverish design competitions, the "building race" of recent years. A sound, well-maintained, well-sailed boat, long-since "outmoded" by rule-beating theorists, could still come up with the biggest prize in ocean racing (even though she was once tabbed a rule-beater herself, as we shall see).

For Fales, a New York banker, it was the grand climax to a career assumed fairly late in life. Until 1938, his interest in yachting had been confined to cruising. After owning two other cruising boats, he bought *Niña* in 1935 when she had been laid up at Nevins Yard in City Island, N.Y., for several years. She had gained fame by winning the race for which she was built, the ocean race to Spain in 1928, under her original owner, Paul Hammond, as well as the Fastnet Race of that year in England. She also won the New London-Gibson Island Race in 1929. Then she lay idle for several years, and had one interlude in which she almost foundered on the way to the Bahamas on a cruising passage after having been bought by the noted English ocean racing skipper, Bobby Somerset.

Fales had *Niña* reconditioned in 1935 and has been improving her ever since while keeping her in the most immaculate condition. His first racing was in the 1937 New York YC cruise when, Fales says, he "found out the things I had to do." From then on he began to race her seriously, and her first major win was the Astor Cup in 1939, repeating in 1940. Before World War II halted activities, she became "the boat to beat" in any event around Long Island Sound, and the Stamford-Vineyard Race became her private specialty. She has won this event or placed high in it more than any other yacht has ever dominated another event of similar stature. After World War II, she was NYYC flagship for three years, and she began her Bermuda Race career in the 1946 event. Her best two races, until this year, earned a third in Class A in 1948 and first in A in 1956.

At 34, *Niña* was the third oldest boat in the 1962 race—*Cotton Blossom IV* and *Chicane* were built in 1926—and she has rightfully earned the nickname of Grand Old Lady of ocean racing, just as her skipper, oldest in the race, is known as the Grand Old Man. In her youth, however, she was looked on in quite a different way. In his book "Ocean Racing" commenting on her entry in the 1928 race to Spain, Alf Loomis (who, incidentally has a longevity record to make *Niña* look puny and was on his 15th Bermuda Race in 1962) has this to say. "For the first time in transatlantic racing, handicaps were allotted . . . and so it follows that for the first time, a boat was built to beat the rules." Later on, in writing of *Niña's* Fastnet victory, Alf states: "The effect of *Niña's* performance was profound. She was berated as a racing machine, and, in truth, with her double staysail rig she required a large crew and was anything but a comfortable cruising boat."

Her plans were published in the June, 1928, YACHTING, and the commentary with them mentioned that her short ends were because of the rule to which she had been built. Incidentally, the Cruising Club rule change put in effect this year only altered *Niña's* rating by one-tenth of a foot.

Whether or not she was a rule beater in 1928, Starling Burgess, who designed her, produced the ultimate in the then-popular schooner rig, a much closer-winded boat than the traditional fisherman types of the day. Her original rig was even said not to be a schooner at all, but a "two-masted cutter," since there was a straight line down her stays from the mainmast truck to her bowsprit. The foremast could have been removed without changing the line of the stays. Since then, Fales has heightened her foremast and shortened her bowsprit, but she still has an immense "fore triangle" ahead of her mainmast, and she makes full use of it both on the wind and off it. She has an assortment of jibs, staysails, genoas and fisherman staysails in her complement of 23 sails that allows for many different combinations. Most effective for reaching are the big fishermen, called golliwobblers, carried between the mainmast and foremast. The two biggest are known as the Monster and the Grand Monster. The latter is so big that its clew trims all the way to the end of the main-boom and could actually be pulled through the sheave there if trimmed too tight.

While *Niña* now rates as a big boat, and big boat devotees took heart at her victory, first by a Class A boat since *Argyll* did it in 1950, she was thought of quite differently in 1928. Designed for the race to Spain, she was also named especially for it, since there was also a *Pinta* entered, and for a while a *Santa Maria*, which didn't start. She was built by Reuben Bigelow of Monument Beach, Mass., on Cape Cod, a craftsman who had never built anything bigger than a catboat before. Her construction is double planked, mahogany, with teak decks.

There was a great fuss over "small" boats going in a Transatlantic race for the first time, and the account by Weston Martyr of her arrival off Santander in 1928 made much of the drama of such a little boat being first to finish. The small boats had started a week ahead of the 180-200 footers, such as *Atlantic* and *Elena*, in the big class. When *Niña* was finally identified Martyr's account says " . . . we look at each other dazed. For instead of the great, redoubtable *Atlantic* that we had come out to greet, it is the *Niña*, the little *Niña*—the smallest boat in the fleet."

Another finish spectator was excited too. He leaped to the cabin top of the launch he was riding, waved his cap and shouted, "Well sailed, *Niña!* I congratulate you. I am the King of Spain."

And so *Niña* has had a long career of causing furores and gaining respect. From a "rule beater" and a "small boat," she has evolved into the champion of the traditionalists and the savior of the big boats. The excitement surrounding her entry into Hamilton Harbor was equally as high-pitched as her arrival off Santander 34 years ago, even without royalty to greet her. Officials of the Royal Bermuda YC hastened out to welcome her as she powered through Two Rock Passage into the anchorage. At the time she was only a strong possibility as a winner and smaller boats had a chance to catch her, but there was a growing feeling that she had done it, and the crowd watching the results being posted on the RBYC bulletin boards cheered every time a new batch of finishers failed to dislodge the old girl.

Finally, shortly after midnight, early Thursday morning, when *Lancetilla II*, the top time allowance boat, had failed to finish within her time, the popular result became official.

As far as the racing went, there was nothing dramatic or unusual about *Niña*'s performance. She had "schooner breezes" for perhaps 75 percent of the time, with a golli-wobbler up. She never was within a plank of putting her rail under, carrying full sail, and she made runs of 200 and 214 miles in the first two days. Perhaps the key to her victory came Sunday night when she had several Class A boats in sight ahead. Instead of holding high of the rhumb line to make more westing while crossing the Gulf Stream, Fales decided to slack sheets a bit and drive her off, paralleling the line.

By this decision she got a bit to the east of many of her rivals and suffered less from the great calm that caused so many boats to go dead after two days of glorious sailing. *Niña* had it for about 12 hours, starting Monday evening, but she was dinghy-raced through it, with every zephyr played for what it was worth and constant sail changes to catch what catspaws there were. Drifters, gollies, spinnakers, genoas and other light sails in varying combinations were worked carefully and she never lost way, gradually moving into better air by Tuesday morning, while the bulk of the fleet had to wait until much later Tuesday for it. She saw no other boats after dropping *Petrel* astern on Monday afternoon until she sighted *Stormvogel* on approaching North Rock.

Niña's gear is as modern as the newest racing machine. Despite the complexity of lines needed to handle a schooner rig, she has remarkably uncluttered decks, and her winches and fittings are right up to date. There is a clean efficiency about every inch of her, and her hollow mainmast, built with the boat, looks as new as it did in 1928.

Fales, who stands watches and handles the wheel often, has naturally been able to collect a topnotch crew to sail with him, and he gives full credit to them whenever he is congratulated. The watch captains were Peter Comstock and Capt. Arthur Schuman, USN, and Dan Bickford was the navigator. Also in the crew were: Howard L. Payne, John Sinclair, Harold Wilder, William Close, Tony Hogan, Radley H. Daly, Charles L. Stone, Dr. Paul Sheldon and Capt. Trygve Thorsen.

Grand old girl that she is, and as wonderful a chapter in her career as this popular victory was, everyone who races knows that *Niña* has many more winning races ahead of her.

From *The Best from Yachting* (1967)

VI

Racing in its Varying Forms

Many sailors live only to race. Over the years, I was deeply involved, and these are some experiences and events that stand out.

The Fun of Club Racing

The sort of racing that most of us do

STATISTICALLY, THE most popular form of sailboat racing, club racing, is the least widely reported and publicized. The local fleet competition is truly the backbone of the sport. More people engage in it than in any other form of boating competition, yet their efforts are only memorialized by some agate type in the local paper, if at all, or perhaps a belated mention in a local news column in *Yachting* if they happen to win the season championship.

This is the fate of nonchampionship caliber competition in golf, tennis, squash racquets, bowling, and all the other sports with heavy local participation. It is a natural enough situation, but the sports would not be the same if it were not for these loyal and relatively unsung devotees. And they wouldn't do it if they didn't have fun. They might dream of going on to a class national title, an individual NAYRU crown or an Olympic berth, but meanwhile, they'd like to pin back the ears of the guy down the street when they get out on the race course of a weekend.

The SORC and an occasional long distance race are a touch of the "big time" and provide glamour and excitement, but the weekly battles in our local fleet are the real focus of my competitive instincts. I have these in pretty good supply, but only at the moment of battle—not for long periods of preparation and anticipation. Some one-design sailors become deeply involved with the care and tuning of their boats, with the development of go-fasts, the polishing of bottoms, and the constant search for new gadgets, but I don't have the time (or inclination) for this phase of the sport. I like to step in the boat on race day knowing I have an even chance, race hard, and then relax afterwards, so the more one-design the class the better.

We have therefore ended up in a rather unlikely "racing machine" that suits our purposes exactly. This is the 18′ Sanderling catboat, a fiberglass replica of the classic Cape Cod cat. She was never intended by her developer and builder, Breck Marshall of South Dartmouth, Mass., as a race boat. He thought of her as a roomy, comfortable day sailer and overnighter, but she actually has all the elements that make for good, strictly uniform, one-design competition. She is an able, responsive boat, and all Sanderlings are from the same mold, with sails and spars from the same manufacturers. The boats are basically identical, and our local fleet at New Jersey's Shrewsbury Sailing and Yacht Club has agreed on no alterations to the stock boat. The rudder and centerboard cannot be changed, and all fittings must be approved by fleet vote. The intent is to keep the boats completely one-design, and the policy has been successful. The only variables are the rake of the mast and the condition of the bottom (and possibly age of sails, which may not be replaced until after two years) and in the eight years the fleet has been racing, no one boat has had demonstrably better boat speed.

People laugh at us when we get in our big, beamy cats to go out to race, but we laugh right back. What we have is a bunch of oversized fat man's dinghies, and we have consistently had the very closest kind of competition. No one worries about someone else having a "rule-beater," and there is a minimum of fussing over boats, which is what really counts. The class is popular with younger marrieds, who must spend a good deal of time with growing families, and they can get a lot of use out of their "racing machines" as picnic boats and overnighters. It is also ideal for middle-aged types (present company included) who can no longer perform the acrobatics needed in less sedate vessels. It's a great husband-and-wife boat, as the crew has very little opportunity to louse up. The main crew functions are stopwatch reading, centerboard tending, placing the butt correctly, and moral support. Under these circumstances, there is virtually no reason for the skipper to scream at the crew, and a pleasant, team-like rapport can be established.

There is no national championship to aim for, and only a few special open regattas in which we're included, as there is no national class organization and only a few isolated fleets in other areas, so our local competition is the complete, and intermittently fierce, focus of our efforts. And so, as a tribute to all who sail in the same relative circumstances, and as a come-on to those who have problems sailing in other ways, here is how, distilling in its particulars the generalities of this form of competition, a recent race day went for us.

A race day morning always has an aura about it. There is a sense of anticipation, a pre-kickoff feeling and a working up of competitive juices as we check the weather outlook and get ready for the two-mile jaunt from our home pier to the sailing club. Part of the ritual is a scrub of the bottom with a long-handled brush, our only "tuning" each week, and I put on a bathing suit and old sneakers to wade in and go to work. The tide is low, and it isn't quite the effort needed at high tide. About an hour before the 1:30 race time, we put the ice chest aboard and cast off. Hors d'oeuvres and cocktails take up the passage to the club (training for this kind of competition doesn't preclude the amenities) while we look around for weather signs.

It is a warm, hazy day, with very few clouds and a strong, 18–22 knot west wind, a rarity for the Shrewsbury. Usually, a fitful morning westerly gives way to a sea breeze from just east of south at about one o'clock, but this seems to have enough strength to last through the day. There'll be tricky lifts and erratic puffs in a land breeze like this.

"Pretty strong westerly," I pontificate. "Don't think there'll be a sea breeze."

At the club, we put the outboard and gas can ashore, check the boom and gaff outhauls and the entire set of the big 265-foot sail, and head for the starting area. Excitement builds inside as we case the rest of the fleet—nine boats today—check the stop watch, set the centerboard depth according to the still-low tide, exchange a few wisecracks as we swoosh past other boats, and get the feel of the breeze.

The course is a triangle with three beats, and the starting interval is three minutes. Sanderlings go second, after the Comets, and the horn goes for their warning gun as the white flag snaps out in a freshening puff.

Jane calls off the half-minutes, and I stay close to watch

the Comets start and to see how the line lies. It favors port tack a bit, but the shifts are erratic enough so that you can't count on it. It's still favoring port when they go off, and then a shift blows in that squares the line for a while. Will it last or shift back? I don't think it will last, and I plan it that way.

"Two minutes."

Jane starts calling every 15 seconds now as we head away from the line on port, fairly high, jibe over at 1:30 to go, and head back, sail luffing while we take stock. There's a new shift, and it favors port again. We're closest to the flag. Good! No one to leeward, no one too close astern, clear air, and the whole line to play with.

"One minute."

I start sheeting in, and Jane hikes over the coaming, fanny on deck, as we begin to move. Sanderlings don't accelerate like a dinghy, and it's fatal to wait too long to get up to speed.

"Forty-five." We gather speed; then, "Blue down," Jane says, and we pass the leeward-end flag. Still no one bothering us.

"Twenty." Charge the line, bearing off along it to build up speed. "Fifteen." Start sharpening up. "Ten—nine—eight—seven—six—five—four—three—two—one—GO!"

This is when the semi-relaxed maneuvering, the gradual build-up suddenly becomes hard-nosed and all-out, like the first hard block on the kickoff, the first ace of the tennis match—everyone means business, and the sense of intensified action is electric. Nobody's giving an inch or a nickel now.

We're two-thirds of the way along the line and right on it with the horn, hard on the wind and driving into a fresh header. There's room to tack. Let's flip.

"Ready about."

We swing over onto port in the lift, with the fleet below us.

"Holsey's over. Waterbury's over," Jane reports, as I concentrate on using the lift. "Stives is still on starboard."

"Can't cover 'em all," I mutter. We feather up in the fresh puff, edging to windward of the boats that have just tacked, and Jane hikes out as far as she can. The course legs are short today because of low tide, and we can't go too far on the port side of the leg because of the Gooseneck Point shoal, but fortunately this is still the favored tack, and we're doing OK. All but Stives are tucked away below us, and I play the little lifts and headers, waiting for a major shift. I don't want it yet. Wait till we get nearer the lay line, and it should come around the point behind the windward mark (to be left to starboard).

"There it is," I say, and Jane exhales happily as she senses it. We stand on for a couple of hundred feet to make sure, then flip to starboard almost able to lay the mark. We can lay if it lifts us any more.

"Stives has a lift," Jane says, frustration edging her voice. He has skirted the shoal and flipped to port over there on the other side of the course in a beautiful shift off that point, and it's better than ours. He has us by two lengths at the mark, and we up-board and bear off trying to get on his wind. We go high in the light spots and drive off in the puffs, gaining a bit, but we can't quite make it before the jibing mark. Here's where the workout comes in a Sanderling in a fresh breeze. That's a big sail to get across, and a lot of sheet to go through your hands. Both boats slam over, just under control, and Stives goes high, protecting his wind. I stay up there, and he keeps going higher, fighting me off, and Holsey, a few lengths behind, heads straight for the leeward mark and takes over first. I miss getting buoy room by a few feet, but how important they are just then, and we round third. It's hot going down wind, and I've worked up a sweat and a dry mouth. I fight the sheet in, and as soon as we're close-hauled we flip to port to get clear air.

"They let us go!" Jane reports.

"Good.—Hike!" as a puff hits and we ride it for all its worth. We stand out on port all by ourselves, heading for that same starboard tack lift near the windward mark, we hope, and it looks good. Holsey and Stives have gone way off on starboard, but Waterbury, a close fourth, has gone to their side and flipped sooner, and he's charging across now in a big lift on port. Will the hoped-for starboard lift be enough for us? No. It's there, but not a sharp one, and he has us by about the same distance Stives did the first time. What musical chairs! Stives and Holsey are well behind now and the big task is to catch Waterbury. We can't on the run and reach, again by a few feet after a lot of sweaty effort, but he lets us tack to port first after rounding the leeward mark and doesn't cover on the instant. From then on it's just sail her hard, hike and feather in the puffs. He's off our port quarter, and it's really close. Despite the over-the-shoulder fascination, I concentrate on boat speed, with a few reminders from Jane to "sail your boat."

Just at the right spot short of the lay line, the blessed starboard tack lift comes through with an extra favorable angle to it, and we tack. Any further and we might overstand and let him tack inside us. We skin across his bow by a length. It's only a couple of hundred yards to the finish and we're laying it now. No headers! Please no headers! We have him if we don't have to tack again. There's a momentary lull and a dropping off to leeward, and our stomachs sink but there's another good, fresh lift right behind the lull, and we slice up to the line sharply, two lengths ahead holding her down and driving, and finally there's the wonderful sound of the horn.

"Yee—hooooo. Break out the beer."

That should be the dramatic way to end the story of a race day, but we always have two races each day of our championship series, and our glow of triumph can only last through a short breather over the beer. Soon we are out there banging way at the starting line again in an even fresher breeze, and this time my start is not a good one. It's a port tack line again, and I can't get far enough up it because of boats controlling me from leeward. We're fourth most of the way round, finally pass one boat on the run, and salvage a third behind Stives.

A letdown, yes, from the bang-bang excitement of the first race, but, as we hoist a long, tall cool one and head home on a swooping run with the afternoon light slanting against the sedge banks and ocean front cottages off to the eastward, there's a wonderful sense of having been thoroughly involved, of tired muscles relaxing, of teamwork and excitement shared, of challenges met and at least partially mastered, and of a day of all-out competition that gave us just about everything we want from sailboat racing.

From The Sailing Life (1974)

The "Old Man" and the Sea

The strains of crewing for a 12-year old son in a Comet

The "Old Man" in this case is not a Cuban tuna fisherman, but the author, and not just because he is pressing 40 a mite close. Age is a question of how you feel, and I never felt like an old man before. Then I took to crewing for my children in sailing races, a new career that has me hopping in and out of various small craft, and I have an aching midriff, a bursitic hip, spavined shins, fingers and back that won't straighten out, and a general stem-to-stern creakiness that qualify me well for the title.

I have discovered muscles I didn't know I had—ones that are never needed in handling a tiller, driving a car, bending an elbow, or even playing squash racquets. Then there are other muscles I never knew I lacked, plus a certain agility and sense of balance. This showed up in the very first minute of my new career. It was embarked upon as a way of helping the three children along as beginning skippers, and it started when my son Robby graduated from a staid, stable 13^1/$_2$' Wood Pussy Class catboat to a 16' Comet sloop for his twelfth birthday two years ago.

We launched the light, slender Comet for the first time, pulled her over to the bulkhead, and it then became the crew's duty to go aboard and rig her. I stepped down on the foredeck, started aft around the mast, and—you know what happened. You might say that I started my crew career with quite a splash.

At least I showed the proper loyal instincts by letting go of the mast before I pulled the boat in on top of me, though the skipper was laughing too hard up on the bulkhead to express his appreciation. From this damp beginning I was seldom dry again all summer, and other adventures were not long in following.

Our first sails were in mercifully light air, as we found all the shoal spots that never bothered a Wood Pussy, and there were other interesting developments. In our first race, we came about off a reach to beat to the next mark. I switched the backstays with fair timing, managed to trim the proper jib sheet (I had been just as likely to grab the windward one), and scrambled awkwardly over the centerboard trunk to the other rail. Catching my breath as we squared away on the new course. I looked up and to leeward to see how Robby had the main trimmed. It wasn't there!

"Hey!" I cried. "Where's the main?"

In sudden bewilderment I reared up to look around and hit my head on the boom directly over me on the windward side of the boat. The boom vang was still set (my job to cast it off).

For a while, the father-crew role was a mixed one, leading to exchanges like this:

Skipper: "The other tack looks good. Do you think I should come about?"

Crew: "If it looks good to you."

Skipper: "I'm not sure."

Crew: "Well, make up your mind."

Skipper: "Ready about, hard alee." (Silence, except for heavy breathing of crew as he tends backstays and jib sheets and scrambles to opposite rail—then, a few minutes later) "Darn. Eddie Ryan picked us on that tack."

Crew: "You must have come about into a header."

Skipper: "But, Dad, you *told* me to come about."

This sort of thing gradually lessened, as Robby realized he actually was skipper, with the responsibility for decisions. I figured my being skipper in everything but the hand on the tiller would not do him any good, and I tried not to revert to being a father too often.

Sometimes parental pressures were too strong to resist. When we hit a buoy in an important race because Robby let the tiller go, I sounded off with a lecture on carelessness in everything from cutting the grass to algebra exams, not to mention rounding buoys. As a father I was sometimes a help, though.

One reason I was tolerated as crew despite advanced decrepitude was that Comet competition in New Jersey means a lot of trailer work. The boats are dry-sailed and driven from regatta to regatta. Since 12-year-olds can only operate hot-rod boats, not cars, this became an important function for father-crew when it came time for our first away regatta.

In the good old days, the fat catboats I raced sat on a mooring all summer. You just hoisted the sail and were ready to race. Now, keeping up with the march of science, we had to arise at the crack of dawn, unrig the boat, lash spars and rigging with loving care, load the car with gear, hitch up the trailer, drive through weekend traffic, unhitch the trailer, manhandle it across a crowded parking yard, unlash all the gear we had just lashed, set up the rigging, wait in line at a hoist and finally lower away, fending her off the bulkhead in mid-flight, before we even got her in the water. I was ready for bed, and we hadn't hoisted sail yet.

The regatta was on Raritan Bay, a wide, breezy body of water, and the usual southwester was blowing. As we swooped out of the yacht basin, planing swiftly between seagoing tankers in the ship channel, I became increasingly conscious of a Comet's slender proportions, not to mention those of my 100-pound skipper. To an old-fashioned eye, the modern "piano wire" rigging and lightweight race fittings on the boat looked as fragile as Christmas tree ornaments no matter what anyone said about their strength. It was with an anxious eye on the weather, then, that we headed for the starting area with 25 Comets and boats from several other classes.

There was a sultry feel to the air, a dirty look on the western horizon that was more than the usual Jersey smog, and the breeze bounced off the shore in uneven puffs. As we planed along on a broad reach with a white wing of water arching out to windward between my legs and blowing back on me with remarkable precision and thoroughness, I was introduced to my single biggest problem as a crew.

"Hike, Dad!" Robby called, as an extra puff hit us.

I leaned well out to windward, or so I thought, with my legs wrapped around the hiking straps in the cockpit, and Rob stretched his slender frame out until only his toes seemed left in the boat. Despite this effort, we heeled over, spilled our wind and fell out of the plane in an ignominious wallow of wake. All around us other Comets zoomed on ahead, planing flatly as they skittered over the wave tops, their crews leaning far out, parallel to the water.

"Gosh, Dad, why didn't you hike?" Rob asked as we collected ourselves.

"Why didn't *I* hike?" was my injured reply. "I practically fell out of the boat."

My midriff muscles were still quivering, and I could feel pains shooting up and down what I'd always thought of as a fairly serviceable pair of legs, but I got out there again and managed to hold it long enough for us to pick up on a plane again in the next puff. It had better staying power than I did, however, and once again there was a question of my straightening up or breaking in two backwards. The old abdomen went into a critical quiver, sort of like a jet plane hitting the sound barrier, and I sat up.

As we slewed out of the plane in a shower of spray, another boat shot by us to windward with two college athlete types, muscles rippling on their bronzed "Greek God" torsos as they leaned far out, whooping and hollering like cowboys. Robby watched them go with mournful eye.

Once the race started, excitement pumped enough adrenalin through the old system for me to hang out at the proper angle well enough for us to be in the first 10 at the mark. The excitement also made us forget the weather for a while, but it brought itself to our attention as we cleared the buoy and planed off on the second leg of the triangle. A rumble of thunder sounded over the course, and we looked up to see a wall of black clouds, with the sky a dirty brown between them and the horizon, moving our way rapidly. The breeze took on new authority, and we had a wild ride to the next mark, with my sinews twanging like old rubber bands at every puff.

As we neared it two boats jibing the buoy tangled masts, and there was a horrendous ripping of sails and cracking of spars. Their predicament left precious little room for us and the three or four boats near us to squeeze by.

Comet routine for jibing is for the skipper to handle

tiller and mainsheet, with the crew working vang, sliding backstays and jib, then the centerboard, but suddenly I found myself thinking, in the habit of years, like a skipper, worrying about buoy room and looking for a hole for us to shoot through. I was also thinking like a father, wondering how the skipper, now all at once just my little 12-year-old child, was ever going to handle sheet and tiller and find an opening at the same time.

As a result, the 12-year old child did his job beautifully, easing her through an eyelash of an opening and bringing the main over just in time, while the crew, all father now and watching him anxiously, forgot to take up on the windward backstay as the boom swung over. Robby yelled "Backstay!" as the mast bowed dangerously, and I slammed the slide home on the track just in time.

Now the weather was our main concern as we surfed along on a run. We kept ahead of the squall line to the lee-ward mark and hardened up for a second lap just in time to see a brownish curtain over a line of foam race away from the shore to the northwest and head for us like an avalanche, with streaks of wind blackening the water ahead of it. The rain line sent out a roar like a jungle waterfall as it sped toward us, and we saw the boats ahead engulfed by it.

"Let her luff," I cried, slacking the jib sheet, and the main spilled wind just before the big blast hit.

It was more than 50 knots and loaded with icy rain. All around us boats flipped over in a wild panorama of careening sails and hands clutching gunwales, but we had just had enough time to be ready for it. Robby kept the tiller hard over and her bow held up as the sails thundered like maniacal machine guns.

Not trusting the light rigging (overcaution, as greater familiarity proved), we were sure it would give under the shattering vibration of the sails, so we freed the halyards and fought main and jib down, running off before it once they were under control.

It proved a thin squall despite the vicious front of it, and we were soon looking at its backside as it raced off to leeward, the mutter and roar diminishing like the sound of a train moving away. More than half the 70 boats in the regatta were capsized or dismasted. Twelve other Comets had been able to luff through it with their sails up. With ours down we had been blown so far to leeward that we finished 13th, but it felt like a winning race as we crossed the line.

Our teamwork improved with the confidence gained in this one, along with the tone of my muscles, though I found it difficult to stand up straight before Wednesday of each week, and a whimsical friend sent me a booklet put out by his insurance company entitled "How to Enjoy the Aging Body." I also decided to buy stock in a company making small adhesive bandages, having become their best customer.

I never could match the football heroes in sustained hiking, but we did enough of a job to qualify for the territorial regatta from our club and then for the International Championship Regatta via the territorial. All this was by mid-July, with the International not until September. We planned on all of August to perfect our teamwork for the big event, but we reckoned without the feminine three-fifths of the family. They had been racing the Wood Pussy with 10-year-old Martha as skipper, Mom as crew, and 7-year-old Alice an occasional third crew and severest critic. They were doing well enough, but Mom came up with a point.

"It isn't fair," she said, "for you to spend all your time with Robby. Martha has more to learn than he does, and I can't teach her. Now that you've qualified for the championship, how about crewing for Martha for a while?"

Translated, this meant that Mom, who was brought up a horsewoman and had never been in a boat until she was married, felt a lot more confidence in taking a horse over those fence things than in trying to tame a boat. After all, a boat doesn't eat lumps of sugar. Much as she now loves boats, she feels that understanding the mysteries of racing, much less having to explain them to a 10-year-old, is a man-sized problem with which no grown woman should have to cope.

So, naturally, the change was made, and I was back in Wood Pussies, only this time as a crew. The physical change was a delight. No backstays, no jib sheets, a wide comfortable cockpit, no hiking, and no wall of water shooting over you in a plane. In a week or two my bruises actually began to disappear and I was able to stand erect while walking.

Now my troubles were social. Martha had a fine touch on the tiller, and an instinctive grasp of the basics of sailboat racing, but an ideal course for her would have been about a quarter of a mile. The attention span of a gregarious 10-year-old female is short, and the river seemed to be entirely populated by friends of hers in other boats. No matter what the stage of a race, she never snubbed a single one, waving gaily to them all. I fully expect her to be the first lady mayor of our town some day.

The antidote was a monotone from me of "Look at your sail, Martha . . . look at your sail, Martha . . ." Repeated at frequent enough intervals it managed to get us around a course in good order, though once I stepped up the frequency a bit in a tight situation and got this exasperated reply.

"I just *did* look at it, Daddy."

The comfort of a Wood Pussy cockpit also gave me more time to think of other things, such as the perpetual running battle I've enjoyed with certain race committees for years. In one regatta run by a committee whose ways have always seemed especially mysterious to me, although I know them well and have even worked with them on their side of the fence, there was a real rhubarb of a mix-up in a recalled start, and my stack suddenly blew. I was unable to restrain a certain measure of vocal criticism. (I'm told that it was heard downwind for three miles.)

Martha was mad, too, to start with, but I noticed a change in her expression about the third time we sailed by the committee boat. Finally, as we neared it again, she spoke in that special tone children get when they wish their parents were two other people.

"Daddy, please stop. You're right, but it won't do any good to yell at them any more."

Martha now has a stalwart male classmate as crew and gets along fine on her own. I'm sure natural processes account for her increased ability to concentrate, though I hope she sometimes hears a voice in the back of her mind repeating, "Look at your sail, Martha."

That soft session in a Wood Pussy set me back physically for returning to the Comet for the International Regatta on Lake Erie that September. Instead of lolling in the Wood Pussy's big open cockpit, I should have been working out with some football team to get in shape for three days of a Lake Erie northwester. At least I felt as though I'd played a full football season, and under water at that, by the time the regatta was over. It was an incident during it that made me realize my Comet crewing days were numbered, even though I lasted through the next season.

With Lake Erie lumping up in a vicious slop no self-respecting body of salt water would ever be a party to, dropping every other wave top down my neck, we were back to the old routine of "Hike, Dad, *hike!*" and the muscles were back to their old quivers, with a few brand new twinges. As my effective periods on the hiking straps grew shorter, while the muscle men all around seemed able to hang out ad infinitum, Robby grew more and more outspoken.

"But they're all young athletes, Rob," I said. "Remember your old man's age."

Just as I said this, a boat went by us with crew and skipper barely hanging by their heels, their torsos bending downward toward the water in a fantastic show of acrobatics. I knew the skipper was in his mid-20's, but he happened to have parted company with most of his hair at an early age.

"Look at them," Robby cried in scorn. "Look at that guy hike, Dad, and he's *bald!*"

Well, the signs were right. Robby, now 45 pounds heavier himself, has a fellow footballer as crew, and I am seldom needed in a boat. In a way it's even tougher to watch from the shore as a parent than to sit in as crew, though a lot more comfortable. I'm not through yet, though. Alice got a 10′ Turnabout catboat for her birthday this year and has just started to race.

I'm happy to report that it is almost never necessary for a 185-pound adult to hike in a Turnabout.

From *The Sailing Life* (1974)

The King's Dragon

Colorful competition in Denmark, and an unusually stressful relief situation

When I sailed with King Constantine's Olympic crew in *Toxotis* in the Aegean Rally in 1966, we found that after the rally we were all going to Denmark for the festivities in connection with the centennial of KDY, the Royal Yacht Club of Denmark. A Transatlantic Race was ending, which I would be covering, the One Ton championships were being held, and a great many one-design classes were conducting regattas. One of them was the Dragon Gold Cup, the world championship of that class, which was then an Olympic class, and Odysseas and his sidekick, Yorgo, were going right from the Rally to trail Constantine's Dragon to Copenhagen.

When we had a reunion there, I found out that Constantine had not yet arrived, and Odysseas and Yorgo asked me to crew with them in the tune-up race for the Gold Cup. Top sailors from all over the world were in the regatta, and it would be a great experience. Fortunately, this was not the race in which printed instructions, which were handed out in either Danish or English, contained a lulu of a mixup. The Danish instructions had the fleet rounding the first mark to port, and the English ones called for a starboard rounding, and the resulting confusion was one of the classic shouting matches of all time (the race, of course, had to be canceled).

We had a very exciting race in a fresh, puffy land breeze, and rounded the last leeward mark in first place. Right behind us were two of the top class hotshots, the Americans Bobby Mosbacher and Buddy Friederichs, and we had to make the unavoidable decision on which one to cover. We chose Mosbacher and held him, but Friederichs naturally split tacks, and he took us both.

It had been a hard race, and we were glad to break out a beer and relax a bit as we jogged back to the KDY smallboat club at Skovshoved. I knew the beer was going to tax my bladder after a long afternoon, but I figured we would soon be in, and it tasted great. Halfway back to port, we saw a powerboat heading for us at top speed with a man standing on the bow wigwagging madly, and suddenly Odysseas and Yorgo braced up and looked sharp (what they said to each other in Greek I have no idea), because it was Constantine, tall, dark, youthful, and very excited. He wanted to come aboard.

Jumping over eagerly from the powerboat, he greeted his crew with joyous cries as they handed him his sailing jacket. "Ah! My boat. My lovely boat!" he said, laughing happily. "I am so glad to see her again. It is so long since I have sailed her."

We had met briefly when he came to wish *Toxotis* luck at the Rally (and his first sentence was "How is Bus Mosbacher?"), and he shook hands warmly now and asked about the race. As he shrugged into his sailing jacket and grabbed the tiller, he turned to me and asked, very politely, "Do you have any plans, Mr. Robinson? I would love to sail my boat for a while if you are not in a hurry to go ashore, but we can take you in if this is inconvenient."

So how do you answer a request like that? Tell him your bladder is about to burst?

Instead, I mumbled what I hoped was a polite and diplomatic version of "Go ahead, King. Sail your boat," and settled onto the cockpit sole with my legs crossed, wondering about the protocol of taking a leak over the side of a royal yacht.

I knew he was far from stuffy and had a sense of humor, judging from a story Bus Mosbacher told of a time when he was crewing for Constantine in the Dragon at Piraeus. Bus was tending the spinnaker sheet, and there came a time when he wanted to trim it and found that Constantine was sitting on it. With the diplomatic tact that kept America's Cup crews at top form for him and earned him the job of Chief of Protocol in the State Department, Bus asked, "What does one say to a King who is sitting on the spinnaker sheet?" and Constantine's answer was "Tell him to get his royal ass off it!"

Still, I didn't have the guts to stand up and use the lee rail, so I suffered in silence while we ranged through the fleet, and Constantine renewed acquaintances with his friends and competitors in the class. Finally we came to Prince Juan Carlos, at the time the designate to the throne of Spain in Franco's plans, and now the King of Spain, who is Constantine's brother-in-law. English is their mutual language, and they greeted each other with glad cries. Juan Carlos is slender, blond, and so handsome as to be almost pretty.

"Hello, brother-in-law," Constantine called. "How's my sister? How's the folks?"

"Everybody's fine," Juan Carlos said.

"How did you do in the race?"

"Don't ask."

"What's the matter?"

"Last night!" Juan Carlos cried, holding his head. "The Spanish Ambassador came aboard the yacht for one drink at nine o'clock, and would you believe FOUR O'CLOCK—" He held his head again and rolled his eyes.

After some more banter we sailed on, and Constantine chuckled over Juan Carlos' plight.

"What yacht is he staying on?" I asked.

"My father-in-law's. The royal yacht of Denmark."

"Why does he live there instead of ashore?"

Constantine laughed and gave an expressive shrug. "If he lives ashore, we can never find him," he said.

In my condition, laughing was difficult, but I kept up a brave show, and finally we made it ashore. I departed with what I hoped was not too unseemly haste, not knowing the protocol for going ashore from royal vessels, and safely managed a stiff-legged walk to the place I had been dreaming of for the last hour.

From *A Sailor's Tales* (1978)

Man Overboard!

A dramatic incident in the Bermuda Race

"Unless I had been through it, I would never have believed it. I didn't think anyone could ever have been recovered under those conditions." This was the way Jack Weston characterized his experience in the Bermuda Race aboard Charlie Ulmer's Block Island 40 yawl *Scylla* when he fell overboard at the height of the storm in the early hours of Thursday morning, June 23.

Weston, who spent between 40 minutes and an hour in the water (everyone was too busy to keep an exact log) said there were several keys to the happy ending to his fantastic experience. Most important was the new type of water light made by Guest Products.

"Without the light, it never would have been possible," Weston said, "and to think that I kidded Charlie about spending all that money when he showed the light to me before the race. The light costs about 80 bucks, but I'll have to say it was well worth it."

Other factors in the successful rescue were the extremely thorough preparations for the race made by Ulmer, excellent organization and cool performance, with no element of panic, by *Scylla's* crew, a spare engine battery among her stores, and the fact that Weston is a strong, experienced swimmer. Although he played down this part of it, it is obvious that he is a better than average swimmer. He was a football player and competitive swimmer in college and has been around the water all his life. The battery, incidentally, was Weston's pre-race present to the boat.

Weston is a 35-year-old salesman from Eastchester, N.Y., married and has three children. Although this was his first Bermuda Race, he has been sailing out of the City Island area all his life on Long Island Sound around-the-buoys and major middle distance races. He has specialized in sail handling and foredeck work. He is stocky, muscular, youthful-looking and in very good physical condition.

The story of his ordeal starts with the buildup of stormy weather through Wednesday afternoon and evening. As the storm increased, *Scylla* went through a series of sail changes, shortening down gradually. Like almost everyone in the race, her crew thought the storm was a short squall that would soon be over, and were reluctant to shorten down too much. Weston was on the foredeck almost constantly from 1600 to midnight, when everyone was finally convinced that the blow would last at least all night.

Weston decided to go below about 0100, as he had stayed up through one watch off. Dressed in pants, shirt, knee boots and foul weather gear with a hooded parka, and with a safety belt on over his parka, he detached his lifeline, which he had been using constantly, and started down the hatch to the cabin. *Scylla*, under small jib, heavily reefed main, and mizzen, was heaving and jumping in wild, erratic fashion in short, steep and very confused seas, with winds estimated at about 50 knots.

When he was hip-deep in the companionway, *Scylla* lurched violently and fell away from under him, down and sideways. Weston was catapulted out of the hatch, slid over the trunk and down to the leeward rail, where a rush of water along the deck washed him underneath the lifeline and overboard. Dazed by being knocked down, he had no idea what had happened and felt nothing to grab or hold onto. The first realization that he had actually gone overboard came when he saw the transom disappearing away from him over a wave. Then the masthead light dipped out of sight, and the awful awareness came over him with full impact that he was alone in the water.

"My first feeling was one of terrible sadness," Weston described it. "I gave myself up completely. I had no hope that they could get back to me in those conditions, and I just drifted without conscious effort, thinking of my family. I kept afloat almost automatically, but with no hope, and wondered how long it would take to drown and what it would be like."

Meanwhile, on *Scylla*, although there was little hope that a rescue could take place under such conditions, all hands turned to the man overboard detail with dispatch and efficiency. Each man had a sick, gone feeling that they would never find him, and yet they had to make every effort. The first move, and the key to the whole operation, was made by Ray Kaufman, Snipe sailor from Port Washington, Long Island, who was tending the mizzen from a position abaft the cockpit. He saw Weston go and immediately threw the waterlight overboard. Unlike waterlights previously in use, the Guest light, developed for air-sea rescue use, shows a bright flashing light rather than a steady one. It is a strobe light that pulses with great brilliance.

Chuck Wiley, of Oxford, Md., on the wheel, immediately made note of *Scylla*'s heading so that she could be turned back on a reciprocal bearing. She was jibed over as soon as possible, and the sails were dropped as an attempt was made to start the engine. *Scylla* has a diesel. The battery was dead, so the sails were hoisted again while Ulmer went to the heaving, crashing forepeak to get the spare battery out. It was buried under spare sails and bags and lines, but he finally wrestled it out. Meanwhile the navigator made a plot of *Scylla*'s position for the moment Weston went over.

After considerable wrestling and heaving, the new battery was hooked up to the engine and the motor kicked over. The sails came down again. Through it all, the light in the water, or at least the glow of it against the clouds, had remained visible from the boat for all but a moment or two.

It was the light that changed Weston's situation. He was not aware of it for quite some time, estimated as perhaps 15 minutes. He had merely been keeping himself afloat, with no effort to do anything else, and no hope of rescue, until the glow of the light gradually impinged on his consciousness.

"It took a while for me to wake up to what it was," Weston said, "and then my actions became almost subconscious. I don't remember planning out any steps to save myself, or any orderly thinking on how I should act, but the glow of the light started me acting. I guess I realized that as long as it was there, there was some chance of my being found. It sort of beckoned me to it with the pulsing beat of its signal.

"I don't remember stripping my clothes, and I couldn't tell you exactly how I did it. I know I'd have trouble enough getting out of a hooded parka in a country club pool, but I got out of it somehow."

Trying to get to the light, Weston found that he could not make any progress on top of the water because of the size of the waves and the roughly cresting tops, so he started swimming under water. He would take a breath and dive deeply, and the water was so clear that the glow of the light penetrated beneath the surface to guide him. He doesn't know how long it took, or how many dives, but he finally made it, approaching the light from underneath. He came up from below, with the glow shining eerily down to him, and grabbed the light by its weighted bottom.

"Once I got to the light, I felt some hope for the first time," Weston grinned. "I really felt that they might see me, now that I knew how bright it was. I did some pretty irrational things, like picking the light out of the water and waving it over my head, and I never did realize that there was a life-ring attached to the light by a line. Don't ask me how I missed it. I just didn't know it was there.

"When the boat showed up, I almost expected her and I knew I was all right."

Under power and with sails down, *Scylla* worked her way back to the light, and there was unbelieving joy aboard when they sighted Weston's bobbing head. One pass missed but on the second time around they brought him alongside the lee rail and Ulmer grabbed him by his safety belt and manhandled him aboard, still clutching the light in his hand. When he landed on deck, the whole crew fell on him to make sure he didn't slide back overboard.

Weston's physical reaction was to go into a profound sleep almost as soon as they got him below, and he felt few ill effects when he woke up the next day. He was, however, in a state of shock most of that day, weeping without warning on occasion, and unable to go on deck and face the waves. By midafternoon, after some more rest, he did come on deck to help with a sail change, and he was practically back to normal on arrival in Bermuda. The emotional after-effects on the rest of the crew were almost as shattering as on Weston for the first few hours, but they kept sailing *Scylla* as hard as they could. She finished 10th in Class E and fleet. (There is no penalty for emergency use of the engine.)

Weston did not relish the thought of the return passage, and almost took a plane home, but decided, on the "get on the horse after you're thrown" theory, to stay with the boat.

"I'd go in the race again, sure," was his answer to the obvious query, "but I'm going to be even more careful how I handle my safety line. Now we all keep it fastened until we get down the hatch and then have someone on deck detach it.

"And I'd never go to sea with someone who didn't take the advance care that Charlie Ulmer did. I can thank that for my being able to talk about it now. As I said, I'd never have thought anyone could have lived through the experience if I hadn't done it myself."

From *The Best from Yachting* (1967)

The Night the Storm Hit

Our experience in Barlovento that same night

It has been frustratingly calm, but now we get our weather change. The clouds thicken and begin to spit light rain in late afternoon, and we get more of a breeze. It's from east of south, however, almost dead ahead.

Another boat comes close enough to be identified, and

as she crosses our bow we make her out to be *Manitou*. In four days of drifting she has gained 400 yards on us! She tacks on our bow, and, in increasing breeze, we decide to change from light to heavy genny. There's nothing like another boat close aboard to liven things up for the crew. Capt. Jackson keeps up a constant fight talk as the switch is made.

Ross has the wheel, and looks as though the change was perhaps not fast enough to suit him. John and Walter secure the halyard and Capt. Jackson comes back to check with the skipper. It is raining harder now as we crank in the new sail on the coffee grinder and stow the old one in the dinghy. *Barlovento* likes the stronger air, perhaps 16 knots and we drive powerfully by *Manitou*. She has tacked on our weather quarter and has now fallen far off to leeward. If this holds maybe we won't do so badly after all. *Manitou* gives us a few minutes.

It holds all right!

Through the early hours of Wednesday evening, increasingly severe rain squalls lash across us from the southwest. Down below, *Barlovento's* husky steel hull is quiet as we eat dinner, and the motion, which has been like a church since the first night, is only beginning to make itself felt.

On deck, though, the sting of rain on the cheek and the hum of wind in the shrouds, with a background of ever-increasing wave and wake noises, are all signs that the "light southerly" breezes predicted by the Bermuda radio have been misnamed. By 2100 the electric anemometer is registering a steady 30 m.p.h. for the apparent wind, and the needle spurts higher when gusts hit. *Barlovento*, still under full sail, is standing up to it stiffly and driving powerfully through the night.

We all feel that each rain squall will be the last, a "clearing shower," but when, about 2200, a puff sends the needle up to 60, and the rain turns colder, the rail buries and we know it is past time to get the genny down. The bow is an eerie maelstrom of wind and water under the spreader lights as we drop the big, madly flailing sail into the water and wrestle it aboard from there. By the time we get the staysail on, we know we are in for it.

For the rest of the night the anemometer stays in the 60s and we plunge forward in a world of blackness and hideous sound. The wind is a steady shriek, the waves crash and surge along the hull, and, above it all, is the most awesome sound of all, a steady bone-jarring, ear-splitting rat-a-tat from the leech of the mainsail. Sounding like a machine gun gone mad, it shakes the whole ship. Every moment for the long hours of the night we wait for the rending rip that will signal the death of the sail, but somehow it never comes; just the continued, unbelievable shaking.

There is no sleep aboard as we rear and plunge over the now steep and cresting seas, but we are on course for Bermuda and still driving. It may feel like a battle for survival, but it is still a race. Through it all, the skipper maintains a stoical calm, and no one says much. Thoughts, however, are very active and imaginative.

The sight on deck at dawn is a wild one of waves towering over us, their steep crests tumbling and crashing. Miraculously the mainsail, carried all night without a reef, is still there, still vibrating the whole ship like a rough engine. The anemometer needle never goes below 60 for the whole 0400-0500 wheel trick, and twice we watch it spurt to the top of the dial, past 80, as the first blast of a gust hits us, tearing off the tops of the waves that rear over us and blowing them straight out.

Smashing ahead in the rain that stings like shotgun pellets, throwing spray over her whole length as she rears and plunges over the steep, tumbling waves, *Barlovento* drives on for Bermuda. Gradually, though the seas stay high and the wind still has vicious weight as it streaks across the hard, bright water, the weather improves with the day. The worst is over by 0600, and by mid-morning we can think of adjusting the sails again. The strain of the night shows on all hands.

From *A Berth to Bermuda* (1961)

The Replica America's Only Race

An exciting sail in OpSail in the Baltic

The most glamorous yacht I have ever raced in is *America*, the 103-foot replica of the schooner that brought the cup that bears her name home from England in 1851. The replica was contracted for in 1967 by Rudi Schaefer as the centerpiece of a TV documentary about her sponsored by his beer company. Her launching at the Goudy and Stevens yard in East Boothbay, Maine, on May 3, 1967, the hundred and sixteenth anniversary of the launching of the original *America*, was a colorful ceremony as her black hull glistened in the slanting light of late afternoon, flags fluttered, and bands played.

Schaefer, a Bermuda Race-winning yachtsman himself, had her copied in every detail abovedecks, and her lines were taken off the old plans and adapted for modern boatbuilding by Olin Stephens. Belowdecks she is a modern yacht.

When Schaefer retired, *America* was sold to Pres Blake of Somers, Connecticut, for use as a private yacht. He cruised her in New England and the Caribbean for several years and then decided to take her to Europe for OpSail 74, which was to go from Copenhagen to Gdynia, Poland, and then back to France and England, ending up in the Solent, scene of the original *America*'s triumph.

I joined *America* in Copenhagen as she lay alongside a quay in the inner harbor of that colorful seaport city, surrounded by tall ships and by hundreds of small craft there for an antique boat show and parade as part of OpSail. There were Viking ships, *botter* boats, trawlers, converted fishing smacks, rowing shells, an old 12-Meter (the British *Evaine*), and many sail training vessels of every size and description from all over Europe, but we were the only American representative.

America attracted tremendous crowds of the curious, and it was like living in a boat show exhibit or a museum to have hordes of strangers ogling you from a few feet away and asking all sorts of questions. Anyone who had an American connection let you know that he had a cousin in Brooklyn or Minnesota or whatever, and a surprising number of American tourists came to pay homage to the Stars and Stripes.

Blake, who made the money necessary to support *America* as a private yacht from the Friendly Ice Cream Company, which he started in 1937 with a loan of $530, was well aware of her symbolic role, and he played "American Ambassador" to the visitors with genial patience, answering all sorts of questions. He also enjoyed going ashore and testing the product of the street vendors selling ice cream to compare it with "The Product."

"Not enough butter fat," was his usual verdict as he licked a cone or bit into a popsicle.

The day of the start of the race to Gdynia, which was to be preceded by a marine parade out of Copenhagen's harbor, was overcast and blustery, but there was no way that any more vessels could be crammed onto the water or more people along the banks. The focus of the parade was the Danish royal yacht, an immense, white, clipper-bowed vessel that loomed over the spectator fleet like a mother hen over chicks. Somehow, she reminded me of *Corsair*, years before, dominating the boats around her at the Yale-Harvard crew race.

The Queen of Denmark stood on the top deck and took the salutes of the vessels as the cadets on the tall ships manned the yards, whistles blew, horns tooted, flags fluttered, ensigns dipped, and the crowd on shore cheered, and it was a lively, dramatic spectacle under swiftly blowing clouds and an occasional pale patch of sunlight.

The start was outside the harbor in the Oresund with a reaching leg of fifteen miles to a lighthouse, which had to be rounded to port as the start of a long leg to the eastward out into the Baltic. The tall ships, six of them, were to start from anchor an hour before our division, which contained the smaller sail training vessels. These included *Evaine*, a Swan 48, sister ship of the boat that had won the 1972 Bermuda Race, and several big schooners about the same size as *America* from Sweden, France, England, and Holland. It seemed interesting that *America* was to race a Twelve in the only formal race she's ever been in.

The Russian *Tovarich*, the German *Gorch Fock*, and the Polish *Dar Pomorza*, graceful white full-rigged ships, blasted away from the anchored start and were soon dark towers on the horizon, but the big Russian barque, *Kruzenshtern*, was slower in getting her hook up, as were two smaller ships, the Danish *Georg Stage* and the East German *Wilhelm Pieck*. The wind had piped up to about 25 knots, freighted with rain, as the square-riggers started.

When our time came, it was still blowing as hard, with a few stronger gusts, and we charged out beyond the windward end of the start intending to run back outside the line, then dip it and harden up on course. The sailing master was having trouble locating the other end of the line, and he was also preoccupied with the crew's work on the sails, since we had three young Danish naval cadets aboard just for the race in order to qualify as a sail training vessel. Pres was having a real wrestle with the wheel, and we kept riding up to windward instead of bearing off for the line. The sailing master was not really aware of this, and, at the last minute, he picked out a boat that was not the other end of the line, thought that it was, and that we were behind the line, and gave the word to Pres to harden up as the gun went off. As a newcomer aboard, I was only spectating, but I was sure that we had never dipped the line. I hoped that the Sail Training Association, which runs OpSail races, would not be too strict with us, but I had no way of knowing.

When we squared away on the reach, with the breeze still a good 30 knots and spitting rain, *America*, under main, foresail, and working jib, took off like a Le Mans racer. I know I have never been faster in a sailboat, even a planing catamaran, as she smoked along at perhaps 13-14 knots, and the most amazing part of it was that she didn't seem to be straining or laboring. She made so little fuss going through the water, and her wake was so flat, that you had to look straight down over the side at the water rushing by to realize just how fast she was going.

Two powerful Swedish schooners that were close astern dropped back quickly, and the skipper of one later told me that no vessel had ever sailed away from his ship like that before.

We caught *Kruzenshtern*, *Georg Stage*, and *Wilhelm Pieck* soon after jibing the lighthouse (jibing *America* is a man-sized job, but the crew did it well), and their rigs made a striking pattern against the western horizon in the lingering July twilight of that latitude.

It was glorious sailing through the night and into the next day as we followed a zigzag course eastward in the Baltic. The breeze moderated and the sun came out, and, on a direct run, wing-and-wing, we were not moving the way we had on the reach. Modern boats like the Swan 48 caught up under spinnaker.

We rounded a mark off the south end of Sweden's Oland Island for the last leg of about a hundred miles southward across the Baltic to the finish in the Bay of Gdansk. We had been under a vast cloud of 10,000 square feet of sail, everything *America* can carry in the way of topsails, gollywobbler, light genoa, and staysails, an impressive amount of Dacron. Now, with the wind still west and piping on again as the day waned, we had visions of a roaring reach to the finish and an arrival in early morning. We began to pick up the boats that had passed us under spinnaker, as no one can reach like *America*.

The Baltic is a fickle sailing ground, however, and its breezes seldom hold a pattern for long, and our dream ended shortly after midnight with fifty miles to go. The westerly quit, and in its place came a soft southerly off the Polish coast, a fitful breeze blowing through haze, and we took until the next evening to finish, tacking back and forth at about 110-degree angles as the modern Marconi-rigged boats made their close-winded way past us again. Through the haze, we could see *Gorch Fock* and *Dar Pomorza* making lazy progress tacking through about 160 degrees, with glints of sun occasionally highlighting their sails as they dropped behind us.

We charged across the finish shortly after 2000 in a freshening lift off the Russian shore of the bay, not too sure of how we'd done, but thoroughly impressed with *America*'s sailing qualities. Considering her schooner rig, long keel, and oversized three-bladed propeller, her progress to windward had been pretty satisfactory, and there is nothing like her when it's blowing fresh on a reach.

When I checked in with the Sail Training Committee ashore the next day, Colonel Richard Schofield, the very proper Englishman who conducts the races, pulled at his moustache a bit and made a few noises in his throat.

"Ah, yes. *America*. Hmmm," he finally said, then paused for a while. "Are you aware that you never started the race?"

I didn't like the sound of this, as right as I knew he was.

"Well, yes," I said cautiously. "Some of us thought there might have been some confusion over the off-line mark."

"Exactly. Exactly." He made a few more "Hmmmms," then spoke again. "We have had to assess you a penalty of 2.7 hours for not making a proper start, but I'm happy to say that this does not affect your standing as the winner of Class B." He then flashed me a small smile. "Congratulations."

And so we had saved our time, and the penalty time, on *Evaine*, the Swan 48, and all the other modern boats in our class. Not bad for a 124-year-old design on the only occasion the replica was raced. And no matter what happened, the first miles of reaching after the start would have been worth the whole thing and more.

From *A Sailor's Tales* (1978)

The Aegean Rally
The Greeks have a special way about them

Man's first "sea stories" came from the ancient world of which the Aegean Sea was the center, but it is only in recent years that the modern sport of ocean racing has taken hold in these fabulous waters. It was bound to happen. Yachting interest is very much on the increase in Greece, a nation of long maritime traditions, and one result has been the establishment of an event that could very well become one of the top glamor dates on the international yachting calendar.

This is the annual Aegean Sailing Rally, held this year

July 6–10, a two-part affair on courses threading through the dramatic, history-drenched scenery of the island-studded sea. The first part was 113 miles from Piraeus southeastward to the primitive island of Ios, with an overnight layover followed by a 147-mile eastward leg to Rhodes, much larger and more cosmopolitan. A new club, the Panhellenic Offshore Sailing Club, sponsors ocean racing in Greece, and this was the third annual Rally.

The fleet of 17 boats was divided into Classes A and B, with 45′ l.o.a. as the dividing line, and all boats had official RORC certificates. Handicapping was by the RORC time-on-time method and the point system was interesting and eminently fair, if somewhat unusual. Old-style Olympic place points were awarded for each leg and then multiplied by the distance of the leg to weigh their importance.

My invitation from POSC to cover the rally luckily included a berth on the boat that won, the 50′ cutter *Toxotis III*, owned by John Sikiarides and manned by a topnotch racing crew, three of whom had Olympic experience. Two had sailed with the then Crown Prince Constantine when he won the Dragon Gold Medal at Naples in 1960. They still sail with him now that he is king, and they brought a "round-the-buoys" alertness and drive that showed to great advantage when changeable conditions called for constant sail drill. Almost too appropriately, it seemed, since the poet Homer lies buried on a remote hillside of Ios, our sailing master was named Odysseus (although in modern usage it is spelled Odysseas).

It was perhaps the noisiest and most argumentative crew I have ever sailed with, but each argument ended in cheerful shrugs and smiles and the quickest and slickest kind of execution. Language difficulties kept me in ignorance of the gist of most of the discussions, but I did pick up a few "Greek" words fairly rapidly, such as "genoa," "chart table," "handicap," "time-on-time," "walkie-talkie" and "boom vang."

These became my special province, as they were the only items I could always pick out from the welter of words that flew around during maneuvers. The rest of the terms had not been adapted from the English as had these, but I did soon learn that a spinnaker is a *baloni*.

Weather conditions played ideally into the hands of a good sail-handling crew. The vast arch of blue over the very blue Aegean was not marred by a cloud for the two weeks we raced and cruised there, but the wind played every kind of trick under this endlessly azure cover. For the Piraeus-Ios leg it was fluky and fitful for the entire route, shifting constantly and never going over ten. The second leg started in the same way but ended before a fresh meltemi, the north or northwesterly "trade wind" of summer in the Aegean. We swooped down on Rhodes and its modern hotels, smiling beaches, crenellated Crusader castles, and soaring mountains on a wild *baloni* sleigh ride that was a fitting climax to a challenging three days of competition. It was bathing suit racing by day, hot in the calms, delightfully cool in the meltemi, and a sweater at night.

Not only was the racing fascinating; the scenery was a constant wonder. We were never out of sight of the Aegean's endless supply of islands, reminiscent of the Virgin Islands in outline and in the arrangement of their peaks and the stark barrenness of fawn-colored grass and rocks, terraced for cultivation in the most unlikely places. On most of them, a slash of white lay on top of a hill like an improbable snowdrift. These were villages, perched there since ancient times for the best defense against marauders.

A color card of the Aegean would be dominated by the deep blue of the sea set against the glaring white of the isolated villages, churches and monasteries, with softer supplementary tones of gentle blue sky and dun-colored land, splotched here and there with the dusty green of an olive grove or the single dot of muted color where one gnarled tree stands against the wind.

Like *Toxotis*, built in England in 1935 as *MacNab* and a successful distance racer there, most of the race entries traced their origins to other countries but are well-maintained and equipped by their Greek owners. Many of them are available for charter part of the time. Sikiarides, a textile executive who is a Harvard Business School graduate, uses *Toxotis* for extensive cruising and an occasional race. She is well maintained by a fine paid hand and has all racing gear, some of it old but all in good shape. Although aboard for the race, he turned race management over to Odysseas and crew.

Two former American boats were the big 102′ bronze-hulled yawl *Alexandra Lisa*, ex-*Thistle*, once a queen of the New York YC cruise with her rival *Manxman* and scratch boat of this affair, and the 92′ ketch *Aries*, last boat owned by the late R. J. Reynolds. Smallest boat was the 28′ Controversy, *Hara*, built by Mount Desert Yacht Yard in Maine and sailed to Greece several years ago by her owner, Savas Georgiou.

There were half a dozen boats with excellent gear and sails and well set up to give a good battle, and *Toxotis*, heavy now for topflight racing, had to be coaxed along with expert handling to keep up with them. When near some of the slightly bigger boats in equal conditions, she obviously lacked their boat speed, yet she was third boat-for-boat on the first leg and fourth on the second, taking Class A both times, first-in-fleet the first time and third-in-fleet the second time for a combined first-in-fleet for the whole rally. Second was a handsome new Illingworth and Primrose 36′ sloop *Christina*. She easily took Class B and was first in fleet on the Ios-Rhodes leg but had been fourth on the first one. *Alexandra Lisa* was first-to-finish at Ios, and Markos Keusseoglou's svelte 69′ Swedish-built 12-Meter cruising yawl *Ivanhoe* was awarded a special trophy in memory of British yachtsman Bobby Somerset for being first-to-finish at Rhodes. Somerset, world famous for years, lost his life at the entrance to the harbor at Rhodes a year ago when his boat hit the jetty. Alan Paul, secretary of RORC, came from London to make the award.

There were several key spots in *Toxotis'* victory. By continuous sail drill, she was maneuvered from a dying southerly to a feeble attempt by a meltemi to come in from the north, and then back into a new southerly, to work by Cape Sounion south of Athens and break away from the bulk of the fleet soon after the start. The edge of the meltemi was marked by a swarm of butterflies and bugs blown out from the land, and Odysseas, spotting them, worked her over there to get the little boost needed to break free. Throughout an almost calm night, we ghosted between the black peaks of Kithnos and Seriphos, gaining three miles on a big yawl that lay immobile for a whole watch, and played wind streaks all the way into Ios while boats remained becalmed nearby.

On the leg to Rhodes, some of the bigger boats got the meltemi quicker than we did and romped on ahead to a commanding lead. There was one hole in the otherwise fresh northwester, however, and, noting them wallowing to a stop ahead, Odysseas headed down a live streak. We changed from spinnaker to genoa and back to spinnaker within ten minutes in the one soft spot we hit, and came up abeam of the leaders as the meltemi resumed with new strength.

So competitive was our crew, who had been personally wished well in a surprise visit by the king just before the race, that they acted as though they had been badly defeated when the enormous *Alexandra Lisa*, allowing us hours, managed to beat us by the length of her tremendous bowsprit as we converged on the finish off the entrance to the harbor at Rhodes. Though intensely competitive, the crew was full of laughs and horseplay, and "happy hour" on ouzo and bouzouki records was right out of "Never on Sunday" each afternoon. The food was exotic to my American tastes but ample and filling, with such items as candied apricots, spiced meatballs, cheese pies, octopus, vine leaves, cucumbers, bouillabaise, and goat cheese, plus beer and ouzo, the clear aromatic liqueur that turns cloudy when water is added.

It was rewarding sailing to be with such an eager and accomplished crew, and the shore rewards were equally as much fun. The whole event was beautifully organized and was run without a hitch. Excellent arrangements were made for the boats in both harbors, and the formal festivities were gay and gala.

At Ios, as we ghosted into the narrow dogleg harbor between towering cliffs, fireworks filled the blackness overhead, and the town quay, backed by a few shops and open air cafes, was a blaze of lights and alive with shouting, cheering people. Donkeys and chickens milled through the crowd and the peculiar haunting strains of Greek folk music drifted out from the cafes. A reception on the big training schooner "Tall Ship" *Eugene Eugenides* (spectator escort for the Rally) was the only formal festivity here, with visitors given medallions of Homer's tomb.

At Rhodes, a bustling resort city dominated by the castles of the Knights of St. John who based here during the Crusades, the wind-up festivities were more varied and formal. Prizes were awarded in the ancient city hall, once the palace of the Knights, followed by a reception in a big modern beach hotel that would not be put to shame in Miami Beach, and a final burst of fireworks and folk dancing in the town square. There couldn't possibly be more colorful surroundings for ocean racing.

From *The Sailing Life* (1974)

The Loss of the Mary E

A dramatic series of events in the Miami-Nassau Race

When we went to bed the night of February 22, 1976, in our hotel overlooking Biscayne Bay, thunder and lightning filled the air outside and rain squalls clattered against the northern windows. In the morning, awakening to the rustle and slash of palm fronds and the glimpse of a flag at the marina across the way giving off little machine-gun-like *whaps* as it vibrated stiffly in a norther, I was stirred by a sense of foreboding and an unhappy, long-remembered feeling in the pit of my stomach.

I knew what it would be like in the Gulf Stream that afternoon when the Miami-Nassau Race started, and deep down inside I knew I didn't want to be there. Too many times, on subchaser duty in World War II and on eleven previous Miami-Nassau races, had I seen these big mountains of blue water building against the northward thrust of the Stream, looming at eyeball height on the flying bridge of a subchaser or spreader height on an ocean racer, before hurling cascades of white water against the topsides to burst over us with the always surprising reminder of Gulf Stream warmth that only makes the wind seem colder afterward. I knew what it would be like clinging to the windward rail of *J & B*, alternately prey to stinging but warm hosings and cold wind blasts, muttering, "What in hell am I doing here?"

Even when I'm not reluctant because of conditions of the day, I'm never particularly happy to leave Jane for sea, a feeling that goes back, I guess, to the many subchaser sailings of the war. This time, as I listened to the nervous rattle of the palms, there was a heavier than usual reluctance to forsake the comfortable companionship of the double bed and the luxury trappings, no matter how impersonal, of the room. This was our first travel since she had recovered from a serious illness, and even though she was fine and would be with the other *J & B* wives, old and good friends all, I would have liked to be with her on the plane to Nassau. And, purely selfishly, that inclination grew ever stronger as we drove up Bayshore Boulevard to Miamarina under the lash of palm fronds against a sky that had that hard, blue look of air straight from Canada.

Too late to chicken out, though. I had sailed with Jack Sutphen and Mort Engel, veteran co-skippers of *J & B*, for several years now, and despite that stab of reluctance deep in my gut, I knew there was no way to back out gracefully. A few years ago, such thoughts would hardly have crossed my mind, but the fifty-seven-year-old body remembers those Gulf Stream thumpings in a different way.

Miamarina was aquiver with last-minute preparations. *J & B* lay alongside the seawall in front of the marina office, where long lines of race sailors queued up for the two pay telephones. She surged uneasily, with ensign and burgee flapping and slapping noisily and the breeze humming in her shrouds as I kissed Jane goodbye and clumped aboard with my gear. The name *J & B* has nothing to do with Scotch whisky, by the way, although the distiller did wake up to the promotional possibilities and send her some of the product when she did some winning. Jack and Mort's wives are Jean and Barbara, and the boat was originally to be called *B & J*, until someone remembered that there was a female whose nickname sounded like that who had been rather well known around the SORC fleet for quite a few years. To avoid any confusion, the initials were reversed, and the Carter 39 sloop could identify with well-aged Scotch, not an ocean-racing groupie of somewhat the same description.

Gradually, around the marina, crew members working

high up on masts were lowered in their bosun's chairs, wives gave last kisses and waves (and some came along), and, amid noisy banter, the mutter and rumble of engine exhausts, and the skitter of dark wind gusts across the protected water of the marina, the fleet unscrambled from slips and berths and headed for Government Cut in a long, irregular procession.

I munched a sandwich and drank some iced tea, reflecting mournfully (and so correctly) that it would be the last real sustenance for some time, as we struggled into foul-weather gear and sniffed the fresh, uneven puffs sweeping across MacArthur Causeway from the north. We headed into them at the Miami Beach Channel to hoist a reefed main, and Peter Wilcox, the "do-everything" man in the crew, jumped overboard to put a rubber band on the folding propeller at the correct alignment. With droplets blowing off his matted hair and beard, he was shivering with duck bumps as he climbed back on deck and quickly got into his foul-weather suit.

"Hey, the water's great!" he said, laughing, "—but, oh, that wind!"

J & B bore off and surged toward the entrance of the Cut, where pale green breakers frothed across the darkly jagged rocks of the breakwater. The boats ahead of us could be seen rearing their bows high and crashing down through wings of spray as they met the first seas outside the tide-roiled Cut. Soon we were bouncing along with them out of the lee of Miami Beach in the unhindered sweep of the wind, close-hauled and jogging toward the starting area. With somewhat misplaced optimism, we decided on the No. 2 reefable jib, and the deck apes scurried around surefootedly setting it up.

Class by class, the fleet got away, big boats first, close-reaching through the powdery green of the short, steep inshore seas toward the line of blue lumps that marked the edge of the Gulf Stream about a mile to the eastward. Jack makes as good starts as anyone I've ever sailed with, and we settled down to the business of it as our time came. We were in a class for stock boats, a new division in this series designed to bring back this type of boat to Southern Ocean Racing Conference competition. Ten years ago, stock boats had been dominant, but the change to the IOR Rule and the development of super-fancy, custom-built racing machines had driven stock boats from the circuit in the past few years. There were only six boats in our division, but they had been engaged in intense, closely fought competition over the previous four races, with at least four of the boats still holding a shot at the class SORC title, and everyone was very intent on the starting process. This race would probably be the clincher.

Jack is such a competitor that tension always hums across the deck while the time ticks away, called by Mort in fifteen-second intervals. Jack, his voice rising and edgy as the minutes narrowed down, fired questions about the other boats and the location of the buoy at the far end of the line. We were a little early, and we had to slack sheets while Jack sashayed *J & B* on a zigzag course to slow her down. With only six boats, we could get away with a tactic that would never have worked in a crowd, and we hit the line a second or two behind the gun, with *Mary E*, a Standfast 40 and our closest competitor, right on our stern, and the Tartan 41 *Vagary* and our near sister, *Phoenix*, the other two boats in the running, right alongside us to leeward.

As we charged and leapt eastward within a few boat lengths of each other, bows soaring high and crashing down in great clouds of spray, with crews huddled to windward and lee rails awash, the sun, in its low winter path over the receding silhouette of Miami Beach hotels, was blotted out more and more by clouds marching in from the horizon in close order formation. Watery shafts of light slanted through breaks in the pattern, picking up the tiny, heeling splinters of black that were the class behind us.

On the rail, with the cockpit coaming jammed into the small of my back, I spent the first hour trying to keep dry under the repeated onslaught of wave tops, but finally gave up as the Gulf Stream gradually worked its way down my neck and into the legs of my foul-weather gear. My dry areas slowly contracted into a small panel below each arm, but those didn't last long. From then on, immersion was as total as that of the most devout Baptist wading into a river. All the while, I couldn't help remembering the various dismastings and rigging failures I had witnessed in this area on previous races, plus the dismasting of a previous Engel-Sutphen boat, *Bones*, in the Nassau Cup, and visions of disaster dodged through my mind as I sat on the cramped, damp panel of deck space—just too narrow for one sideways buttock to find a perch that could be lived with—and automatically dodged the showers of spray, even though it no longer did any good.

It was no surprise when the reefed jib, rolled and tied so that the reefed section faced inboard and therefore filled with water whenever the jib scooped, which it did quite often, began to rip at the reef points and had to be replaced with a No. 3—plenty of sail anyway for the way the wind and seas were building. Clouds had completely taken over the sky before sunset, and twilight was gray and unfriendly, making the seas look bigger, blacker, and more menacing. By now the wind was well over 30, and an occasional gust had more authority. It began to feel lonely out there as the other boats washed out of sight in the dusk.

There was no thought of a real meal at suppertime, and, after some extra exertion on a winch on a sail adjustment, I had my first experience with seasickness in fifty years of sailing. On powerboats and subchasers, yes, and often, but never before on a boat under sail, and, perhaps because of this lack of experience, I didn't handle the usual position of ignominy at the leeward rail very well. In fact, I lurched out of sync with the boat, and the genny track jumped up out of its smother of foam and gave me a good whack on the mouth. From then on I had a fat and tender lower lip that didn't really cure itself for a couple of weeks, but it was also the end of mal de mer. There was too much else to think about.

In darkness, the only relief from total inkiness was the bob and blink of running lights of the other boats, the luminous rush of whitecaps out of the wall of night, and the pale, wavery ghostliness of our starboard running light reflecting back off our bow wave in uneven, occulting flashes.

I had no intention of going below no matter what the watch schedule, and I happened to be looking off to starboard when a blob of red arced up briefly from the nonexistent horizon, followed by a couple more.

"Flares off the starboard bow!" I called, and almost simultaneously the VHF radio crackled with a clearly heard "Mayday" from *Mary E*. Then there was another flare. The time was 2040.

Twice before, Jack and Mort had had SORC races interrupted by rescue operations, once to stand by a sinking tug off Key West, and once to help a competitor in trouble, and from Jack at the wheel and Mort below at the radio came the absolutely simultaneous cry: "Oh, shit! Here we go again!"

Aside from my natural reaction of excitement and concern, the thought popped up that here, after thirty years as a sportswriter and boating editor covering predictable, scheduled events, was the "real thing." The old phrase "This is it!" also jumped into my head. I remembered having the same reaction, with the same phrase, the first time I saw Zeros coming directly at us in the Southwest Pacific. It wasn't something from a movie or novel any more, and I felt like a cub reporter chasing his first fire engine.

Mort immediately started to talk to *Mary E*, and I gave the approximate bearing of the flares I'd seen. We eased sheets and headed over that way without any definite point to aim for, and Channel 16 came alive with other yachts in the race responding to the message. *Mary E* reported that she was leaking badly and that the water was gaining faster than they could pump. She had eleven in crew, including two females, a large complement for a forty-footer. As we drew closer to her supposed location, a swarm of running lights began to flock together like lightning bugs gathering in a garden—some windy, dark garden—and we had no idea which one was *Mary E*. At least five boats were in the area, all but one of our class, but, gradually, it was sorted out that *Phoenix* and *J & B* were probably closest and would take over the duty of standing by.

Someone had the bright idea of telling *Mary E* to upend a man-overboard strobe light so that we could pick it out from the welter of running lights and aim for the right place, and its quick, distinctive flash solved the problem immediately.

Searchlight beams stabbed across the water, picking up the cresting, breaking wave tops and then the mothlike apparition of a white boat lying ahull and wallowing in the seas. Her sails were down and lay messily across her decks, and her jib trailed over the bow and into the water. At first we thought this was just an evidence of hasty action, but we later learned that it had been rigged this way as a drogue to keep her bow on one heading, and it proved remarkably effective in holding her steady, without yaw, and with minimum leeway.

Mort, ever cool and matter-of-fact, had been on the microphone gathering all the information he could and then began an attempt to raise the U.S. Coast Guard in Florida, now about forty miles away, to tell them of the situation. Line-of-sight VHF did not have enough range to make it, but the cruise ship *Emerald Seas*, on her way from Miami to Nassau and just over the horizon to the eastward in the vicinity of Great Isaac Light, picked up the transmissions and reported in that she would notify the Coast Guard.

Meanwhile, Chuck Coyer, Jr., and Denny Sanford in *Phoenix* had reported that they were alongside *Mary E* and would begin taking crew off, ladies first. Both *Phoenix* and *J & B* had taken sails off and were under power, heaving and pitching over the steep seas, and we watched in some awe and trepidation as *Phoenix* slowly approached *Mary E* from leeward. *Mary E* had running and spreader lights on, and flashlights playing over the scene made eerie silhouettes and sudden splotches of brightness as they hit on a white hull. Both boats were gyrating wildly in the seas, *Phoenix* more so than the stabilized *Mary E*, as the bow of *Phoenix* slowly approached the stern of the disabled boat. In the wavering light, we could see moving figures as the two boats came together, bow and stern rapidly rising and falling past each other, and there was a tense moment of hesitation before *Phoenix* backed away. On the radio they reported that both girls had made the transfer safely but that it was much too dangerous to try the maneuver again. By radio conference it was agreed that *Mary E* would drop one man at a time down to leeward in an Avon inflatable dinghy on a long line as a much safer method of transfer, and this was done three times while we watched. *Mary E* had about half her normal freeboard and was wallowing sluggishly, but she did not appear to be sinking rapidly. The word was that the water below was over the table in the cabin and that the pumps were clogged.

Phoenix took on three men, and it was then agreed that *J & B* would take off the remaining six, splitting the load as evenly as possible between the two rescuers. *Phoenix* moved out of the way, and Jack Sutphen maneuvered *J & B* up from the leeward side of *Mary E* as the rubber dinghy dropped down to us with one man at a time. It was tricky boat handling, and he did it flawlessly despite the heave and bobble of the seas and the lash of spray flinging across us in the wind, which *Emerald Seas* reported was now up to 40 knots.

Six times the black blob of rubber bounced downwind to us, and each time Jack put *J & B* close enough for our crew, under Peter's leadership, to throw a line across to the man in the Avon and then haul him alongside. It was like landing a slippery tuna to wrestle someone in foul-weather gear out of the inflatable and over the rail of *J & B*, and it was not exactly a graceful operation, but one by one they made it, landing heavily on deck with a sodden thump. There was remarkably little talk and no aimless shouting or evidence of panic. Jack's orders and the communications between our crew and each man in the Avon were calm and only loud enough to be heard over the whistle of the wind. *Mary E*'s gradually fading spreader lights and the erratic stabbing of flashlight beams from *J & B* cast a flickering half-light over the action, with the bulky, glistening figures of rescuers and rescued, faceless and impersonal in their foul-weather gear in the uneven light, forming a growing blob of congestion in *J & B*'s cockpit.

At a moment when I had no hold on anything and was moving across the cockpit to lend a hand to someone, a *Mary E* crew member, tired and groggy and not sure of himself, lost his balance from a perch on the windward rail and came flying down across the cockpit, hitting me at the waist with the kind of block good enough to be shown on instant replay. With a great "ooof" of escaping air, I was upended and knocked over the leeward coaming. Because of the crowded conditions that made moving around so difficult, none of us had harnesses on, and my instant thought was that I was headed for a swim, but I didn't fly quite that far.

Instead, I crashed onto the leeward deck on the point of my left shoulder.

The pain was immediate and sharp as I landed heavily, and I remember bellowing an enraged "God dammit!"

I was sure that the shoulder was broken, but this proved overly dramatic. From then on (and forever afterward, as a matter of fact) it hurt. Motion was possible but painful, and between it and my fat lip I was far from happy. At least I wasn't seasick any more.

The last one off *Mary E* was her skipper, Chuck Benson, glum and subdued but matter-of-fact as he checked to make sure everyone in his crew was safe. Most of them had brought a duffel with them in the Avon, and these were hurled down to the cabin sole, where they made a great wet mountain of lumpy canvas for the rest of the trip. *Mary E* was equipped with an inflatable eight-man raft, and they had broken this out soon after the "Mayday."

When it popped open, it also had a canopy, a fine idea for protecting survivors if they have to remain afloat for several days in foul weather or tropical sunshine, but a severe hindrance in abandoning ship. Getting into it through a slit in one end of the canopy proved just about impossible as the raft and *Mary E*'s hull roller-coastered by each other on the Gulf Stream seas.

They had ended up loading it with bags and savable equipment and sent it to *Phoenix* on a long line. They did manage to get the gear out and then cut the clumsy raft adrift, as it proved much easier for one person at a time to jump into the open Avon dinghy. Undoubtedly the canopy could have been folded down, but no one realized it.

Now, with the little knot of boats clustered in the wild night, the question was: What to do next? By this time, Mort had word that the Coast Guard had received the message from *Emerald Seas* and was on its way. First would be a fixed-wing patrol plane to establish position, then a helicopter to drop high-capacity pumps, and finally the ninety-five-foot cutter *Cape Shoalwater* to attempt salvage. *Phoenix* was relieved, and we were asked to stand by. With her extra complement of five, *Phoenix* made sail again, wished us good luck on VHF, and disappeared into the heaving darkness in the direction of Great Isaac, whose loom could occasionally be picked up to the eastward, perhaps sixteen miles away. It was the first mark of the course, a third of the way to Nassau, and, oh yeah, there was still a race on. In the back of our minds was the realization that the boat that had rescued survivors of *Wimoweh* after she hit rocks off Isaac and sank in the 1974 race had been awarded such a big time allowance for the rescue that she ended up winning the race, but we had no idea what would happen this time. We weren't through here by any means.

Mary E was a bit lower in the water, but not sinking fast, and we learned the crew's story now as we waited for the Coast Guard while staring across the mess of sea at her half-awash form. They had been doing well in the race, gradually moving out on us, which they had to do, since they gave us some extra time, when the skipper's wife went below to do something about supper at about 1830. She noticed that there was water sloshing around on the cabin sole and commented on it, but this didn't make much impression. Lots of water had been coming aboard, and it was no surprise to find some below. The men on deck told her not to worry and to go ahead with supper, but they did turn the pump on.

After a while, in a sharper tone of voice, she called up, "Hey! There's a LOT of water down here!"

At first the reaction on deck was chauvinistically male—"how silly women are to worry about a little water" sort of thing—but Benson felt there was real conviction in his wife's voice and thought it best to check.

"God. You're right," was his reaction as he stepped into a slosh of water over the cabin sole. It was obvious this was more than anything that flying spray had put aboard, and they got auxiliary pumps going and began a check of all through-hull fittings and other areas of possible trouble. They could find nothing, as the water continued to rise far faster than they could pump with every regular and auxiliary piece of equipment they had. They stopped driving her hard and eased sheets, falling off to leeward to see whether that would ease some strain on the hull that was causing the leakage, but it hardly changed the rate of increase.

Someone on deck, happening to grab a shroud in passing, noticed that the whole rig had gone slack, and this created the suspicion that something had happened in way of the mast step. Her fiberglass construction consisted of two half-hull sections joined at the centerline, and there had been a previous history in this model of leakage on this seam just forward of the keel. *Mary E* had actually been beefed up with extra fiberglass there while under construction in an attempt to correct the propensity.

This might have been the trouble, and in fact was the best bet, but there was no way of checking it while she heaved and lurched over Gulf Stream seas. Gradually, the pumps began to clog, as clothing, can labels, and other paper fouled the intakes, and the water came inexorably higher. There had been a thought to cut the water intake hose of the auxiliary engine and let it act as a pump, but the engine was already under water when this idea came up, and it was too late.

Finally, there seemed nothing else to do but send the "Mayday," and now it became a question of the best way to keep *Mary E* from sinking. Perhaps the Coast Guard pumps, if they arrived in time, would take care of the situation. There was not much more to hope for.

The rescue effort had taken almost two hours, so there

wasn't long to wait before the lights of a plane could be seen dodging through the clouds, and Mort got the message that it was the Coast Guard patrol plane homing in on our transmissions. She began to circle over us and sent word that a helicopter was on its way.

There was an inevitable feeling of "Here come the Marines!" when the brilliant, searching light of the helicopter appeared low in the sky to the west, and the peculiar whickering rackery-rack of its engine and rotors broke through the constant smash of waves and whine of wind. Closer and closer it came in an advancing avalanche of sound and light until it hovered right over *Mary E* just above mast height, flooding the scene with an intense electric-blue bath of light that turned the black water to a frothy, tossing expanse of whipped cream and glinted and reflected in smaller flashes off *Mary E*'s gyrating spar and wet hull. I've never seen St. Elmo's fire, but there was an eerie glow around the edges of the panorama that brought descriptions of it to mind.

Mary E's Avon dinghy had been left attached to her by a long painter, and it was worked out by Mort and the helicopter crew via VHF to put two of *Mary E*'s men back aboard to receive the drop of a high-capacity pump. When she was abandoned, *Mary E*'s radio transmitter key had been left open, and the slurp and slosh of the water in her cabin was a weird background to all the transmissions. Her batteries remained operative all night, though the running lights gradually dimmed and her spreader lights were no longer working.

It was again a tricky bit of boat handling to put *J & B* up against the Avon to transfer the men one at a time, but Jack moved her in unerringly, and they made their way aboard. Over the still-functional radio, they said that the water was higher than ever, completely covering the table, but that its rate of gain seemed slower.

When all was ready, the copter moved in directly over the wallowing sloop, enveloping us in sound, and its downdraft added even wilder swirls to the whirlwind of broken water around her, setting up a dense mist of spray in the harshly glaring light. With breath held, we watched the bulky pump pop out of the copter's belly hatch on an umbilical and start downward in jerks and halts until it landed with amazing accuracy right in *Mary E*'s cockpit. When it was detached, the copter turned off its light and soared upward to circle around us, which uses less fuel than hovering, and its clattering roar continued to engulf us.

After all this excitement, it was a long-drawn-out anticlimax to have the pump not work. Anyone who has played with a gasoline handy-billy knows they are recalcitrant on a warm summer day on dry land, and the heaving, slanting, spray-strewn cockpit of a disabled boat made an impossible working platform. The pump was covered with heavy grease, and the men struggled with it, hauling frantically on the pull cord and priming it time and again, but it never did more than sputter a few times. There were instructions with it, but they were on ordinary paper, which soon disintegrated into pulp, and it seemed that there was also water in the fuel supply that was dropped with it. Whatever the reason, after what seemed an eternity of suspense that probably lasted less than a half hour, there was an admission of defeat from the two on *Mary E*. I hope no FCC official was monitoring what they had to say on the radio about the antecedents and functional ability of the pump.

The helicopter then advised that it had another pump and that this would be dropped on *J & B* for transfer to *Mary E*. Mort knew this down below at the radio, but we had not had the word on deck when the whirlybird suddenly swooped in over us just above the mast. The floodlight came on again, so bright it was like a physical force, the downdraft splattered around us amid a hurricane of sound, and I looked up in fascination to see whether the truck of our mast was safe, so low was the copter above us. There was something hypnotic in the excess of noise, light, and blasts of air, and I had no idea what was going on or why we had this roaring monster hovering overhead, when I felt a moderate thump on the side of my head and found a line draping over my shoulder and down my front. A small sandbag was in my lap, and the line stretched up like the coil of an Indian ropedancer, lost when it disappeared into the blinding brilliance overhead. Although the sandbag hadn't really hurt, I was stunned for a moment before waking up to the fact that it had been dropped from the copter.

Just as I began to make sense, the line went slack and draped over the stern, and there was a big splash in the water at the limit of the circle of light.

"Hey!" I cried. "They're dropping something!" and I began hauling in on the line. Mort then called up that they had dropped us a pump, and a couple of us began heaving on the line as rapidly as we could. It offered suspiciously little resistance the more we pulled it in, and finally we came to a frayed, unattached rope end. Whatever had been attached to it no longer was, and thus ended the episode of the helicopter and the pumps. It had been exciting but unproductive, as their supply consisted of the two that had been dropped.

The helicopter had nothing more to offer, and it and the patrol plane checked out, heading back to Florida and saying that *Cape Shoalwater* was on her way. It was then about a half hour after midnight, and her ETA was some four hours off. We had nothing to do in the interim but stand by *Mary E*, slowly decreasing in freeboard and with more and more waves breaking across her. Would she last until the cutter got there? Her red and green lights still glowed fuzzily, her open radio transmitter still sent us the slosh of water in her cabin, and the jib over her bow held her on a steady heading, but the prospect was not too good.

Mary E's emotion-spent survivors had gradually drifted below to spread out over the great wet mass of duffels in the cabin, and Jack, Mort, and the members of the crew who had done the toughest physical work of staging the rescue and wrestling the survivors aboard were all dead on their feet. I had no desire to descend into the incredible mass of bodies, wet duffels, and seasick buckets in the main cabin despite the lash of spray and cutting howl of the wind. Knowing that I would be next to useless in normal operations with my damaged shoulder, but feeling able to steer with one hand while we stood by under reduced sail, I offered to take the wheel for a while, and Charlie Booz, who evidently shared my feelings about conditions belowdecks, said he would stand watch with me.

For the next several hours we reached back and forth across *Mary E*'s position, keeping the dim glow of her lights in sight and watching her wallow lower and lower, more and more down by the bow. Now and then one of her crew would slip into the cockpit and silently watch her for a while before ducking below again, and Mort kept radio watch below, talking to *Cape Shoalwater* as she pounded her way toward us from Fort Lauderdale through the smashing seas. It was like waiting for the other shoe to drop as we watched *Mary E* settling down. Here was $100,000-plus on the ragged edge of extinction, and it was a morbidly fascinating sight. Sometimes, as we reached the end of an orbit and jibed around, we would lose sight of her for a few moments, and you wondered then "Has she gone?" "Did we miss it when she went under?" Each time, though, the blurred glow of one of her running lights would wink across a wave, and from time to time a late moon would break through a small parting in the clouds to send a beam down to glint off her hull and spars. Our motion was relatively easy as we jogged back and forth on a reach. The wind had never let up in the slightest, and the waves were still steep and nasty, but, whether it was due to the easy reaching course or the long exposure, they didn't seem quite as awesome any more, and our thoughts were constantly on the race for time between *Mary E*'s impending disappearance and *Cape Shoalwater*. As the cutter came closer, she asked us to put a strobe light at our masthead to help her find us, so we put it on a halyard and sent it up, and its nervous blink skittered down on us. Just as the first dim change from inky blackness to a hint of gray began to appear in the east, *Cape Shoalwater*'s lights came over the western horizon and gradually grew sharper. By the time she was alongside, morning twilight had evened everything to gray pallor under a solid overcast, and *Mary E* was still there, her bow barely showing as waves smashed across it. *Cape Shoalwater*, rolling and pitching her underbody halfway out of the waves, checked details out with us, thanked us for our assistance, and relieved us to go on our way. As we left, the cutter was trying to come close aboard *Mary E*, and this was our last sight of them.

The crew struggled back on deck, the No. 3 jib went up again, and Jack took over, squaring us away on a hard beat for Great Isaac. As soon as we started moving into the seas at best speed, the easy jogging motion of the reaching we had been doing changed to leaping, smashing plunges, and the longest, nastiest twenty-four hours I have ever spent in a boat—or anywhere else—followed. We were a glum, physically beat crew who had lost any enthusiasm for competition, companionship, or anything else but survival and the passage of time, and never have the hours dragged slower as we tacked around Isaac and set off on a long port tack toward Stirrup Cay, sixty miles to the eastward and the next turning point on the three-legged course.

Life settled down to considerations such as whether to eat a hard-boiled egg or an apple and how the hell to take a leak, finally a necessity despite almost complete lack of consumption. It became a clumsy balancing act on your knees on the leeward corner of the stern, with more than usual difficulties with layers of soggy clothes and the openings in them, and, with cascades of water streaming over you through the whole process, it was a very good question whether you had been able to clear your own fly, much less the rail of the boat, with whatever you could produce.

The longest day wore on to the accompaniment of constant pounding and clouds of spray, colder now that we were out of the Gulf Stream and into Northwest Providence Channel, a body of water I've never had much affection for and now grew to hate with an active passion. The day remained gray, the wind remained at about 40, and the seas remained unrelenting, much shorter and steeper than Gulf Stream monsters, but, if possible, even nastier. There was not another boat, not a plane, not even a fish or a bird in sight, and the radio told us nothing of the fate of *Mary E*.

Our boat had been built in Greece, *Mary E* in Holland, and, as we slugged through the seas, lower and heavier because of our extra burden and resounding with nasty cracks and crashes as each wave hit, I began to think of *Mary E*'s fate more and more and couldn't help wondering about the comparative boatbuilding skills of Greeks and Dutchmen. If something happened to us out here, we were out of VHF radio range of anyone, we did not have enough life jackets or rafts for the fourteen souls now jammed on board, and we were very far from land. Just a few pleasant thoughts to pass the time as the spray lashed across you, and I couldn't help but be amused at my concern the afternoon before, which now seemed as though it had been in another century, about staying dry under my foul-weather gear. Ha!

I tried it below once or twice, but conditions were beyond belief and description. Almost everyone was being unrestrainedly seasick at frequent intervals, and I won't go into the atmosphere created by this activity plus a dozen or so bodies in wet clothing, the great wet pile of duffels, and the slosh of bilge water. Perhaps a slave ship in bad weather might have had somewhat the same ambience.

We thrashed around Stirrup on two long tacks that took most of the evening, thinking that once we had cleared it and could head off south-eastward for Nassau, reaching would be more comfortable. Another "Ha!" Boat speed picked up, but so did the velocity of the spray, which now smashed across the cockpit with the intensity of a fire hose, and I finally decided that the Black Hole of Calcutta below was the better choice. Also, it had started to rain.

Nursing my shoulder, fat lip, and an incipient case of diaper rash under the salt-sodden clothes, I wedged into a corner of the cabin on a couple of lumps of duffel and listened to the sounds of regurgitation as *J & B* lurched on her way. The sensation, and the roar of rushing water echoing through the hull and clattering across the deck, were akin to being trapped in a runaway subway train in imminent danger of derailment. Jack and Peter kept her driving through the mess, stalwart in the avalanche of spray and showing incredible stamina.

Somehow Nassau finally appeared in the next dim dawn, twenty-four tortuous hours after the one in which we had left *Mary E* and *Cape Shoalwater*, and we still didn't know what had happened. *Mary E*'s crew had kept a very low profile during the ordeal of the sail to Nassau, and we could imagine how they felt. We had all been equally uncomfortable, but we at least had our vessel under us.

Our wives, who had heard about *Mary E*'s being in trouble and knew we had been standing by, but had had no further word for twenty-four hours, even though Mort had asked the Coast Guard plane to relay a message about us, were waiting at Yacht Haven when we straggled in. They had been up all night hoping for some information, and the reunion was subdued but emotional.

Jane had a rental car, and we staggered to it in driving rain, anxious to get to the hotel and a hot shower, as my diaper rash was now in full flower, stinging painfully under the salt-soaked clothes. When we got in the car, there was a sudden strong smell of alcohol and sweat, and I was just beginning to react to it when a form lurched up out of the back seat behind us. For a moment, I thought it was a mugging—just what we needed at the moment—but all that happened was a mumbled "Huh—wha—?" We had awakened a drunk who had taken refuge from the rain in our car, and he quickly opened the door and stumbled out into it before we had time to do anything ourselves.

After all this, it was somehow no surprise that the water in the hotel was off and did not come on until 10 A.M.

And what happened to *Mary E* and in the race? From sketchy reports, we gathered that *Cape Shoalwater* did put pumps aboard, but they were hampered by debris in *Mary E*'s cabin and wouldn't keep working. The cutter tried to take her in tow, but she was too far gone for this and finally dipped below the last blue Gulf Stream mountain to wash over her and sank in several hundred fathoms of water about two hours after we left her. No one will ever know for sure what her trouble was, as the proof lies hidden deep on the floor of the Florida Straits.

As for the race, since five of the six boats in the class were involved to some extent in "Operation *Mary E*," it had not been a real race for anyone in the class. Because the wind kept swinging into the northeast while we were standing by *Mary E, Phoenix* and *J & B* had different conditions from the rest of the fleet, and *J & B*, leaving the scene four hours after *Phoenix*, took five hours longer to get to Nassau because of added windward work. The committee decision, which was generally accepted as a fair solution, was to arbitrarily award *Phoenix* and *J & B* a tie for first-in-class. J & B, incidentally, then went on to win the class SORC title by taking first-in-class in the finale, the Nassau Cup.

As for me, I knew I "shoulda stood in bed" the morning we awoke to the uneasy thrash of palm fronds. If I had obeyed the feeling in the pit of my stomach, I just might have continued ocean racing a little bit longer instead of retiring to the press box as of February 24, 1976. But then, if my twelfth Miami-Nassau Race had been like this, what would my thirteenth bring? I'll never know.

From A Sailor's Tales (1978)

VII

Favorite Cruising Areas

Some of the more colorful and interesting cruising waters as we first enjoyed them

The Bay of Quinte

A quiet corner of charm, with plenty of happy shampooing

IN BRIGHT SUNLIGHT, washed and sparkling in the early morning, we skirted Allen Otty Shoal and reached across the main channel of the Seaway and its parade of ships that appeared as a smudge of smoke on the horizon, grew to a passing surge of bow wave and towering superstructure, and diminished over a bobble of wake and a quick blast of that hot, pungent shipboard smell, as they funneled in and out of the St. Lawrence. A fresh northeaster broke the blue sheen of the lake into eager little whitecaps as we slid along the lee of Grenadier Island and around Point Peninsula into Chaumont Bay, where the mainland stretched in a gentle rise to distant hills capped in cumulus.

The buzzing warmth of fields and forests on an August noon closed around us, and we anchored under a bluff for lunch and a last swim, then closed the log on Lake Ontario by powering the few miles into Chaumont harbor. As we un-rigged the boat for the trailer trip home, we could look back on a week of pleasant discovery, of finding out what it is like to cruise in this isolated corner of the lakes, and to the impressions we would carry away with us.

What was it like, and what were these impressions? Of what were they made? Main Duck, Galloo, Adolphus Reach, the Bay of Quinte, Prinyer's Cove, Picton, Kingston and Chaumont Bay were mere names before, some vaguely familiar, some never heard. Now they were the stuff of memories, of those special associations that go with a pleasant cruise. Some visited, some merely glimpsed in passing, they were the highlights of an area that has its own special charm, and a variety of attractions, in the relatively small northeast corner of the smallest of the Great Lakes.

We chose them for a cruise in *Mar Claro*, when we realized we could reach this international cruising ground in less time by family-car-cum-trailer from our Jersey Coast base than it would take us to get to western Long Island Sound by water. In nine hours of driving we had arrived at the yard of Boats, Inc., in Chaumont, N. Y. (pronounced Sha-moe by its citizenry), where advance arrangements had been made for launching, and after a late afternoon and evening of re-commissioning we were "ready for sea."

It was a cruise of new experiences and new appeals to salt water trained senses, although Chaumont, with its well-run boatyard, large concentration of sail and power cruising yachts and fleets of Dragons and Bantams, had almost the feel of a seacoast town.

Its wooded bluffs and narrow harbor, whose mouth showed a glimpse of open water surrounded by farm fields and rolling hills, were of the north country, however, and, as we went ashore for dinner in the clear cool twilight, there was that strange business of no tide to worry about and no concern with water supply (once outside the harbor) or shower bath facilities ashore. My wife and daughters also enjoyed a week of ecstatic hair care and over-the-side baths. They never stopped comparing the joys of swimming without a cap, of repeated latherings, and of manageable hairdos for shoregoing, to that constant battle with the wiry mop salt water makes of feminine topknots.

As we set forth down Chaumont Bay next morning at over seven M.P.H. (no knots on fresh water, and it makes the passages seem swifter), we were in the lee of the farm fields and hills. We smoked across smooth water in a puffy northwester at more than hull speed until we cleared the tip of Point Peninsula and met the short, steep seas of the open lake. Instead of that sharp tang of salt in the nostrils, there was an aura of meadow grass and lily pads on the strong breeze. As we surged across the dancing blue water toward an open horizon, it had the look of the ocean but not quite the feel of it in the shorter, steeper waves. The "heavy" crests broke less often, and there was no taste of salt when they did break and dashed some spray aboard.

Despite the tricks it played on the senses, or maybe because of them, that sail as *Mar Claro* ate her way offshore on a close reach, was a memorable one. That extra brightness to the sun, sparkle to the water and lively feel to the boat, the sharpness of the horizon ahead and the dun and purple color of the shoreline as it slipped astern, will forever be the mental image on hearing the words "Lake Ontario."

We were launched on a cruise that was stastically unimpressive on a chart, or in a log of the bare itinerary: Chaumont to Main Duck, 24 miles; one day sailing out of Main Duck; Main Duck to Picton, Ont., 32 miles; Picton to Kingston, 33 miles; one day ashore at Kingston; Kingston to Chaumont, 28 miles. All passages were under sail except the last five miles into Kingston. Yet statistics mean little against a memory of hard, spray-flinging sails and lazing along in the gentlest zephyrs, of slipping smoothly through protected water and leaping over offshore waves, of gunk-holing at its quietest, of laundromat and supermarket conveniences so necessary on occasion to anyone cruising on a 24-footer, and of splendid isolation. Main Duck had plenty of the latter, at least on our second night, after the usual Saturday night convention of motorboats had carried on in the Saturday night manner of motorboat crews since time out of mind and then headed for home Sunday.

Main Duck was our first landfall, a narrow little island three miles long that popped over the horizon as separate clumps of trees while we surged past Stony and Galloo, its American counterparts closer to shore. It lies just across the International Boundary in the middle of the lake and is owned by the estate of the late John Foster Dulles, who used it as a refuge between his State Department trips. An ardent conservationist who had visited the island since early boyhood, he kept it in its natural state except for a couple of cabins and a jeep road, and there is a Canadian lighthouse at the western tip. It abounds in duck, deer and small game. Landing is not allowed except by special arrangement.

The harbor is a tiny cove on the north side, with an entrance barely 50 feet wide and perfect protection for about four feet of draft inside. We swept in on a quartering breeze, rounded to anchor just inside the little gravel spit that all but closes off the entrance, and were surrounded by flowers, trees and waving meadow grass while the waves from the open lake shattered their scend a mere 200 feet off the bow.

We had previously secured permission to land, and the children spent fascinated hours of exploration with the caretaker and his wife. A Canadian woodsman of multiple outdoor skills, he gave them forestry lectures, taught them fly-casting, showed them the Dulles cabin in its impressive setting atop a rocky, forested cliff, and took them to the haunts of deer, the duck ponds, the beaches and the lighthouse. When the chance came for them to camp in one of the cabins the second night, we decided to stay over, after a lazy sail around the island in the much moderated northwester.

Mar Claro was alone in the harbor that night, riding serenely on the dark, star-reflecting mirror of the water as the waves rumbled and hissed on the beach off the bow, a renewed breeze from the north whistled a warning of autumn in the rigging, and the aurora borealis flickered to the zenith.

Our 32-mile passage to Picton on successive headings of 330, 225 and 180 was one of those rare ones when the breeze fairs with each course change, and we were on the port tack from pier to pier without one recourse to the outboard. On the first leg, out of sight of the mainland at the start, we steered a compass course across the heave and bobble of the open lake, empty except for steamer smoke astern and commercial fishing boats working their lines, and we swooped along on a roller coaster ride until we rounded into Adolphus Reach.

This arm of the meandering Bay of Quinte is in a graceful setting of wooded hills and farms, once a retreat for Loyalists during the Revolution. From a half to two miles wide, it is reminiscent of some of the Chesapeake's tributaries and has many pleasant coves for gunkholing and overnighting. One of the favorite ones, Prinyer's Cove, just inside the entrance to port, looked inviting as we slid by, but it was too early to stop, and the breeze was too good.

It followed us around as we reached through the Reach, enjoying one of those classic delights of cruising, hull speed over flat water in interesting new territory. *Mar Claro* had been the only yacht on the open lake, but now we began to meet a parade of cruising yachts, mostly Canadian, mostly from Toronto, flying their ensigns at the stern staff under sail. "When in Rome—" so we did too, though it kept surprising me to look back and see it there.

In among them, bluff-bowed, heavily-laden lake freighters pushed by us now and then, and off in the distance cabin cruisers and outboards cut curling wakes as they slipped in and out of the coves. Over all, there was an air of leisurely relaxation and unhurried peace in the hazy afternoon sun. After it had warmed us for an hour or two, we poked around an island into a cove and anchored for a swim. The green-tinged water was warmly pleasant, and the girls lathered and frolicked, while children romped on a beach ashore, dogs barked, boats drifted by and the high hum of a midsummer afternoon filled the air.

Pushing on past the Adolphustown ferry, we reached Picton just at sunset in a mere whisper of breeze, but still fair on the port beam. Shore sounds carried clearly across the water from the wooded hills, and everything stood out sharply in the last bright horizontal light of evening. We cooked dinner underway and ate it in the cockpit as we slid around the little lighthouse on the point and into the valley-like security of the inner harbor.

Picton, and later Kingston, the next port after a quiet return sail up Adolphus Reach, share that drab, stone-fronted respectability that seems to be the hallmark of middle-sized Ontario cities, where the restaurants are all run by Chinese for some reason, and the wildest form of night life is a double feature movie. Approached by water, however, they have their charms, and the visits were worthwhile.

Picton is tucked sleepily away on a dead end of an arm

of the Bay of Quinte. There is a yacht club that sells ice frozen in paper buckets in a freezer, a long public dock, usually filled with cruising boats by supper time, and plenty of room to anchor off. Protection is perfect. It would take a tornado to disturb a boat in this quaintly picturesque setting. Gingerbread palaces, wide-porched and cupolaed to the skies, lend an air of dowdy Victorianism to the harbor hillsides. Customs, when finally located in the Post Office next morning, was a quickly completed formality.

Kingston is a big industrial city with a waterfront of forbidding aspect for yachtsmen, but the yacht club, although badly exposed to the east, is hospitable, and there is a municipal yacht pier farther up the harbor. Some go across the way to Cedar Island on the east side, a small park with a pier under the hill-topping ramparts of Old Fort Henry, a gigantic tourist attraction. In Kingston our weather luck left us, but it was the best place this could have happened. On a day of flat calm, fog and rain, on which we had hoped to head into the Thousand Islands, we hired a car instead and turned tourist, along with laundromat and market visits and a movie. Fort Henry's pomp, circumstance and souvenirs delighted the children.

During the night, a front blew through, clearing the atmosphere, and it was a bright fresh dawn for our return to Chaumont across the Seaway. As we slipped out of the harbor with the rest of the crew still asleep, Kingston's buildings, grim and gray in the rain of yesterday, had an Old World sort of glamor about them in the clear early light, and the open lake was an inviting blue ahead. We rounded Simcoe Island close aboard, where the lightkeeper's children were playing on the beach, and *Mar Claro* squared away for the reach across the end of the lake moving fast under the lee of Wolfe Island.

A fine aroma of eggs and bacon drifted up from the galley, telling me I was no longer the only one awake, and the sun warmed as it rose above the green of the island. We hardened up on course, and a dollop of spray from a wavelet that slapped under the chine bounced up and ran down my cheek. I was enough at home in the lakes now not to be surprised at its fresh taste. Everything fitted into place as we sailed along on this final leg. It didn't seem strange any more to have Great Lakes cruising nine hours away from a seacoast home.

From *Over the Horizon* (1966)

The Aegean
The special qualities of this storied sea

From the battlements atop the monastery of St. Christodoulos, shadows from the shifting patterns of sunset could be seen moving across a great panorama of Aegean land and seascapes far below. A shimmer of light plated the darkening sea in the west, and the hills of Patmos, brown and dusty olive during the day, now glowed with a patina of gold. Scala Harbor at the base of this highest of the three peaks of Patmos was purpling into deep shadow, and a cruise ship at anchor looked like a white toy on its dimming mirror. The village houses, pale cubes clustered at the base of the towering gray walls of the monastery, shone briefly in panels of gold, orange, and crimson until they too fell into shadow, and a soft, mauve twilight spread over mountain and sea.

Next to us at the chest-high, crenellated wall, a monk in gray robes was scanning the harbor through binoculars. His hair was gathered at the back of his head in a small pigtail and his salt-and-pepper beard, riffled by the soft breeze of evening, had a cigar stub protruding from it. As twilight faded into darkness, he led us down a steep, narrow staircase into the chapel, rich with the smell of incense, where the relic of St. Christodoulos, who built the fortified monastery in 1088, was encased in a silver shrine. The walls were ornately and intricately carved and decorated with inlaid crosses, icons, censers, and candles. Cases lining the walls held jeweled presentation pieces, many of them gifts of the Russian imperial family. From the hushed, aromatic chapel we were ushered through a labyrinth of corridors, high-walled courtyards, and a massive gate, across a moat, and out into the dim streets of Chora.

It was on this same mountaintop that an altar of Artemis, sister of Apollo, stood in antiquity. Halfway down the slope a cave where St. John the Divine is said to have dictated the Apocalypse to his disciple, Prochoros, is now a chapel. A hollowed indentation in rock shelving is pointed out as the place where his head lay when he slept, meditated, and had his vision.

Far below, as we followed the curving road in windy darkness, the rigging of yachts at the quay in Scala formed a tracery in the lights of the town; and bouzouki music echoed in the night from a taverna. At an open-air table under the feathery green of tamarisk trees, we had a standard Aegean dinner of eggplant, tomatoes, and *barbounya*—a small reddish fish—after an aperitif of ouzo, served with small black olives, octopus, and feta cheese. *Retsina*, the heavily aromatic, resinated wine often described as "an acquired taste that some never acquire," came with dinner, followed by the sweet, muddy Turkish coffee known as *metrio*.

During dinner, men at the tables responded to the thumping rhythm of the bouzouki, played by an impassive, wrinkled old man. They danced first by themselves, drifting dreamily in circles, a handkerchief or napkin swaying limply in one hand. As the tempo increased they whirled faster, joining others by grabbing an end of a flying handkerchief. Finally they broke free and launched into leaps and midair heel clickings. Throughout, their expressions were enigmatic, unchanging, and remote, no matter how feverish the effort.

This was Patmos, but it was also the entire spirit of the Aegean islands in microcosm, a world that has stirred the imagination of man since earliest time by its physical images, mythology, and history. Nowhere else on earth are these elements combined with such an impact on the intellect, emotions, and senses. The monk, cultivated and worldly in a detached way, fluent in English, graciously hospitable, and proud of his calling, was a link with a strange, remote life, and the dancers in the taverna brought us back to the colorful vitality of modern Greece. The yachts across the quay, ghostly shapes in the light flickering through the tamarisks, fit well with the scene but were also reminders of the world we had left, and of the special excitement of sailing through this most storied of all seas.

Since *The Iliad* and *The Odyssey* and Homer's description of it—"gray-eyed Athena sent them a favorable breeze, a fresh wind, singing over the wine-dark sea"—the Aegean has held a fascination beyond normal reason for all who come to its shores, especially sailors. We had seen it that day, not wine-dark, but a hard, vivid blue, brighter than the richness of tropical waters, setting off the dun hills of Cos, Lemnos, and Calymnos, as we threaded our way through the narrow cuts and channels of the Dodecanese. Against the brown of the hillsides, here and there relieved by a dusty grove of olive trees gnarled and bent with the wind or the spire of a lonely cypress, the white of village houses and monasteries, often high on a mountaintop like a misplaced cloud or improbable snowdrift, gleamed supernaturally.

History and legend crowded in on us every inch of the

way, from reminders of nighttime battles fought in the narrow channels by British and Italian destroyers in World War II, to the ruins of the Aesclipion, the world's first hospital, and Hippocrates teaching his medical students under a great plane tree, in legend the same ancient of days that spreads over the square near the harbor in Cos, although in reality this one is only 500 years old. The Dodecanese have been handed back and forth between nations through the centuries. Ancient Greeks and Romans, Persians, Turks, Italians, and modern Greeks again have asserted ownership in a tangled sequence of invasions, subjections, and liberations. The vacant buildings of a mammoth Italian naval base can still be seen in the spacious harbor of Leros, a reminder of Italian control between the two World Wars. Mykonos, in the Cyclades, was once the private preserve of an elite Venetian family—the deserving rich, evidently—later controlled by Russia, and always a haven for pirates exercising squatter's rights.

There are towns and villages at the harbors, but the major settlements, like the village on Patmos, usually have been located on the highest point of an island for purposes of defense, with seafront buildings considered expendable. The inconvenience of hill travel was outweighed by considerations of security. Also dotting island hillsides, often on lonely points of land or even on off-lying islets, are hundreds of little chapels. Every town has its church standing high above the huddle of square, white houses, and the monasteries are often large and sprawling, following the contours of the hills, but these chapels are private affairs, and usually very small. They have been built by families, or by seamen who, caught in perils at sea, have vowed to build a shrine in gratitude for their survival. One like this stands on a rocky crag off the west end of Cos. The ruins of a Byzantine church look out at the chapel from a point marking the end of a deserted curve of beach. The bone-white little building, just one tiny room, was an offering to St. Nicholas by a grateful seaman who made it safely home, and once a year priests row out to place lighted candles on its miniature altar.

Greeks have always been seamen. The Aegean was a principal highway in antiquity, and control of the seas meant control of the known world. It was through domination of Aegean waters that Athens flourished. Between 490 and 400 B.C., a century including the age of Pericles, the civilization of Athens and the foundations of modern humanism were spread throughout the Mediterranean. The ships they used would not have seemed too archaic to Columbus, or even to Lord Nelson, insofar as the basic techniques of handling the big square sails that gave them their power were concerned.

Islands played a major role in the maritime-oriented ancient world. Delos, where Leto took refuge from the pursuit of Hera, jealous wife of Zeus, and gave birth to the twins Apollo and Artemis, later became a major shipping center and a crossroad of commerce. At one time it was also a religious center that women were not allowed to visit. Today, one wonders at its importance as a port, as it is a relatively small, barren island without water supply, uninhabited, and living with the ghosts of the past—and a daily invasion of tourists. They must all make the short passage across from Mykonos by ferry or launch to see the ruins of the sacred island, dominated by the heavily eroded but still striking row of lions, made of marble from Naxos and dating from the seventh century B.C. They guarded the approach to the sacred palm tree in whose shade Apollo, god of the sun, and Artemis, goddess of the moon and the hunt, were born.

While bare, ruined Delos is a relic of antiquity, Mykonos is a disturbing example of how the twentieth century has caught up with at least part of the timeless ambience of the Aegean. In recent years, Mykonos has become the most heavily visited of all the central islands. As one of the most picturesque, and as the gateway to Delos, it has succumbed to most of the trappings: shops selling gimcrack souvenirs and cheap clothing, bars, tavernas, and fast-food outlets, and an atmosphere of frantic, forced gaiety. This goes on along the waterfront, where the trippers stream off the ferries from Piraeus, but the hundreds of windmills on the hills behind the town flail away against the pure blue sky, and the winding alleys and back streets removed from the water have kept their original charm. There are many who enjoy Mykonos enough to be satisfied with it as their complete Aegean experience.

Mykonos is also the focal point for that phenomenon that so dominates an Aegean summer, the wind known as the *meltemi*. This is a giant thermal action, generated far to the north on the great plains of Russia (so Greeks will tell you) that gathers force as it funnels through the central Aegean. It blows from early July to late August, with variations between the days, and a slackening at night, a fair-weather wind in a cloudless sky, with temperatures in the middle 70 degrees Fahrenheit and all the appearances of perfect conditions, except that its blasts are as high as 40 to 50 knots. As the Aegean widens south of Mykonos, the meltemi fans out from its north-south axis to slant southeast and southwest, moderating a bit, but yachts are often weathered in for days in the crowded harbor of Mykonos, while the windmills spin, and spray dashes high over the windward side of the seawall.

Fortunately, the Aegean experience has included more than the gift shops of Mykonos for us. We came there through a wild meltemi from Patmos, slicing through the foam-streaked whitecaps of the central Aegean, steep, short, brilliantly clear and blue, and surprisingly cold in the sting of their spray, at the end of two weeks of racing and cruising in the 46-foot cutter *Toxotis* (the archer–Orion). I had raced with a crew led by sailors who had been gold medalists in the Olympics when the then-Prince Constantine won the

Dragon Class at Naples in 1960. This was in the Aegean Rally, the major sailing event in Greece, in a two-part race from Piraeus to Ios to Rhodes, which we won. Jane had followed the fleet in a "tall ship," a training vessel used as committee boat, and we then cruised back from Rhodes to Mykonos with the owner of *Toxotis*, John Sikiarides, a cultured Harvard graduate and delightful host, and his professional captain, Markos.

It was one of the highlights of a lifetime of sailing to be shipmates with these Greek sailors. Markos was one of the finest seamen I have ever met, a joy to watch as he went effortlessly about his tasks. He was a native of lonely Orthonoi, the northernmost point of Greece in the Adriatic northwest of Corfu, where men are born to the sea. Heavily muscled, he was bigger and taller than most Greeks, with strong features and a flashing grin that was shy when he tried English words, but bold and beaming when I noticed some good touch of seamanship. Although he spoke almost no English, and my Greek is effectively confined to *parakalo* (please) and *efkharisto* (thank you), we managed to communicate with appropriate laughs and shrugs by sign language, gestures, and the special nautical lingua franca of the Mediterranean that uses a mixture of Greek, Italian, French, Spanish, Arabic, and English words. I had learned some of them, such as *panni* (mainsail), *flocca* (jib), *baloni* (spinnaker), *lasca* (let out), *ferma* (take in) and even *boom vang*, which is English for a strap that helps trim the boom, and is used without translation.

The racing crew was one of the most skilled, and noisiest, I have ever shipped with, captained by the appropriately named Odysseas (the modern spelling—or Ulysses, if you prefer). They were my first introduction to the Greek custom of settling even the most trivial questions in loud, prolonged argument. Whatever the minor detail, the decibels and gestures increase, and everyone talks at once in a great hubbub of shouts. Eyes flash, feet stamp, and knives or fists would seem to be the next step, but suddenly someone gives in, and the loser, no matter what he is doing, makes the ultimate gesture of concession, a great shrug, with hands thrown wide, palms out at waist level, and a grunt that sounds like "ennnh!" If he happens to be holding a halyard or steering, the results can be unnerving, but then everyone laughs and all go smiling about their business.

No matter how serious the racing, we had our "happy hour" every afternoon, with bouzouki music on a portable, hand-wound Victrola, ouzo, and even a quick variation on the Greek male dance in the limited confines of the cockpit. When we won the regatta, the celebrations were long, noisy, and abandoned, and I almost became used to being kissed (on both cheeks) by my shipmates.

On the first leg from Piraeus to Ios, the course took us by Cape Sounion at the southeast tip of Attica, where the ruined pillars of the great Temple of Poseidon stand high atop the promontory looking out over the blue reaches of his realm. It was here, so one version of the story goes, that the Aegean got its name, when King Aegeus, keeping watch for the return of his son Theseus from battling the Minotaur in Crete, sighted his ship approaching under black sails. When he had left for Crete, Theseus had promised to use white sails if he was returning in victory, but he had forgotten the pledge, and Aegeus, thinking his son vanquished and dead, threw himself into the sea that now bears his name.

Although there are legends like this on almost every headland and island, we were concentrating on the racing, and we broke away from the fleet, assuring our eventual victory, through the very special local knowledge of Odysseas. We were almost becalmed in a fitful southerly, the afternoon breeze that blows into the Bay of Phaleron at Piraeus, when he spied a cloud of butterflies not far away in the direction of the land. He knew this signaled the edge of a new breeze, the beginning of a tentative meltemi that had blown the butterflies off the flower-covered hillsides of Sounion, and we managed to work our way into it, the only boat to do so. As the pale wings fluttered across our deck and *Toxotis* heeled over and trimmed to the new breeze, we swept away from the becalmed fleet around Sounion and on past Kithnos and Seriphos in the Cyclades to victory at Ios.

Ios, as much as Patmos, is the perfect model of an Aegean island. It is hilly and barren, with agricultural terracing on brown slopes rising sheer from the sea, blindingly white chapels dotting the hillsides, a drift of village houses across the summit of the highest peak, and a cluster of buildings around the harbor quay. We moored fore-and-aft to the quay amid brightly painted caiques festooned with drying nets, and the whole populace was there to greet the racing fleet with cheers and shouting as each boat tied up. In the evening the waterfront plaza was a blaze of lights, with music from tavernas as a background to the cheers of the villagers along the sea wall. Jane and I spent the night in a tower room of a small hotel at harbor's edge, the cleanest, neatest, sparest room I have ever been in, with the hardest bed and pillows. In the morning, after breakfast at the taverna downstairs with post-celebrants from the fleet, I went up to the hilltop village for a magnificent view of the whole island. It was a whitewashed town of houses packed closely in geometric patterns over narrow, arched alleys, clean and quiet in morning sunlight. The experience would have been a perfect one except for the mode of transportation—a recalcitrant donkey.

Ios is one of the places where Homer is supposed to be buried. Perhaps. Supposedly, his mother was an Ios woman. I hope it is the true place. It seems just right.

From Islands (1985)

The Grenadines

Early bareboating adventures in another immensely popular area

If things came to pass that I was allowed just one more cruise, I think it would be in the Grenadines. The choice between them, the Exumas, and the British Virgins would not be easy, but this unique 60-mile long string of islands in the lower Caribbean has just about everything one could ask of a cruising area. Unless, that is, you are the rugged type of adventurer who enjoys sliding into a Labrador tickle past ice floes. You'll never see an iceberg in this lower Caribbean seascape of perpetual 70s on the thermometer and easterly trade winds of 10-20 (and more) knots.

We had been there before, in 1962, when the venerable schooner *Mollihawk*, complete with professional crew, carried us south from Martinique to Grenada, the last of the Lesser Antilles, with stops in the Grenadines, and the impression we had carried away from that cruise was enhanced, not weakened, by a bareboat charter of 10 days my wife, Jane, and I took this past January. Familiarity breeds enchantment in these islands less than 100 miles from South America.

And the years have also bred change. On *Mollihawk*, on an early April cruise, we had the islands almost to ourselves. When we anchored for the night off the Tobago Cays, we were the only vessel there, and there wasn't a light to be seen on the horizon after darkness fell over the vast expanse of water and islands. When we swept down the leeward side of Grenada into St. George's Harbour, we were one of three visiting yachts, and there was no local activity in pleasure boats.

Six years later, Pan Am could wing us there from New York in one day via Barbados and a connecting flight, where it had taken two to make it in 1962, and the changes on the St. George's waterfront were truly astounding. We were to pick up the 36' fiberglass sloop *Merlin* at Grenada Yacht Services, and she was one of 57 vessels berthed there, with many more at anchor in the lagoon. This is a satellite to the main harbor, and it had been shut off by a shallow bar on our last visit. Now, with a channnel dredged through, it has become the bustling center of yachting for all the lower Caribbean, with a marina, repair yard, brokerage offices, yacht club, and "watering hole."

When we headed north for the magic place names of the Grenadines—Kick 'em Jenny, Carriacou, Mayero, Bequia, and all the rest—we found more changes. Most of them are of benefit to the cruising yachtsman in the way of added facilities and conveniences, and the only thing lost is that sense of magnificent isolation. We never felt lonely. Under way or at anchor there were other yachts around, but anyone used to the normal American harbor on a summer weekend would still feel delightfully uncrowded in these waters. It will be many years before they lose their special quality. Meanwhile, things like fuel, ice, and water are more readily available, though there is still the need of some ingenuity to come by them, and there are now several places to eat ashore.

Most of the yachts in the area are operated by professional crews, and first-time visitors, unless they are very experienced cruising people, should start this way. Bareboating is very much on the increase, however, and will continue to grow. Operating a bareboat here is not the lead-pipe cinch it is in the Virgins, nor is the practice as well organized as yet. Newcomers on boats under 35' would find the going rough in a few of the spots, but the potential is there for larger boats.

Grenada, the base of all this activity, is a spectacular island, one of the truly graceful and distinctive ones in the world and certainly one of the lushest and most scenic in the

Caribbean. Politically it is an Associated State of Great Britain, with an independent local government, but foreign policy and defense are in British hands. Rare in this area, the economy is a prosperous one without depending on the tourist dollar, based on bananas and spices such as nutmeg and cinnamon.

St. George's is a cosmopolitan little city, and the Riviera-like aura of its fine, moled harbor, steep streets, and clustered houses blends with the uniquely paradoxical combination of bustle and languor. Its setting is dramatic against cloud-splotched mountains, and the Trades sweeping across them in uneven gusts bear a specially heady mixture of tropical scents. All this scenery and atmosphere is background for some fine local boating waters. The south coast is a wonderful maze of coves, bays, reefs, and small islands, with the sudden gleam of a white beach glimpsed beneath palms as the bays open and close. It is well worth some exploring, but more of that later.

Merlin first took us northward. She was in her maiden season as a part-time bareboat, a modern fiberglass van de Stadt stock British-built racing-cruising sloop of the Excalibur Class, with spade-rudder, fin keel, a fine turn of speed, good stability, and the seakeeping qualities to handle the rougher passages. Everything was satisfying about her except the size and shape of her main hatch. A contoured bulge atop the cabin trunk permitted an oval opening between cabin and cockpit, with no sliding hatch. An agile racing crew might have thought it adequate, but we and our guests, Mason and Julie Gross, both rather tall, found it a mental and physical hazard, and felt rather like collies trying to get into a dachshund's doghouse.

We provisioned her in St. George's well-stocked markets, and the prize addition to ship's stores turned out to be in-bond Barbados rum at $7 (U.S.) a 12-bottle case, and good scotch at $16, obtained through Customs for shipboard use only as we departed. This seemed to make an especially ceremonious leave-taking out of our 1400 departure up the leeward coast of the 17-mile-long island. Shopping had kept us too long to make the 30-mile jaunt to Carriacou, southernmost of the Grenadines, that day, so we were simply changing the scenery by sliding along to Halifax Harbour a few miles to the north.

Fresh from northern snows and a temperature of 6°F in New York, we revelled in the sunlight on bright blue water, the soft feel and scent of the breeze, and the afternoon spectacle of trade wind clouds piling up on the 3,000-foot peaks in the island's center. It seemed almost too much when a silvery curtain of rain misted down a hillside, washed us briefly, and then centered a semi-halo of rainbow right over the entrance to Halifax.

Feeling our way in slowly, we beat against the fitful leeward-side puffs under main alone to make sure of our bearings while entering the small cove surrounded by steep, lushly forested hills. Suddenly we had a mystery to contend with. In a clearing high on a hill to starboard a group of natives stood in silence, watching us enter. We wondered why they remained so long, and it was even more mysterious when they began to direct us, with slow waves of the arms, to clear the area in front of them. They weren't waving us away, just farther in, and we couldn't make anything out of their actions. It wasn't until the end of the cruise, back in St. George's, that we had the explanation from *Merlin*'s boat boy. They were watching for schools of fish to enter the cove. When fish were spotted, the men on the hill would signal fishermen waiting with small boats on a nearby beach to close off the mouth of the cove with nets.

Halifax, so typical of leeward side harbors all through the Caribbean, had a slow but very noticeable surge, and *Merlin* ranged fitfully around her anchor all night as it heaved and ebbed under her and hissed and rumbled unevenly on the beach. A rooster, another hazard of Caribbean harbors, seemed to confuse sunset with sunrise, but he subsided later, and neither surge nor cock-crow kept us from our sleep.

In the morning we faced the main challenge of Grenadines cruising: Kick 'em Jenny. This craggy lump of land, officially Diamond Rock on the charts, stands in the middle of the 10-mile passage between the north end of Grenada and Carriacou, where the trades blow freely and unimpeded straight from Africa, and the swells pushed before them build up when forced into the confined channel between the islands, to clash with counter currents along the coast. The name Kick 'em Jenny is supposedly a corruption of the French *quai qu'on gêne*—worrisome island—as it was often a rough place to get by in a square-rigged sailing vessel.

Charter boat captains told us to hug the coast under power all the way to the tip of Grenada, which would provide enough easting for a reach past Kick 'em Jenny, but we were impatient to get the sails on and kill the chug-chug of *Merlin*'s little diesel, as the trade was filling in more and more steadily the closer we came to clearing the lee of the island.

Perhaps two miles too far to the west of the tip of Grenada, we made sail and *Merlin* heeled to the breeze, headed northeast, close-hauled on starboard tack. Soon the chop and fuss of surface waves over the long, low leeward-side surge gave way to steep, deep blue waves, capped with white and moving with authority, and *Merlin*, under full main and working jib, which remained our sail combination for the entire cruise, went to work confidently. It was good to be on a real sailboat, as this was serious, spray-flinging windward work, wet and bouncy, with a strong leeward set. *Quai qu'on gêne* took on new significance, but it was actually nothing more than a couple of hours of hard thrashing, perhaps not the best thing for first-day northern stomachs and sea legs, but a good initiation into earning the delights of the Grenadines.

After achieving Carriacou, which we did with one port-tack hitch of about three miles, the course through the Grenadines swings enough to the north to make all the passages a reach. Here and there ocean swells push in from the open Atlantic between the reefs and islands, but everything is a gorgeous reach, and the sailing is magnificent. For several days we crisscrossed the 60-mile chain, moving as far as Bequia, but not on to St. Vincent, Grenada's near twin to the north, six miles beyond Bequia. Between these two lofty islands, capped by clouds and green, thick vegetation, the lower, drier, smaller, more primitive-looking Grenadines are really a world apart. They are split politically between Grenada and St. Vincent just beyond Carriacou. You have to go through entry procedures each time you cross the line, a formality that calls for a little time but no headaches, but the deep blue of the sea, the shape of the hills and cliffs and the quality of the breeze is all one throughout the chain.

Navigation is by eyeball and ever-fascinating as you tick off oddly named islands like Cannouan, Mustique, Mayero, Tobago Cays, World End Reef (a most appropriate name for this lonely, surf-assaulted spot) and many more, but we did bounce lightly on a reef or two when I got a little giddy with my chart reading. Luckily, not too merry, because there's no excuse for it. Communication with GYS by twice-daily "Children's Hour" on radio-telephone is a safety factor, entertaining, and a source of frequent merriment, which reached a peak when we received relay of a cable on business matters that concluded, "This is to be kept completely confidential"—just for us and all the lower Caribbean!

We had evenings ashore, with dinner, at Palm Island, Carriacou, Union, where there is now a commercial "yacht club" at Clifton, and ever-colorful and fascinating Bequia, and only Bequia had had a place to eat in 1962. Palm Island was called Prune Island until John Caldwell, well-known long voyager and charter boat skipper, took a long-term lease on it, changed its name and began the prodigious task of developing a resort colony there. We were among the first to have dinner at the attractive clubhouse on a westward-facing stretch of dazzling sand, which is to serve as social center for the many private cottages being built. John and his wife Mary were gracious hosts despite a demanding schedule of administering to a work force of about 300 Union islanders, and a dramatic moment of their day is the evening "rush hour" when the entire gang departs on a couple of native sloops. We watched the spectacle in some amazement.

Later, while showering in the club after a swim here, a shout of "come quick" summoned us back to the beach just in time to see that hard-to-catch phenomenon, the sunset flash green. Unless the horizon is clear of the usual tumble of multishaped clouds which nightly cavort across the western sky, there is little chance to see this instantaneous spectacle, and that night it was without a cloud. As we gathered towels around us, the red orb was just squatting onto the rim of the sea, and, sure enough, as it slipped from view, a sudden spurt of bright, clear green filled the sky above it, to vanish in a moment. Everyone cheered.

At Bequia and Union we visited with charter boat parties at dinner time, and at Carriacou, after watching the amazing procedure of cattle being loaded from the water onto a native sloop, we ate family-style with all the guests at the Mermaid Tavern, while its proprietor, Linton Rigg, reminisced about his days as a U.S. yacht broker and told of plans for the Carriacou workboat regatta in the summer.

Also at Carriacou, a sunset taxi ride to the hospital grounds, perched on one of the highest hills of this sprawling island, brought us a breathtaking view across a panorama of reefs and islands plated with gold by the lowering sun. This time it sank through the usual panoply of clouds, and there was no green flash.

There were other delights, like a tiny cove on Cannouan

we picked out as a lunch stop. Amid light spits of rain alternating with sun, we had an amusing floor show as great flights of pelicans dive-bombed for fish on the reefs just inshore of us.

Each time we neared Tobago Cays, this colorful group of reef-beset islands had several boats in the small anchorage, and, since we'd been there before, we by-passed them, but they should not be missed, especially by skin-diving enthusiasts. As chartering increases, however, they, like the Baths in the Virgins, Staniel Cay in the Exumas, and all the other choice cruising stops that have been highly touted over the years, will suffer from an excess of popularity. It's hard to keep places like this a secret.

Every sail was a swift delight and Kick 'em Jenny southbound was a piece of cake. We laughed at it and basked in the warm sun as we swept by on a sprayless broad reach, back into the lee of Grenada, ghosting beneath the steep green of its shores as the mountains knocked the trades down to vagrant puffs.

As a farewell dinner with Mason and Julie, who had to fly north the next day, we had an evening of yarn-spinning at the Nutmeg, an upstairs club-restaurant overlooking St. George's harbor, with its proprietor, Carl Schuster, expatriate Long Island Sound yachtsman, who was just starting it in 1962 when we last saw him and has since built it into the yachtsman's "social" center of the area.

On our own with a couple of days of charter left, Jane and I took *Merlin* south around the bottom of Grenada and the starkly dramatic cliffs of Point Saline for some gunkholing and reef-hopping in the fascinating network of bays along a 10-mile stretch of the south coast. A new boatyard at L'Anse aux Epines has brought a number of yachts around from St. George's, and we had a quiet night at anchor there before spending a day of eyeball piloting through the reefs to the eastward. The breeze was the gentlest it had been since our arrival as we lazed over the clear water and its shifting hues of blue and pale green. As though telling us that it was time to go home, the wind quit completely when we neared Point Saline on the way back, a very rare event in these parts in the winter, and we had to power back to Grenada Yacht Services to turn *Merlin* in.

From The Sailing Life (1974)

Les Iles Sous Le Vent

To leeward of Tahiti; islands of charm and glamor

The prospect of visiting the Society Islands of French Polynesia—Tahiti and Les Iles sous le Vent—brought to mind in advance certain images out of Somerset Maugham and Nordhoff and Hall. We fully expected to be skimming across limpid lagoons perched on the outrigger of a sailing canoe or fighting for deck space with a pig or two on a trading schooner, but we were in for a few surprises. The image has changed in these fabled islands.

The scenery is still there, as breathtaking as ever, but the world has caught up with these islands of paradise in many ways. First of all, getting there was a swift overnight flight from California. In dawn stillness just eight hours from Los Angeles, our big Pan American jet eased down to the runway built on coral across the pale green waters of Tahiti's lagoon. I couldn't help but compare this with the 23 days I had spent in a wartime convoy plodding 4,800 miles from Panama to Bora Bora, or with the time taken by many long voyagers who have pursued a dream by sailing out here before the southeast trades.

Tahiti itself has probably changed most of all from the traditional South Seas image. The island is still one of the world's more graceful bits of scenery, but its city, Papeete, is a crowded, hot, over-touristed seaport with all the added disadvantages of being France's big military base for its atomic bomb tests. Prices are extremely high, and what's left of the image is constantly being shaken further by such sights as the dancers for the native floor show at the Hotel Tahiti arriving on motorcycles in leather jackets with cigarettes dangling from mouth corners. They change into grass skirts, go through the motions of the old rituals, then come out afterwards on the dance floor in modern clothes to frug and watusi amid the few tourists young enough to engage in such activity.

One can still be grateful to Tahiti, though, for its jet strip providing such easy access to the delights of its satellite islands. Nearest is Moorea, lying athwart the sunset 12 miles off Papeete—one of the most impressive backdrops anywhere. Moorea is still 99 percent unspoiled and has a valid, thoroughly logical claim to the title of world's most beautiful island. The one percent spoiled is actually a benefit to the visitor, as the only encroachments from the outside world are two modern inns that blend well with the scenery while providing most of the comforts of home. Moorea is reached by a daily boat and by five weekly flights in an ancient flying boat.

The inn accommodations are thatch-roofed bungalows, native style, in gorgeous settings. We stayed at the Bali Hai, run by three Californians with a background of sailing at Newport Beach. Their pioneer was Hugh Kelley, who was bitten by the South Seas bug when he came down on the schooner *Constellation* in the 1959 Tahiti Race and has never really gone back, except to persuade his pals Jay Carlisle and Muk McCallum to join him in partnership.

Bali Hai lies along a white beach under coconut palms, with a northward view across pale blue lagoon water to surf creaming onto the reef, piled up there by the ever-whistling southeast trades. These same trades air-condition the bungalows like no electronic gear ever could, and lend a constant accompaniment of rustling palms to the lap-lap of lagoon wavelets on the beach.

One-day tours do come over by boat from Tahiti for special native "feast day" dances, but the rest of the time guests can enjoy the island's unblemished splendor by themselves. Bicycle or truck are the land transport, and the arrangements for getting afloat are unique. This is where the next changes from the image became so noticeable. Not a sailing canoe or trading schooner was in sight. Almost everything that floats is now motorized in these waters, and Bali Hai's fleet consists of an outboard-powered outrigger, a small launch, and a completely one-of-a-kind vessel dubbed—with feeling— *Leaky Tiki*. She was built by a man intending to navigate her from Tahiti to Hawaii for fame and fortune. Needless to say, all this came to an end just beyond the reef at Papeete, and the Bali Hai boys were able to pick her up cheap. She lends an adventurous flavor to expeditions in the lagoon.

We took off in her one morning with a mixed crew of vacationing airline pilots and stewardesses and unsuspecting tourists, to visit Papetoi Bay five miles to the west of Bali Hai. This is a favorite stop of cruising yachts and the home of the island's only American householders, Mr. and Mrs. Kellum, who came here by yacht in 1925, built a house, and have never left. A visit with them was a delightful highlight of the stay.

Before the trades, even *Leaky Tiki* swept along like a Transpac yacht, and we could turn off the twin Seagull outboards—slightly unmatched in size of props, but somehow effective—and proceed under sail. A marked channel led us through wicked coral heads. Past Cook Bay, a deep indentation backed by peaks that soar amid scudding shreds of trade wind clouds, we rounded a point where thatched cottages string along a golden beach in a frieze of palms, into Papetoi Bay. It is hard to decide whether Cook or Papetoi is more dramatic, but the question is academic. They are both un-matched in the pattern of their peaks and charm of the fore-shore.

After a leisurely couple of hours of gamming aboard a visiting yacht, the Heilman family's *Merrywing* out of Beth-lehem, Pa., via Raritan YC, Perth Amboy, N.J., splashing in the shallows and picnicking, we flailed *Leaky Tiki*'s steering oar around and got her headed out of the bay and back to Bali Hai—and someone actually intended to steer to Hawaii with it! The trades were at their freshest, well over 20, and it was an interesting contest between the Seagulls and the el-ements. Despite a few periods of sliding backwards as stronger puffs blasted down the sides of Papetoi's steep peaks, the Seagulls eventually won. Wary of maneuvering through a couple of 90° turns in the marked channel, we de-cided to eye-pilot along the beach, a shorter, more protected route. At our speed any dangers would be thoroughly evi-dent before we could come up on them, and we threaded our way successfully.

In many places, this snail's pace could have been a te-dious trip, but Moorea's splendor can hold the eye for hours. The slow unfolding of perspectives between the peaks, the gradual opening up of Cook's long slit, and the sparkle on the water astern as the sun lowered to due west from di-rectly overhead (at 17° S. lat. in February), were delights that could have been enjoyed for hours more.

It was with a feeling of triumph, and of a great adven-ture completed, that we "secured all engines" after *Leaky Tiki* groaned around the corner at the entrance to the little cut off Bali Hai and slid her ponderous bows onto the beach.

Leaky Tiki's unique characteristics at least had a Poly-nesian flavor, but our next adventures afloat showed even more completely how changes in the image have been ef-fected. From Moorea, we again took the flying boat further *sous le vent* (to leeward) 100 miles to the north to Raiatea.

The Bali Hai Hotel has a branch here, even more informal. The setting is less idyllic than Moorea (nothing could be more so) but Raiatea is a bigger, more varied island. It shares a large lagoon with the island of Tahaa, both high, rugged, and good examples of modern-day Polynesia minus tourist influences. Snorkeling and scuba diving are excellent, the latter especially on a wrecked square-rigger in 60 feet of water off the Bali Hai.

Bali Hai's few bungalows are the only hotel, but 20-mile-long Raiatea has 10,000 people on it. Many of them have no road connection with Uturoa, the main town. This was once, before Captain Cook and American whalers made Tahiti important, the religious and commercial center of this part of Polynesia. Tahaa has several thousand more inhabitants along its roadless shores. Vanilla, copra, fishing, and farming are the economy of both these islands. Raiatea has an airstrip with daily DC-4 service to Papeete, in addition to the once-a-week flying boat visit. Night life at Bali Hai consisted of the kitchen help and gardeners singing native songs after family-style dinner at one big table for everybody.

There was a 16' Boston Whaler with a big Johnson outboard off the Bali Hai dock, but Hugh Kelley said that it would be better to hire the "Chinaman's boat" for the day-long circumnavigation of Tahaa we planned to take with two other couples from the hotel. Aha, we thought; here would be South Seas color, conjuring a vision of some rugged work-boat with fish heads hanging here and there and some sort of canvas canopy over a scarred and peeled-paint hull.

Well, there was a Chinaman running the boat, but it was a four-month-old 20' Glastron fiberglass cabin cruiser from Austin, Tex., complete with vinyl upholstery and powerful outdrive. South Seas color, no; but a fine boat for the trip. A good turn of speed and shallow draft were both needed to do it up properly.

It was a day of gusty trades and thick, black clouds tumbling down the peaks of Raiatea and Tahaa, parting now and then to reveal Bora Bora's distinctive flattop peak 20 miles to the northwest, and occasionally sending sheets of rain down the valleys and across the reef. Between showers, the sun burned down hotly and the pale colors of the lagoon sparkled to life.

Our first stop was a curve of white beach at the tip of a little palm-studded island in the lagoon off Tahaa. Snorkeling and swimming in the warm, clear-as-glass water was great before lunch by a driftwood fire. Isolated little towns on Tahaa, each with a dock for the trading boat, a church steeple peeking through the palms, and a few thatched cottages and tin-roofed stores, made interesting stops. At one, the mayor (he would have been the chief not too many years ago) had enclosed some pools along the shore and all sorts of exotic fish were impounded, as well as turtles and sharks. Each village had a rickety wooden Chinese store selling a bewildering array of goods, from soda pop to kerosene lanterns and freshly baked bread. One had a coin-operated pinball-type machine with a soccer game in it, and several of the village sports were operating it intently.

Chickens, pigs, and dogs wandered along the dirt track between the houses, along with naked children, and the only traffic was an occasional motor scooter. Not a sailing craft was in sight in any of the harbors. Outrigger canoes and small launches were all powered, mostly by American outboards.

The last stop, after a rough pounding inside the reef on the windward side of Tahaa, through a kaleidoscope of sunbursts and hanging curtains of rain, was a tiny motu, just an acre or two, perched on the inner edge of the reef. Surf pounded on the other side, where a confused sea surged through a pass in the reef, as we nosed toward two thatch huts on the beach under an overhang of palms. Around a little point, the third side of the triangular island was fenced in by a large trap filled with fish. A youngster ambled up to us and he and our Chinese driver netted a few, but the only other person on the island remained asleep in an open-sided hut all the time we were there. Dozens of pigs of all sizes had half the island to themselves behind a wire fence, and they all came lurching at me when I ventured along the beach on their side. Probably the chorus of grunts and squeals meant that they thought it was dinnertime, but I didn't linger to communicate.

In contrast with this sample of reef and lagoon living, our last bit of outboard yachting in Polynesia was the next day via the Boston Whaler up a river cutting deeply into the mountainous heart of Raiatea. Planing across trade wind chop ruffling the lagoon, we moved into a bay of still, dark green water at the mouth of the river, headed inland through the ever-narrowing channel.

Children waved to us from a few huts set amid a riot of flowers along the bank as we throttled down and idled around the bends in the river. The water turned from green to a steely gray and the palms closed in overhead. Through them there were glimpses straight up to the face of cliffs soaring into the clouds, and the banks alternated with tangled brush and vistas of open fields. There was no sound except the low hum of the motor, and the water was flat and still. Finally, perhaps a mile inland, fallen trees blocked the channel and we nosed into the bank. With a line on a palm trunk, the Whaler nestled quietly under the bushes, and we took a swim in the cool fresh water. It was more refreshing than it looked and balm to sun-scorched, salty skins.

Backing and filling to turn in less than twice the Whaler's length, we slid back downstream to the lagoon. As we moved out onto the bay, now ruffled to silver by a sudden gust around the point, two native children paddling a tiny outrigger canoe along the shore paused to watch us go by and raised their paddles to us, the old saluting the new changes that have come to marine transportation in this idyllic corner of Polynesia. If it hadn't been for modern power, we wouldn't have seen so many fascinating things in such a short time. No doubt Somerset Maugham himself would have been grateful, too.

———

From *The Sailing Life* (1974)

Out of This World

The waters around Phuket, an island on the Andaman Sea coast of Thailand, are about as exotic a cruising area as can be found

After a spray-flinging thrash to windward into 25 knots of northeast monsoon, we left the deep-water blue of the Andaman Sea and entered the pale green of Phang Na Bay. At noon the monsoon began to fade and we shook the reef out of the main and glided smoothly toward a panorama of surreal shapes shimmering in the heat-haze. Islands with sheer cliffs, tall peaks and limestone pinnacles eaten away at the base formed what appeared to be an illustration for a Gothic fairy tale.

The southwester riffled lightly in from the sea across the island known as Ko Phuket (pronounced *pooket*) in southern Thailand. We anchored off an island named Ko Yao Yai, its perpendicular cliffs towering hundreds of feet over us. Taking to the dinghy, we ranged its rocky shores, finding a tunnel, sea-scoured and exposed only below half-tide, that led to a lagoon within the heart of the island. Perfectly circular, the lagoon was ringed by sheer walls of rock with scrubby trees hanging improbably from crannies. We had entered a silent, secret world. Little silver fish skittered in panic at our approach, a few landing in the boat. Onshore, a monkey scavenging along a rocky ledge spied us and shot up the cliff in perpendicular panic.

Back on *Singa*, our chartered Sparkman & Stephens-designed Hylas 47, we had a relaxing dinner of curried chicken, rice and prawns in the evening calm before the northeast monsoon freshened after sunset. So ended the first of nine days of discovery in a cruising ground that seemed literally out of this world.

Few North Americans have experienced the unique appeal of Phuket, but each year more sailors come under its spell, which is not hard to arrange as more than 30 charter boats are available there. All are crewed, because both area and language are too strange for successful bareboat operations. The charters are based on Phuket, a 32-mile-long island on the Andaman Sea connected to the mainland by a causeway. Phuket is better known as a winter resort for European jet-setters, who are less than 10 hours from its beautiful beaches lined with luxury hotels. Air service to Phuket, only an hour from Bangkok, is direct from Europe.

We boarded *Singa* at Phuket Yacht Club, a luxury resort at Nai Harn, a beach-lined bay at the southern tip of Phuket on the edge of the Andaman Sea. There are no marinas or yacht harbors here, and all boarding is by dinghy from the beach. Aboard were owner Tony Kozad, a transplanted Californian who operates a charter service in Singapore; Captain Pascal Trouvier, a Frenchman with an impressive resume of long voyages; and Tony's wife Tulimah, a charming Malaysian, who was cook, hostess and delightful shipmate.

That first day was a marvelous introduction to the charms of Phuket sailing. As we absorbed local lore—*Ko*, for example, means island and *Ao* means bay—we ranged through that fantastic seascape, always marveling at the odd island shapes, stopping frequently for more cave exploring and beachcombing. Under the eroded bases of the islands, the limestone stalactites were a perpetual source of amazement.

We saw few yachts, but numerous fishing boats while under way. The bigger boats, with live-aboard crews, have towering deckhouses aft like seagoing pagodas. Great booms lined with light bulbs are extended at night for squid fishing, and offshore after dark the fishing fleet looks like a city at sea.

Even odder craft are the "longtails," a breed we had first seen dashing about the klongs (canals) of Bangkok as water taxis. Here they are day-fishing boats, and on our second morning a fleet of them was on a tiny beach under the cliffs of Ko Hyai. Longtails are slender canoe-hulled 25- to 30-footers. Their outboard motors ride at 70-degree angles, with shafts extending 10 or more feet behind the boat. Accompanied by a cacophony of engine sounds, great rooster tails shoot up from their propellers. Some of the longtails tried to sell us prawns before we set sail, but bargaining broke down over price.

Before leaving Ko Hyai, another dinghy expedition took us to what is known informally as Paradise Island. Here, a small cruising sloop was in a Scandinavian moor with lines from bow and stern tied to trees under rock cliffs that stretched out of sight above her. There were more caves to poke through and a succession of gasp-evoking perspective through openings between cliffs. Ko Hong to the northeast offered another cliff-framed anchorage, and we stopped here for lunch. Another landlocked lagoon materialized: sheer walls, mangroves growing around the edges and a kingfisher eyeing us from a lone tree clutching at the cliff wall.

We powered southeastward in the noonday calm. Long, slithery gar fish skipped across water that grew increasingly more green and clear. The northeast monsoon returned earlier than usual, just as we anchored under another cliff castle at Ko Dain Hok far out in the middle of Phang Na Bay. Here, near a small group of camping huts, we found a place to dispose of refuse properly, so our dinghy expedition under stalactites and onto an idyllic beach was dual-purpose. Tulimah prepared a fine dinner which we savored, cooled by a backwind that curled off the cliff. The open water between us and Phuket looked like a lively metropolis that night as a galaxy of fish boat lights flickered along the horizon.

We ran before the morning monsoon back to Phuket and a fuel and water stop at a fuel boat in Ao Chalong, one of the main yacht harbors on the east side of the island.

From *Singa* we transferred to *Stormvogel*, the legendary 73-foot ocean racing ketch that once campaigned all over the world. It was a thrill to sail on her, having competed against her years ago in ocean races. Her charter crew consisted of two New Zealanders, skipper Graeme Henry and mate Andy, and Françoise, a charming and able French cook. With *Stormvogel*, we headed northwest before dawn into the Andaman Sea to a small group of islands called the Similans almost 60 miles offshore. We had "all five" up—two jibs, main, mizzen staysail and mizzen—as the old lady took a bone in her teeth on a lively broad reach, until the monsoon faded just as we anchored for lunch in a graceful little bay. These islands are a special target for divers, and we found diving boats and a camp there.

After a lunchtime laze, we moved on to the next island north in the three-island chain and anchored in a rock-ringed bay reminiscent of Virgin Gorda's Baths in the British Virgin Islands. Here, Françoise presented a memorable dinner of snapper calamari, salad and fruit.

The next morning, returning to the mainland, the monsoon faded and we powered back to Nai Harn arriving under a gibbous moon. Dinner of lamb Bretagne, salad and chocolate mousse was followed by a blissful sleep.

Raden Mas (Golden Prince), a 59-foot British-built motor sailer, was our last Phuket charter offering. By now the monsoon was fitful even in the morning, so junkets in *Raden Mas* were under power, and we were sorry not to see her red sails raised. Her skipper was Charles Daley, another expatriate Californian, and he had two Thai lads and a Malay as crew. As usual, service was ever-present and with a smile.

Raden Mas took us out across Phang Na Bay, with a lunch stop at Ko Mai Thon halfway across, where longtails buzzed about like bees at a hive, to Ko Phi Phi, an island in the middle of the bay. Phi Phi is a major tourist attraction with its gorgeous beaches and spectacular cliffs, caves and rock formations. In contrast to the lonely islands we had visited in *Singa* and *Stormvogel*, Phi Phi had a small cruise ship in her outer harbor, many boats at anchor, tourist launches moving in and out and longtails by the dozen.

It was warm enough for us to sleep on deck here, waking to a bright, clear morning and a final look at the bizarre scenery of Phuket. Weird pinnacles of rock rose high above satellite islands named Little Phi Phi and Phraya Nak. On the latter, a strange tower of rock was topped with a head-shaped knob that stared up into the blue. From a certain angle, it was E.T. incarnate, which seemed a fitting symbol for our goodbye to cruising in Phuket waters, which truly was out of this world.

From Cruising World Magazine (1990)

VIII

Special Cruising Memories

Over the years, from many wonderful cruising adventures, these stand out above all

---

A Day To Measure By

With no hint in advance, there developed a very special day we will never forget

THAT SUBJECTIVE STATE of mind that is the reward of cruising for most people, is difficult to define. Like late evening hilarity or fine cooking, a successful cruise can be hailed in superlatives, but the why of the success must come in the experience itself. The quality of a breeze, glint of sun on water or rush of waves alongside, and that sense of accomplishment in gaining a new anchorage of a late afternoon, are immediate sensations that blend into a haze of delights without definition. A successful cruise is one in which nothing really happens, and a list of log entries is only a framework for the personal nostalgia that evokes intangibles.

And yet there can be a day that becomes a special one, assuming a quality that leaps from the haze of memories and sets a standard for defining and measuring the joys of cruising. Its charm is that it develops without warning, and the surroundings need not be exotic. In fact, the familiar waters of Long Island Sound, always looked upon by us as a mere passageway to greater delights despite the many advantages they provide for the millions who live nearby, gave us a day of that special kind, the one that takes on definition and spells out, as much as it can ever be done, the intangibles of the joys of cruising.

It was August 28, 1964, a Friday. I had to check the date in the log, but its details are in the mind with a brilliance that will last. Jane and I had cruised to Newport, R. I., to watch the America's Cup trials, and fog and lack of breeze had caused postponements that held us there a day longer than planned. Now we would have to keep moving to get *Mar Claro* the 150 miles back to the Shrewsbury by Sunday night.

After watching the start of the Thursday Cup trial, we had broken off from the spectator fleet and reached westward across a gentle, fading southerly to Block Island, its cliffs and lighthouses silhouetted black against the lowering sun. Staying in the favorable reverse current that flowed northwestward behind the island toward the general easterly set of the ebb, we had eased up to Block Island North Reef making better progress over the bottom than a 72′ yawl out in the ebb. In shallow water at the bar, perhaps a foot or two beneath our 2′4″ draft, an overfalling rip marked the meeting of reverse current and main flow of ebb. As we hit it, the wind died, and we powered the three miles down the west shore into Great Salt Pond in the shimmering stillness of twilight.

At 0630 Friday, the dawn air was cold, clear and completely still, a heavy beading of dew lay over cockpit, decks, spars and pier, and breath frosted in the air, as I slipped out of the warmth of our double berth forward, leaving Jane sleeping soundly, pulled on a sweater and windbreaker and prepared to get underway with as little fuss as possible. Since Jane's approach to a new day is more oblique than mine, I mentally allowed her two more hours of sleep and fortified myself with orange juice, a piece of bread and a peach until she would be ready to cook a regular breakfast.

The flat calm was as much as we could hope for, as I felt we would have to make a long day of it. The tide would be favorable into the Sound in another hour or so, and the prospect was for a long session of purring along under our 5.5 hp. Johnson in its well aft. No hard westerly was the hope from a forecast of light, variable air. Freely translated into Long Island Sound-ese in August, this usually means a windless morning and an afternoon sou'wester.

No other boats were moving, only gulls piercing the hush with plaintive cries as the early sun shone on the undersides of their wings, while *Mar Claro* cut a path across the mirror of the harbor and, at 0715, passed between the jetties onto gently heaving, unruffled Block Island Sound. The mainland was a thin line to starboard, and the sun began to warm my back as I stood at the tiller on course 310°M for Watch Hill. The usual dilemma of where to enter Long Island Sound—The Race, Fisher's Island Sound or Plum Gut—was simply solved. Fisher's was much the best way, since the flood turned an hour sooner there. We would not have to fight any ebb and would be in a favoring current more than an hour earlier than on the other routes.

For almost an hour, the wake's whorls, bubbles and wisps of smoke arrowed off astern to melt into the flat sheen of the water, as Block receded to a dark outline. Then, soon after 0800, dark patches began to pock the reflecting surfaces to the eastward, and in five minutes the silvery sheen had become a gently ruffled blue. Despite the forecast, the day was coming alive with a rare easterly. I waited to make sure that this was more than a temporary catspaw, then turned off the motor and made sail in the blessed silence, broken now by the easy luffing of the sails. Back in the cockpit, I sheeted in main and genny for a broad reach, and *Mar Claro*'s new surge forward had the entirely different feel of the pull of the sails.

Looking to windward to gauge how the breeze might develop, I noticed a smudge of woolly white off Point Judith and said to myself in sun-warmed smugness that Newport seemed to be having some more of its fog. With my eye over the bow again, the quality of the sunlight suddenly changed, and I glanced up to see a gray finger of the stuff moving swiftly in on us. In no time at all, the land was blotted out ahead and astern, and the sun became a lemony balloon suspended in haze. The water turned to yellow-flecked steel for the small radius in which it was now visible, and I carefully rechecked the course as we scudded on through the mist.

Abruptly we sailed through a hole in it, and a long clear corridor opened up all the way to Point Judith before we plunged into another fast-moving bank. Then, just as suddenly, it all blew by, the shoreline was a sharp line to the northward again, and a brownish smudge to leeward, like the smoke of a departed ship, was the only reminder.

The water was a dancing blue again, and whitecaps became a part of the pattern. The breeze was now about 14, and *Mar Claro* heeled to it nicely. This and the warmth of the stronger sun on the convertible canvas hood that covers the main cabin, stirred Jane awake, and we both started the day in the way we like best—I with an early departure and she with a relaxed awakening. Eggs and coffee soon followed, the hood came off and was stowed forward, and the day was in full swing.

The big Victorian houses and hotels on the bluff at Watch Hill changed from skyline silhouettes to collections of cubes, curves and towers in color as we closed with the beach and swept into the passage past Napatree Point. The first buoy had that wonderfully gratifying tail of current gurgling off in the direction of our course, and buoys and beach slipping by near at hand added to our sense of speed. Once in Fisher's Island Sound, a new course of 270°M brought the wind dead aft, and out came the spinnaker pole for winging out the genny, a good rig for making all speed required under cruising-style concentration. The day had now resolved itself, with the questions of early morning answered. It was a rarely beautiful one.

The easterly held steady at 12-16, its hint of autumn warmed enough by the brilliant sun while dead before it to persuade Jane to change to a bathing suit and me to strip to the one-shirt level. Visibility had that remarkable range and clarity only a fair weather easterly can bring in this part of the world. Distant landmarks like the radar on Montauk Point 14 miles to the south stood out on the sharply edged horizon, and details of nearer shorelines had definition, depth and sparkle. Beach sand was yellower, water bluer, greenery greener, and distant sails of other boats now making their appearance caught the eye as bright flecks of white. Several big power yachts with Aurora Syndicate flags at the spreader sped past on the way from Fisher's Island to the America's Cup course, their high bows throwing spray as they ploughed into the easterly.

The visual sharpness was matched by a heady, sea-born quality to the air. The breeze, blowing from miles of open ocean, held a tang of salt, with now and then a hint of bayberry on a warmer gust when under the land.

As I checked the chart steadily for the rocks and ledges in Fisher's Island Sound, Jane brought out a just-started crossword puzzle saved from Sunday's paper and poked a pencil at it now and then. At 1100, with Fisher's West Harbor sliding by to port, it was time for one of our favorite cruising rituals, followed only when the sun is warm and the air is salty, an "elevensies" beer. Right from a bed on ice, the cans were frostily beaded as I punched them open (we use the flip-top for sinking them—a punched hole is kinder to the lips), and the first swig had that good, biting-cold sting.

Soon we were out in the wider expanse of Long Island Sound, with *Mar Claro* almost steering herself as she swept along. Boats headed east were hard on the wind, strapped down and throwing spray, with crew in jackets or foul weather gear, as they slanted across our course, but our decks were dry and steady. The following seas were crested with white now and then and clashed with the wake in a fine, hissing, criss-crossing welter of foam, but they slid under the hull easily, and the motion was gentle.

With 1230 approaching, Jane looked up from her puzzle—all but a couple of "East Indian sandarac trees" she said—and made noises about a martini and lunch. The former was cold and dry, the latter a favorite specialty, shrimp in a mixture of mayonnaise and chili sauce, surrounded by slices of hard-boiled egg and tomatoes, with fruit for dessert.

The miles and hours slipped away as the sun moved from the port quarter to abeam, and on toward the bow. We were out in a wide part of the Sound now, and Long Island was a blue pencil line to port. New London's smokestacks and bridge had faded astern, and we scudded on past Black and Hatchett Points toward the mouth of the Connecticut. Looking ahead when at Block Island, this would have seemed a good day's run on a 20' waterline, but here it was only 1400, with hours of good sailing remaining.

To stay in the strongest current, we skirted the outside of Long Sand Shoal, where the big whistler had a rooster tail on its western side. The breeze had eased a bit, but the added current kept our over-the-bottom average at about the same six knots it had been for most of the day. Jane, whose favorite cruising pastime is reading, picked up a book for a while but soon put it down and sat back to enjoy the exhilaration of motion in the sailing. The sun in my eyes brought on a drowsiness, and Jane took the tiller while I put my head down for a snooze. When I sat up again, the jetties at Duck Island Roads could be picked out against the mainland to starboard, another good stopping place we would have to pass by with this kind of sailing.

Ahead, the stark lump of Falkner Island stood out against the gold-rimmed horizon. As we came abeam of the long bathing beach at Hammonasset, the breeze picked up again, and by the time we closed with Falkner the flow past the bell there confirmed that the ebb had begun. Almost immediately, the seas changed from gently sloped ones with whitecaps here and there to a much steeper tumble of crests, and the boat began a livelier dance.

With 55 miles under her keel, the civilized hour of 1700 coming up, and a slim choice of harbors further on, Sachem Head, a couple of miles off the starboard bow became the anchorage for the evening. The Thimble Islands, just beyond, would have a surge in this easterly, and Sachem was in the lee, so we jibed the main, took in the spinnaker pole and broad-reached toward the rocky promontory on Sachem's eastern side. In the uneven chop, nun buoys on offshore ledges reared and plunged and were slanted against us now. The rocky shoreline sent a backwash of counterwaves into the bobble, but it soon smoothed out as we came under the lee of the point and hove to to drop the sails and start the outboard.

A narrow slit running northeastward between rocky ledges, the picturebook harbor opened up to a vista of tightly packed boats, mostly auxiliaries and one-designs, swinging to moorings. A red-sailed dinghy drifted among them, and the backdrop was a montage of comfortable houses, many of weathered shingle, with clipped lawns and flower-filled gardens edging down to pinkish brown rocks. Topsides and spars of the boats glinted in the slanting sun, shooting back momentary flashes of brilliance as they swung, and white walls of houses shone brightly.

As we eased slowly in, wondering about a mooring, a man in business clothes, cocktail glass in hand, stepped off the verandah of a house on the inland side and megaphoned a cordial instruction to take a mooring close to the club. We waved our thanks and were soon settled snugly at the mooring, anchor cup in hand.

Outside, the waves from the easterly dashed against the rocks, and the flag at the rambling, be-porched yacht club on the point stood stiffly in the breeze, but here the wind was gentle, barely filling the red sail of the little dink, and the light mellowed slowly as the sun sank to a quiet, cloudless demise behind the Thimbles.

Corned beef hash and string beans made the right supper for this kind of landfall, and we ate in the cockpit while twilight faded to darkness. The end of a day that can long stand as a measure of what cruising ought to be, and so often is, came with music on the radio and a nightcap under stars that began to dim beyond the softly humming rigging, while clouds finally moved in as a foretaste of the routine day that the next one would be. When the last star was blotted out, we went below.

From *Over the Horizon* (1966)

Gulf Stream Crossing

*The challenge of a round trip to Bimini;
the full story of the "Landfall" chapter
cruise*

The next real brush with the Stream was in our own twenty-four-foot Amphibi-Ette class sloop *Mar Claro*, which we had trailed to Florida for the winter of 1958-59. Jane and I were messing around in the Keys in her in April when we took a notion, on a day of bright sun and a fresh southerly breeze, to head across the Stream from Ocean Reef to Bimini. We hailed a charter fishing boat out of the Ocean Reef Club working the edge of the Stream, told him we were heading across and would check back with Ocean Reef on arrival, and sailed away from his openmouthed amazement.

Under full working sail, we sped across Hawk Channel and met a steep, lively sea at the edge of the Stream. The breeze held a special promise, and had enough weight to move us along well despite the sea; the day was bright blue and white. The radio spoke of 15- to 25-knot southerlies all day, just right for angling across the Stream.

The rhumb line course was 067° from Turtle Reef buoy off Ocean Reef to Gun Cay Light in the Bahamas, the best landfall to steer for, and I figured a compass heading of 090° would take care of the Gulf Stream drift. The Stream's speed averaged out to about two knots for its whole width, stronger on the axis near the Keys, and weaker on the Bahama side.

The promise in the breeze soon turned false, and in no time, we were slatting over lumpy, confused waves on the axis of the Stream. The sea was covered with the purple sails of Portuguese Men o' War as far as the eye could see, and once we saw a big sea turtle chomping avidly on one of the highly poisonous jellyfish. We wondered what his stomach would be like with that dainty load in it, and didn't envy him his meal. Getting nowhere and jumping around very uncomfortably on the short steep seas, we turned on the five-hp outboard, and soon we were putt-putting across the roller coaster seas of the axis, feeling a bit foolish, but making progress.

We alternated sail and power as the breeze came and went, and by midafternoon, the waves had subsided to a gently heaving surface as calm as the Shrewsbury. Peering far down into the inky depths, we could see thousands of jellyfish floating along, and now and then a school of fish would flash by in the clear blue void beneath us. As our progress slowed with the light breeze, I readjusted our course farther south to offset the longer time the Gulf Stream would have to push us to the north. Whenever there was enough breeze in which to sail at all, we shut off the motor, because I didn't want to run out of gas far offshore. We could run eight hours on our two tanks of gas, but I wanted to have a safety margin for any necessary maneuvering when we neared the islands.

At nightfall, the breeze came back, and I decided to change from genoa to working jib for after-dark safety in case it breezed on heavily. Jane, who has never had much confidence as a helmsman, took the tiller, and I went forward to make the switch. As I was tacking down the working jib and had hands full of shackle parts and a cotter pin in my mouth, I called back something about "be careful not to come about," as I thought she was a little high, and only the last phrase, the "come about" part, got through to her. Suddenly I was whapped against the pulpit by the genny and found myself in a pretty precarious position for a few minutes, with no hands to hold on with and a cotter pin clenched in my teeth.

The pulpit kept me aboard, and I gradually collected myself and the rigging parts and finished the job, all the while hurling rather caustic remarks back to the helm.

Through the long moonless evening hours, we drifted slowly eastward, occasionally under power; sometime after midnight, I began to get the feeling that the Bahamas had disappeared. We had been under power for a while, but then the breeze freshened from the southeast, and I stepped to the cabin top to hoist the sails again. The added height of this position was just the difference needed for me to catch a sudden glimpse of Gun Cay's pin prick of light exactly on the horizon, and as the last quarter moon rose ahead of us, we romped into Bimini on the starboard tack.

When we finally swept in over that luminous white water at the bar, and felt the atmosphere of the islands all around us, my career as a boat-owner was complete. I don't expect ever again to feel quite as much like a millionaire, and taking a gratified backward glance over the years of dreaming and hoping, I was entirely satisfied with the months of planning for the boat, the added months of working out the details of this trip, and finally the long jaunt by trailer. It was all very much worth it now, and somehow New Jersey seemed a million miles away. We were not exactly the first sailors to have made a landfall on a tropical island, and Bimini was no Bali Hai, but to us it was a symbol of the success of the whole venture.

Feeling smug at negotiating it, I relaxed a bit as we turned to port and headed up the harbor toward the marina lights. Suddenly I was aware of some change in the water color ahead, a darker darkness in the dark, and started to say "What's that thing in the waaa—ter," which is as far as I got before we ran aground.

Mar Claro had a two-foot-four draft, so it was a simple matter to hop out and push her off, but I had strayed from the channel at a bend and ran aground again right away.

There was a stringpiece just inshore of us, so I decided to ease the few feet over to it and tie up for the little bit of night remaining. It was narrow, with no railing, and I teetered along it making the lines fast before tumbling back aboard and into the sack. (We straightened out the "come about" business the next day.)

In daylight, I poked my head into the cockpit to see just what kind of place we'd ended up in, and it was something of a shock to gaze through a heavy wire netting that was underneath the catwalk we were tied to. We were at the Lerner Marine Labs, and the catwalk I had teetered on at 0300 was the outer edge of the shark pen at the Lab. Great gray monsters, at least a dozen of them, were lazily nosing around the sandy bottom behind the wire, which was only a couple of feet from the hull.

We didn't stay there very long, moving to the nearest marina.

After clearing into the Bahamas with the commissioner, a polite young man, who came aboard about 9:00 A.M., it took us most of one morning to get a phone call through to Florida to report our arrival; Bimini is no less casual than any place in the Bahamas in matters of communications. Finally, we had done our duty, and could spend the rest of the day enjoying the place.

Another brilliant day greeted us on the second morning, and we were ready to go sailing again. Cat Cay is the only other island in the area, and since it is 90 miles across the Great Bahama Bank before you reach another cay, we headed for Cat, 12 miles away, over the incredibly-clear water of the Bank. The bottom is as visible as the palm of your hand, and the water has a sparkle and clarity I've never seen anywhere else in the world. I don't ever expect to have a much better sail than this one.

Cat is really an American island, a sort of Fisher's Island with palm trees, and everything, from dockage to shower baths to drinks at the yacht club, is outrageously expensive. There is no Bahama atmosphere in the buildings or people, but, in a way, it was fun to moor amid dozens of glossy yachts, where stewards in white coats served drinks on the fantail. In the evening, Zed-N-S, the Nassau radio station, played George Symonette calypso songs and a soft breeze drifted in from the Bank over sand flats and seaweed. This was enough atmosphere for us as we sat in the cockpit and sipped rum on the rocks.

Unfortunately, we couldn't enjoy it any longer, as the weather seemed right for heading back to Florida, and it would not have been wise to leave the crossing until our last day. We sailed away from the pier at Cat at 0430 in darkness and a damp, fresh southerly, which was supposed to last all day (at 15 to 25 knots, Miami radio said), in sharp contrast to our eastbound trip.

Just as we reached the trickiest part of Gun Cay Passage in a cross sea from both the Bank and the Stream, and a course change to be made close to the cliffs of the cay, the jib outhaul chafed through. It was no spot to give Jane the helm. I hesitated to send her forward, but the pulpit made the foredeck a relatively safe spot; she inched her way up there, and soon had the jib under control. If only for these two occasions, the pulpit had more than earned its keep.

Maybe I was thinking of our experience on the way over when I decided to stay at the helm!

For nine hours *Mar Claro* charged across the uneven seas, short and quick, close-reaching toward Miami, and a fast passage was in prospect when we began to see the towers of the beach hotels popping over the horizon. The wind was gradually heading us and swinging southwest; however, a big ring was building around the slowly dimming sun, and the western horizon had a dirty, orange-brown look. The front had evidently stepped up its timetable, but the Miami radio stations were not changing their prediction of a day-long southerly.

Evidently no one was looking out the window, as the wind was now well around in the west, and we could not lay Government Cut close-hauled any more. I kicked myself for not holding higher on the crossing, but I had originally aimed for the south end of Key Biscayne, which seemed enough of a margin for error.

Since I was keeping a weather eye on the weather to weather as *Mar Claro* buried her rail and charged shoreward, I was able to spot a line of white foam and a darkening of the water behind it as soon as it moved out from the beach. There was no curtain of rain with it, but it was moving rapidly in our direction and kicking up quite a fuss, and we wasted no time in getting sail off. We had just gotten everything furled and stopped when the squall line hit us with a blast like the blow of a fist.

The water was a froth of whitecaps and wind streaks at right angles to the daylong southerly chop. I've never been in a maelstrom, but this had to be what one is like, and just as it erupted all around us, someone must have looked out the window at the radio station, because there were now sudden high-pitched warnings about "possible tornadoes" coming over the air. Thanks a lot.

Mar Claro had a convertible canvas hood over her main cabin, a feature which earned her the nickname of "floating covered wagon" in some quarters, and this seemed to provide enough windage to act something like a storm sail. While Jane secured everything in the cabin that could possibly move, I sat at the tiller and held it to leeward, and the boat lay to the howling northwester at an angle, making some leeway and a little progress to windward, and handled the jumping mess of sea beautifully by herself. She never took solid water on deck, though the motion of a light-displacement boat corking around on top had to be experienced to be believed. The clouds were low, black, twisting, and ominous in the dirty brown light, but there was almost no rain.

As we were hanging on patiently at the height of the onslaught, I was startled to see something bright blue leaping across the wave tops in the wildest kind of abandon, heading across our stern, and for a moment I thought it must be some marlin or sailfish gone suddenly berserk in the storm. Uncertainty changed to laughter when it came close enough in its hurtling, bouncing progress to be identified as a beach mat that the front had picked off the sand and was sending rapidly on its way to Bimini.

The radio was making noises about 55-knot winds, which I could easily believe, and still had tornadoes as a possibility, but the cool air behind the front didn't have the look of those conditions. (Actually, the tornadoes did hit up near Melbourne, in a mobile-home camp, as usual.) The temperature had dropped rapidly and there was a gradually widening band of gold in the west and a barely noticeable lessening of wind strength. After three hours or so, we were about seven miles north of where we had been hit by the squall, as we had not quite got out of the Stream, and finally I decided that she could handle the working jib and a reefed main. The wind had settled down to about 25-30 from the west, and by sunset, which now blazed yellowly on a clear horizon, we had beaten our way back to the spot we'd been in about 1430 when the front hit. Twenty minutes more at that time would have put us inside Government Cut before the front. Now, as we came into the lee, I tried to start the outboard in its well aft, but the bouncing around and slop of sea had been too much for it and it refused to cooperate.

So, for the finish of our adventure, we had to beat dead to windward up the four-mile channel of Government Cut, four hundred feet wide (and against an ebb tide to boot), before we could turn to port off the old Clyde Mallory piers (where SCTC had been located) and reach down Biscayne Bay to Dinner Key. I've never been happier to have a self-trimming jib than on that multi-tack session. We were both very hungry, but cooking was impossible in the constant flipping, so Jane handed up sticks of celery, raw carrots, and hunks of cold cuts to keep me going.

When we finally eased into our slip at the Coral Reef Yacht Club, it was close to midnight and the boat was a wet shambles that took two days to dry out, but we fell into the sack as we were. We had only been to Bimini and back, but it sort of felt as though we had been at least once around the world. If we had felt like millionaires sweeping into a Bahama port on our own boat, we felt like Magellans now that we were back.

From New Boat (1961)

Odd Moments

A few silly incidents: these do happen when you cruise

Mystery Port

Cruising in the Bahamas with Martha, her first husband, Hank, and their daughter Julie, then four months old, as crew, we were on our way from Nassau back to Florida via the Berry Islands, Grand Bahama, and Palm Beach, and were making the long hop across Northwest Providence Channel from Stirrup Cay to Grand Bahama. This time, that so often unfriendly body of water was calm and serene on a lovely

May day, and we were approaching Grand Bahama in late afternoon, thinking to make Lucaya for the night.

Against the lowering sun, landmarks in the west were hard to identify, but we could see the occasional high-rises that dot the Lucaya-Freeport area as black silhouettes up ahead. We came to an unmarked sea buoy off two big concrete jetties, with a high-rise building inshore of them, and I asked Hank and Martha, who had been to Lucaya several years before, if this was it. I'd never been to it myself, but it didn't look right. Also I thought we had come on it too soon, but they thought it probably was, and there was no other place on the chart or in the *Yachtsman's Guide to the Bahamas* that had a sea buoy and jetties, so we turned to starboard and powered in.

Once inside, we realized it couldn't be Lucaya. There were big dredged lagoon fingers extending off into empty brush on each side of the main channel as we came in, but none of the facilities or buildings of Lucaya so clearly indicated in the *Guide*. There was just one lonely high-rise, evidently occupied, but with no sign of life at the moment, well up the channel.

There was definitely no such place in any navigational reference we had on board, but it looked snug, darkness was descending, and we decided to stay right there. We anchored in the first lagoon inside the entrance for a quiet, completely undisturbed night in what we could only log as "Port X," thoroughly mystified.

In the morning, we found that Lucaya was a few miles to the westward, and we still had no clue as to where we had anchored. It was a complete mystery, but I thought I could ask Harry Kline, editor of the *Yachtsman's Guide*, when we got back to Florida, to solve the riddle of Port X. I called him, but he was just as mystified as we were and had never heard of the place. He said he would check into it, and he eventually discovered that it was a real estate development that had been started after the last charts were printed and that had failed before it was given any publicity.

Now it is official. It is called Grand Lucayan Waterway, described in the *Guide*, and it is no longer possible to "discover" it the way we did. How often can you find an undiscovered harbor in the middle of a busy cruising ground in this day and age?

Crash Landing

Tanagra, our Out Island 36 sloop, has pretty well followed the dictum that not much is supposed to happen in cruising boats, but there have been a few oddments in her career, like the first time we ventured into the Gulf of Mexico with her from her base during her first winter, Clearwater, Florida, heading for St. Pete.

Clearwater Pass (a "pass" is an inlet in Gulf of Mexico terminology) has a drawbridge at its land end and then runs northwest between extensive shoals for about a mile, with a width of a couple of hundred yards between the shoals, before reaching the open Gulf.

Right after we cleared the draw under power, with the mainsail up as a "safety valve," heading directly into a fresh northwester of about 18-20 knots, the Perkins diesel coughed a couple of times and died. On a lee shore, with shoals on both sides of us, there was no time to mess with the engine (it turned out later to have dirt in the fuel), and it was a question of sailing her out of there or anchoring. I didn't want to sail back through the draw, and it was no place to anchor, as the onshore breeze was kicking up a good chop, so it was up to *Tanagra* to prove herself by clawing out of there under sail.

"Let's see if she can do it," I muttered to Jane as I put the wheel over to fill the main. And she did, making progress to windward under main alone for a couple of tacks. Then, when I had my bearings, we broke out the roller-furling jib (a lazy old man's delight) with a simple tweak of the sheet, trimmed it, and really began to move. *Tanagra*, whose hull mold was originally for an ocean racer in the days of the Cruising Club Rule, tacks quickly (which some Out Island models do not), and she makes little leeway, so it turned into a routine sail to tack our way out the channel to open water.

With a favoring wind, we flew south on a fast reach and negotiated Pass-a-Grille Channel and a drawbridge or two on our way into Tampa Bay and the Sheraton Bel-Air Marina, where we were to meet friends. It was all reaching and running until the last mile, which was directly to windward to the marina entrance, and we beat slowly toward it in the last gasps of the northwester that was fading with the afternoon.

We almost made it, but not quite. In the narrow entrance to the marina, the wind quit completely, and we barely drifted up to a stake marking the other side of the channel, about a hundred feet short of the first pier, so near and yet so far. As we hung on there with our hopes for a spectacular entrance under sail dashed, the marina attendant came out on the pier and called over, "Why don't you use your engine?"

I would have thought any idiot could tell I wouldn't be in this position if I had one, but, trying to keep my voice mild and free of sarcasm, I said, "If I had one I would. It doesn't work."

"Oh," he said, thoughtfully scratching his head for a moment. "I see—Well, I'll come tow you over in the Whaler."

After our brave start, it didn't seem right to end with just a "whimper" this way, but that's how we finally arrived, in tow of a Whaler.

The End of a Perfect Day

At Easter time, Jane and I went back by ourselves and had nine days of cruising the Exumas that were about as perfect a cruise as anyone could ever hope for. The weather was ideal, we had reaching breezes everywhere we went, mostly at hull speed, and everything fell into place beautifully.

We alternated anchorages between spots with some life, like a revisit to the Current Club on our way back, or Staniel Cay with a lively touch of activity at its yacht club, with splendid isolation in the hundreds of coves and cuts that abound throughout the Exumas.

By day we would fly across the pale pastels of the Great Bahama Bank, whose great shining expanse spreads westward from the Exumas, through water so clear that we seemed to be in air rather than liquid, marveling at the subtle changes in color as the bottom changed, here a powdery blue, here a pale, pale green, here almost pure white, and then a ribbon of brilliant blue winding in from the deeps of Exuma Sound off to the east.

It was glorious sailing of the most romantic kind, and after one of the best days of all, we beat our way up to the northern end of Warderick Wells and turned to starboard to reach along a deep blue channel between banks of blinding white to a protected pool well inside, surrounded by small cays. We had it to ourselves, one of the most perfect settings imaginable for a cruising anchorage, and I was filled with the beauty of it as we had a cool anchor cup of Mount Gay Rum on the rocks, and sat in the cockpit watching the sun go down, changing the colors around us as each new hue blazed into the sky.

The colors faded, it grew dark, and the sky filled from

horizon to horizon with the brilliance of the stars. Not a human light could be seen as it came time for supper.

Jane's system for cruising meals when we are away from sources of fresh food is to put the makings of one meal of cans in a plastic bag so that one grab in the locker, instead of a lot of fumbling and label reading, brings it all out at once.

And what, on this most romantic of nights in this most perfect of settings, at the end of this glorious day, was the ambrosia suitable to the occasion that was in the bag she pulled out? Just the two things I really don't like to eat if I have any choice, all wrapped together—spaghetti and beets.

From *A Sailor's Tales* (1978)

The Perfect Cruise

Despite beets and spaghetti, this was the prize one of all

"This is the best sailing I've ever seen."

"Quiet," Jane said, "you'll scare it away."

"I don't care if it rains for the rest of the week. I've never had a better sail. It's worth the whole business," was my answer.

We were reaching across Exuma Sound in a fresh norther, with *Mar Claro* lifting easily to each deep blue wave as she scudded along at hull speed. The sea was alive, the boat was alive, and the air was alive. Ahead of us, the sun lowered toward a string of black silhouettes on the horizon, plating the dancing waves with a sparkle of gold as we neared the Exumas. Once again, April, a great month for cruising in the Bahamas and West Indies, was giving us beautiful cruising weather, and we had been reeling off knots at a fine pace since a mid-morning departure from Davis Harbour on Eleuthera. This was the last cruise of *Mar Claro*'s winter in the Bahamas. Just Jane and I were aboard after a quick flight from New York to Nassau and a DC-3 puddle jump to Rock Sound on Eleuthera, and nine days stretched ahead of us.

Luckily Jane was wrong. Each day I repeated my enthusiastic paean to the joys of this cruise, each day she verbally knocked wood, and each day seemed better than the beautiful one before it. We have never had a cruise that was a failure, but this was the one that topped them all, the perfect one that would seem impossible to exceed or even duplicate, not that we will ever stop trying as long as we can make it over the gunwale.

What are the ingredients of a perfect cruise? These were ours.

Friends had left *Mar Claro* at Rock Sound, Eleuthera, which was where we found her after a taxi ride from the airport, bobbing and surging to a cat's cradle of lines at the end of the long town pier. Extremely atypically, it had been blowing fresh from the west for several days, and her berth was an uneasy one. Rock Sound's settlement is nicely protected in the prevailing easterlies, but the harbor is wide enough to kick up a good chop on its eastern side when a westerly blows. She had been securely moored and was in no danger, but it wasn't comfortable aboard her, and we had gone ashore for dinner and then spent an uneasy night bobbing and pitching.

Rock Sound, bleak and a bit scruffy, is not one of the most charming harbors in the Out Islands, but it is a fine spot to take on supplies, and this we did the next morning before setting forth. The market had fresh fruit, vegetables and meat, all the canned goods we needed, good Pauli Girl German beer in cans, and Mount Gay Barbados rum. We were also able to load up with ice, so all was in good shape for the cruise when we finally cast off from the pier and powered across Rock Sound to its entrance, flinging spray into the teeth of the westerly.

In typical first-day fashion, I had been a bit worried about the navigational hazards of negotiating the shoals and heads between Rock Sound and Powell Point, the barb of the "fish hook" on the southwestern end of Eleuthera, but their terrors seemed much less when face-to-face with than when reading about them in the "Guide." I had thought that we would have to power over the route because of lack of maneuvering room, but soon realized that it was much less confined than home waters on the Shrewsbury River, and we shut off the noise after 40 minutes or so and made sail. As it turned out, this was the last of the motor for the cruise, except for a few moments of dockside maneuvering in a couple of places, and it was also the last windward work.

In a couple of hours, we had threaded our way through the bared sand bars around the prominent radio mast on Powell Point and had then borne off on a broad reach to Davis Harbour. It was too late to cross Exuma Sound, and we didn't relish thrashing into the brisk westerly anyway. By reaching the 10 miles down to Davis, we hoped to give ourselves more choice of routes for crossing to the Exumas in the morning. If it held in the west, we could close-reach down to the Staniel Cay area and then work our way back up the islands. If it started to swing with the clock, as every well-behaved Bahamian breeze should, we would have a wide option of landfalls on the 35-40 mile crossing of the 800-fathom deep Sound.

It had been a fast reach down to Davis, a man-made refuge for sport fishermen tied to the Cotton Bay resort complex developed by Arthur Vining Davis. A quiet, pleasant night there at the concrete piers of the marina, as modern as anything you could find in the States, allowed us to get shaken down and comfortable on board.

This did turn out to be a well-behaved Bahamian breeze, and it very nicely veered into the north by morning, another bright blue day. There was an un-Bahamian nip in the air at first, but the sun soon dispelled it. We made sail right at the marina, zipped out the tiny man-made cut onto the heaving blue of the Sound, and *Mar Claro* jumped to life at once under main and working jib as we headed due west toward an empty horizon. The only thing to appear on it for hours was a special U.S. Navy buoy 12 miles out. This gave us a good check on our progress, which was maximum plus for a 20-foot waterline, and after the buoy dropped astern, we were alone on the heaving blue for several hours. It wasn't hard to feel that we were half way between Panama and Tahiti, or doing well on the Canaries-Barbados route, from the rich blue of the waves and the clean emptiness of the horizon for 360 degrees, and it was one of the memorable sails of all the good ones. At 1100, a Pauli Girl, beaded with frost and tingling cold, was the perfect complement to warm sun and salt air, and our enjoyment was almost tangibly visible as we settled into the feel of being aboard *Mar Claro* and sailing beautifully. Where else in the world could anyone want to be, and I couldn't resist my enthusiastic outburst.

After lunch, company appeared on the northern horizon, and we identified Bill Norton's converted trawler *Empress*, one of the charter boats we knew well. She stayed almost hull down, the only break on the empty circle around us until some dark dots popped up in the sun path in mid-afternoon. I had set a course for Highborne Cay, where we had been on *Alpha*, and where there was an easy entrance from the Sound into a well-protected harbor, but the lumps and bumps ahead of us didn't quite fall into the expected pattern as they grew larger. As I've said, once you lose positive identification in the Exumas, everything looks exactly alike, and you can talk yourself into all sorts of tentative identifications without much conviction. All I knew for sure was that the Exumas were ahead. I was taking no bets on which was which.

Gradually, as the land changed from black silhouettes to beaches, trees, hills, and a house or two, we decided that the lump ahead of us must be Saddle Cay, four miles south of Highborne, and we went on that assumption. Later, checking with Bill Norton, I was gratified to hear that he had been set to the south too on his crossing. The north wind had evidently had an effect on the hard-to-predict currents in the Sound. And Saddle Cay it was.

Late afternoon is a poor time to make a landfall in the west in the Bahamas, since water color is so important to piloting. Nowhere is this more true than the Exumas, where the colors are as definite, and as brilliant as anywhere in the world. In the path of the lowering sun, though, they blended to dancing gold, and I became confused heading into the narrow cut to Saddle Cay. I headed the wrong side of a pair of tiny islets and suddenly we eased to a stop on sand. Looking straight down, it was easy to see how shallow it was, but over the bow it had been plated over by the sun. Grounding is no problem in *Mar Claro*, and I was just about to hop over the side and push her off, when a Boston Whaler loaded with half-naked men shot out from behind one of the islets and headed for us.

Just a week before, a Cuban group had been arrested by the Bahamian police at Norman's Cay, the next island south, while trying to stage a raid on their ex-homeland, and this bunch looked as though they might be more of the same. They were badly in need of a shave, and the first sounds we heard from them were in Spanish. Walter Mitty-like visions sped through my head of *Mar Claro* being commandeered for an expedition against Cuba, but they didn't last long.

"You missed the proper channel," someone called out in very un-Cuban English, and before I knew it, about four men had jumped in the water alongside us and were pushing *Mar Claro* afloat.

"The other side of that rock, mate," one of them pointed, and with a cheery wave, they sloshed back in the Whaler and sped off through the channel they had indicated, waving us on. Later, we found they were a bunch of British office workers from Nassau, with one Latin friend, who were spending the long Easter weekend holiday in Saddle Cay's one house.

I tried to anchor in a shallow bight on the south side of Saddle, but she didn't ride too well, and I was still standing on the bow watching how the anchor tended (and not pleased with it) when a native appeared on the beach and called to us to move around the point to the west of us marking the end of the bight. Once through a narrow cut off the point, a whole new vista opened up. There was a narrow roadstead with several native sloops at anchor, overlooked by a house perched on the brow of a good sized hill that crowned the cay, and a vast expanse of bank water spreading beyond a couple of low islets on the western side of the anchorage.

Before I had fairly settled her at anchor, the same native sculled out in a dinghy and politely asked if I'd like help in anchoring. A little embarrassed, I said yes, and proceeded to get a valuable lesson in anchoring in a tideway Bahamian style. With an anchor at each end of a long rode, one a Northill and the other a four-pronged Bahamian grapnel (a surprisingly effective anchor in sand), he set one up-tide, dropped back to the end of the rode to set the other, then pulled us back to the middle. With the anchors at a slightly veed angle, the boat stays on the same side of them, and swings first to one, and then to the other, as the current changes. No bridle is needed, and it is a very simple, effective rig for at least one night. A boat left for a longer time might swing in a circle too much and foul the rode in twists, but we anchored this way for several nights in various Exuma anchorages and had no trouble. Almost every anchorage is in a swift current in a narrow cut between the cays.

And so we were in the Exumas. A soft sunset had colored the west before we were settled at anchor on arrival, so it wasn't until morning that we got the full effects of the incomparable water colors. No matter how often you see them, they bring gasps of disbelief on re-acquaintance, and Saddle Cay has the full kaleidoscope. The anchorage is a brilliant bottle green, bordered by pale shallows along the shore. A palette full of pastels shades off into powdery blue on the open Bank to the westward, and across the reefs to the eastward, the indigo of Exuma Sound is set off by breakers on the reefs. *Mar Claro* seemed suspended in air at anchor, and the underbodies of the native sloops were graceful outlines under the water. The breeze had moved a bit to the northeast and was still brisk and fresh. With a flood tide holding us bow on in its grip as it swept around the point south of us, she rode stern-to in the wind and the ensign whipped stiffly in over the cockpit.

Our anchoring instructor sculled out to invite us ashore, where the Britishers were packing a native sloop converted to yacht use for the sail back to Nassau, and we climbed the rough stone steps to the house for a breathtaking 360 degree view.

Up here the bright hues were even more startling than when riding amid them in a boat, and the islands strung off to north and south in a color-riddled pattern. It was a glorious spot, but it was also a glorious day for a sail and by midmorning we had retrieved our anchors and were under sail around the reefs to the west, headed down the bank side of the chain. With 2-foot-4 draft and a bright sun high overhead, our only piloting difficulty was in being too chicken. The heads were obvious. Black ones wouldn't hurt us. Greeny-brown ones were to be avoided, and the dirty yellowish ones were almost breaking the surface. It was over the sand that we had trouble believing what the colors meant. So beautifully clear was the water that it had to look like virtually uncovered sand before *Mar Claro*'s keel would bump. At first we were overly cautious, but gradually confidence built up, and after all, what did it matter if we did run on sand. By the end of the week, this was the way we explored gunkholes. We would simply run into a spot until she could go no farther. Small boats have a lot of advantages, especially in this country.

On our way south, with the breeze fresh on the port quarter, we skimmed the beach of Norman's and took a turn through the harbor to look at the pier and airstrip that had been built since our previous visit, and sped onward over the shifting hues toward Warderick Wells. Opposite each cut in from the Sound, there were fantastic strips of color, centering on a royal blue ribbon of Sound water in all shades of blue, green and yellowish white.

Hardening up in late afternoon, we close-reached eastward to the northern anchorage at Warderick Wells, a north-south channel as definite as a blue asphalt avenue between shining white flats. Heading off again, we followed it toward the heart of the island until it widened into a cerulean pool, where we bridle-anchored and settled down for a happy hour of Barbados-on-the-rocks, alone in the world.

Jane's meal system while cruising is to put a complete menu for one dinner in a plastic bag, which saves rummaging through the stowage compartments for various ingredients. Even when she came up with that bag that contained spaghetti and beets, it couldn't take away the perfection of where we were and what met the eye as the sun sank and spread a gentle glow over it. Not a light could be seen in any direction as we swung beneath the stars, and the only sound was a faint hum of the breeze in the rigging and the chuckle of the never-still tide curling around the bow.

The next day was more social. From our splendid isolation at Warderick, we reached out the blue boulevard in a breeze now around to the east, jibed over, and skimmed southward across the gleaming flats to investigate Compass Cay. Again the Pauli Girl ritual added to the sparkle of the morning, and we tacked into the snug little pond at Compass Cay just after lunch to find Harry Kline, editor of the much-used, often blessed "Yachtsman's Guide," alongside the pier in his home-afloat motorsailer *Spindrift*, with his usual crew of wife Nancy Anne and baby daughter. After a pleasant gam and a glimpse of the dramatic view of the Sound and cays from the hilltop clubhouse of Compass Cay Club, we set sail again for one of the very special delights of all the ones in the Exumas, Pipe Creek.

This is really just a winding channel 20 or 30 yards wide between a series of little cays, with surf from the Sound battering the rocks and flinging spray a few yards across the ones to port, and the great calm sheen of the Bank smiling under the sun beyond the ones to starboard. To enjoy it more, we were under main only, and *Mar Claro* glided effortlessly through the ever-changing montage of new perspectives and shifting water hues. Rocky points reached out to us and dropped astern, beaches half hidden up a cove beckoned briefly and slid by, and here and there a few flowers decorated the gaunt shrubbery in this fantastic nautical "nature walk." The peace of our effortless progress over flat, lovely water seemed the more miraculous against a subtle awareness of the open sea and its restless surge and power just a few yards away.

This unforgettable, though short passage, ended at Staniel Cay seven miles south of Compass, and here, at this crossroads of the Exumas, the world was very much with us again. A dozen yachts were in, including old friends like

Traveler II, Empress, Teresa, and *Pocahontas* of the charter fleet, and the partying was in sharp contrast to the lonely delights of Warderick Wells the night before. We rafted at the one pier at Staniel Cay Y.C. alongside *Traveler* and *Empress*, with much visiting back and forth, yarning, cocktailing and a buffet dinner ashore with close to 40 people having a fine time. A calypso band made appropriate noises and the table offered grouper, conch salad and crawfish from the surrounding waters. This was Out Island gaiety at its best, and in its own way just as memorable as the nights of silent isolation under the stars. Both were helped by the contrast of the other.

Staniel is the place to buy bread, and we explored ashore in the village until we found some. It lived up to its reputation for taste and texture, and lasted the rest of the week without turning moldy. By mid-morning, with the breeze obligingly a bit south of east now, we were itchy to sail some more, and we slipped away from the pier headed north in company with *Teresa* and *Traveler*. We were only half way down the fabulous chain, and much more exploring lay to the south, but time was a factor, if not on these wonderful days of sailing, at least a few days ahead at Nassau Airport.

This was another great day, and again I couldn't help but exclaim about it as we sped along. By now, even Jane's superstitions had been lulled by the Exuman weather. If we had wanted to continue south, the breeze would have been forward of the beam by now, but for us it was another broad reach, and we have never sailed faster for as long a time. For over five hours we averaged 6.5 knots in an effortless, swooping surge, lifting easily over the pale green wavelets in the lee of the cays. The convertible hood was rolled at the sides, the usual Bahamian rig, so we could alternate in the sun and the shade, the ice we had picked up at Staniel made the Pauli Girl as bitingly cold as ever, and the final kicker came in staying right with the 43' *Teresa* and 68' *Traveler* all day. True they were under cruising sail and towing dinks, while we had full main and genny, but the 16-18 knot breeze was enough to lift *Mar Claro* up on her chines, continuously over hull speed, while the heavier, deeper big boats would need more to reach theirs.

We had planned a rendezvous with Bud Gieselman, his wife Ricky, and charter party on *Teresa* at Shroud Cay, merely a lee on the western side of the chain, 35 miles north of Staniel, and it was a better anchorage for a heavy boat like *Teresa* than for a little, light displacement one. Though the surface was flat and unruffled through a quiet night, *Mar Claro* heaved and lurched on an imperceptible surge. This was especially noticeable after returning to her from a wonderful dinner aboard *Teresa*. While there, we watched a Haitian sloop tack slowly up to the anchorage from the westward. Unbelievably rough looking, she was on her way to Nassau and had stopped to get water from the well on Shroud Cay. Her skipper sculled over to ask for cigarettes and an aspirin for "a lady with the fever," and said there were 18 people aboard.

Our last full day in the Exumas was spent at a lazier pace, as the breeze eased a bit, once again in the southeast. It was still a perfect sailing one, and there was one section of water we crossed in late morning that was the most beautiful, and the most unbelievable, of all the stretches that had assaulted our senses day after day. A pale, powder blue, it was so clear that it seemed to have no substance at all. *Mar Claro* was flying, not sailing, suspended a few feet off the white sand. The bow wave and wake were like water in a crystal goblet as they sparkled away from the hull, and there was a sense of motion and exhilaration far beyond the six knots or so we were making. Exumas cruising is like this. You think you have experienced everything it has to offer, that the remaining delights will merely be repetitions, and then a new shade of color, a new quality of clarity strikes the eye and brings yet another sensation. I have never been on another cruise of such continuous sensual stimulation.

Noontime was for gunkholing, as we ranged Norman's, with the white expanse of the large shoal called Norman's Spit spreading off to port onto the limitless bank, and the arrow of beach marching along to starboard. The familiar brilliance of the Saddle Cay anchorage slid by, and we dropped the jib to poke along Long Cay, looking for a luncheon gunkhole. Feeling our way around reefs and rocks, we eased into a bight on its north side until the keel touched sand lightly, then moved off a bit to anchor and waded ashore. The sand had a dazzling brilliance under the high sun, and tidal pools along the beach held the whole spectrum of Exuma colors in microcosm. Near *Mar Claro*, I found a reef with some pleasant snorkeling (we do a lot more of this when the younger generation is along), another secret little world in microcosm, and a Barbados-on-the-rocks tasted great when I came back on board.

It was an easy sail up to Allan's Cay, last seen on *Alpha* in 1959, now with a house or two on it to change its sense of loneliness. We poked into a shallow bight of S.W. Allan's Cay where bigger boats can't go, as there were several of them in the regular anchorage, and, suddenly snorkel happy after our noontime success, found a couple of nice little heads to poke around before supper. After cocktails, an early dinner and some sunset watching, we turned in early and were almost asleep when there was the gentle thump of a dinghy alongside, and Bill Norton's unmistakable New England twang filled the night air.

"Hey, aboard *Mar Claro!* Come on to a party." *Empress* had come in at last light, and once again we had an Exuman example of primitive isolation contrasted with pleasant gamming with other cruising people.

We probably should have gone straight to Nassau while the southeaster lasted, but we had two days left and didn't want to waste one in port. Instead of heading the 30 miles directly across, we decided to pay a last visit to The Current Club, 45 miles to the north across a section of bank that is completely blank on Chart 26b and not covered in the "Guide." Bill Norton had said there wouldn't be much to bother us in good light, and we slipped out of Allan's after an early breakfast, with the faithful breeze still out of the southeast. The last of the Exumas dropped astern, with their northern sentinel, the Sail Rocks, a line of black dots on the starboard quarter, and we were alone again on a vast expanse of pale green bank, liberally sprinkled with heads. Sailing close to them, we estimated that there was at least six feet on all but a couple of them.

Toward noon, there was a lull in the breeze, the hottest sailing of the cruise, and the best time of all for a last cold Pauli Girl—we were almost out of ice by now, and it didn't quite survive the day. There was a dreamy, out-of-this-world quality to the empty bank as we lazed along at about four knots. Lonely little Finley Cay showed up on the starboard horizon for a while, and I was just wondering about resurrecting the engine for the first time since a few moments of maneuvering at Compass Cay, when the breeze took on new weight. Finley Cay dropped rapidly aft, the water became deeper, gradually changing to a non-Exuman blue that would appear extremely beautiful to anyone who hadn't seen the Exumas, and *Mar Claro* put her rail down and really began to fly.

It was like Old Home Week when we came alongside at The Current, as *Mar Claro* had been just about their most frequent visitor that winter, and we had a pleasant dinner and visit ashore by way of farewell to the Out Islands. There was even a 10-year-old movie to remind us that there was another world beyond the bright waters we'd been sailing.

As a final incredible fillip to an incredible nine days which had seen us reaching under cloudless skies for all but the first two hours, and at hull speed or better for about 80 per cent of the time, the breeze was around to just east of south the next morning, perfect for reaching to Nassau. We had the current with us through the swift slue of Current Cut as we sailed away from the club pier, and for the next three hours, in a smashing climax to the cruise, we averaged a little more than seven knots over the bottom, the fastest passage *Mar Claro* has ever made. Out now on the 1500 fathoms of Northeast Providence Channel, the royal blue had a different feel to it from bank sailing, even on the gentle ruffle of whitecaps in the lee of the cays. *Mar Claro* rolled along like a deep sea veteran, reeling off the knots in a fine swirl of receding foam, and we were coasting down Rose Island by midday, usually a full day's run from The Current.

Instead of continuing on, we stole a few more hours of drifting over the heads with the glass bucket, stopping to snorkel now and then, until the sun lowering over Fincastle Tower, and the golden shimmer plating the water to the westward, told us that the cruise had ended.

For the last time, as we threaded our way through the Narrows into Nassau Harbor, I made the statement that I had been repeating every day since the sail across Exuma Sound, only this time I changed it to "This was the best cruise I've ever had."

Jane didn't have to "knock wood" this time. She just agreed.

From *Over the Horizon* (1966)

Also from Sheridan House

Destruction at Noonday by Bill Robinson
This novel of nautical peril and adventure
tells of the fate of a big passenger liner
during the Yokohama earthquake.

*Handbook of Offshore Cruising: The Dream
and Reality of Modern Ocean Sailing* by Jim
Howard
The big new reference book for every cruiser.

By Way of the Wind by Jim Moore
Widely acclaimed as "the best sailboat
cruising book to come out in a long time."

*Innocents Afloat: Close Encounters with
Sailors, Boats and Places from Maine to
Florida* by Ken Textor
Unforgettable sailing stories by a gifted
young writer.

Total Loss edited by Jack Coote
A collection of 40 first-hand accounts of
yacht losses at sea with a summary of the
lessons to be learned.

Sailing Alone Around the World
by Capt. Joshua Slocum
The original edition in a fine facsimile
reprint. Hardcover at an affordable price.

America's favorite sailing books